Foundations of Human Development

Foundations of Human Development

A Life Span Approach

Edited by

Asha Singh

Orient BlackSwan

FOUNDATIONS OF HUMAN DEVELOPMENT

ORIENT BLACKSWAN PRIVATE LIMITED

Registered Office
3-6-752, Himayatnagar, Hyderabad 500 029, Telangana, India
e-mail: centraloffice@orientblackswan.com

Other Offices
Bengaluru, Bhopal, Chennai, Guwahati, Hyderabad, Jaipur,
Kolkata, Lucknow, Mumbai, New Delhi, Noida, Patna, Visakhapatnam

First published 2015
Reprinted 2020

ISBN 978 81 250 5907 3

Typeset in
Electra LT Std 10.5/12
by PrePSol Enterprises Pvt. Ltd. Haryana

Printed in India at
B. B. Press, Noida

Published by
Orient Blackswan Private Limited
3-6-752, Himayatnagar,
Hyderabad 500 029 (Telangana), INDIA
e-mail: info@orientblackswan.com

Table of Contents

Boxes

Tables

Figures

Foreword

Welcome to this comprehensive and lucid introduction to Human Development!

The family as an institution is universal. There are differences, of course, in the types of families, but FAMILY is an integral unit of all living communities and settlements in the world. Even among the groups of people who live only as religious communities, we find the labels 'father', 'mother', 'brother', or 'sister' given to the residents.

Almost all families ensure that there is a new generation of children. Thus, the continuity of the human race is maintained. The motivation for, and exercise of, reproduction is built into our genetic structure, our DNA. Human life comes to an end naturally, in 80 to 100 years or so, but the genes that make us what we are continue to live through our children and grandchildren. A science, which equips us to rear our children to adulthood, is thus at the root of human survival and human achievement. As you will discover in the course of completing the curriculum, Home Science includes both the art and the science of living, and therefore constitutes essential knowledge for all.

You might wonder how our ancestors managed the family and brought up children without the formal principles and methods presented here. There are many ways of transmitting knowledge. Traditionally, a family of three or four generations lived under one roof or one settlement, cooking and eating together, working together, hunting and searching for food, or cultivating the land and raising cattle. They learned all the required skills by watching how a task was done. Imitation and learning by doing were built into the system. There would have been differences in the speed of learning and the mastery of tasks, and some children may have had special talents. But generally, the focus was not so much on individual achievement, as it was on task completion and getting on with each other harmoniously.

Modern life does not permit us the luxury of extended families or the freedom to go at our own pace. Technology has reduced the drudgery of much of the work our families did 100 years ago. It has speeded up our communications and brought the whole globe within our reach; it has made our lives easier and healthier. It has given us a broad spectrum of choices in everything we read or do. Our universities bring the Universe into our lives, serving the roles of teacher, parent, grandparent, neighbour, healer, and counsellor. Make full use of this wonderful opportunity with energy and enthusiasm, with diligence and devotion.

As you learn new facts and understand new explanations of human behaviour, develop your own interests and talents and believe that you are not only absorbing information, but by thinking about it critically, creating new knowledge. Discuss your ideas with your friends and teachers. Maintain a notebook for each discipline, jotting down your thoughts or observations, attaching pictures or sketches or selected passages. Your education will be as exciting as you choose to make it, when you realise that the examination result is not the main objective. The adventure of seeking knowledge and using it in your life is both the challenge and the goal. Enjoy it!

An important aspect of this book on Human Development and Childhood is that it sets the theories, principles and observations in the Indian context. In the past, we were forced to depend on textbooks written in the US or the

UK, and would find ourselves explaining and interpreting everything to make it responsive to Indian cultural reality.

You have a great advantage in this material on Human Development and Childhood Studies, written by experienced teachers in the Department. This book fills the need of students to understand the discipline through Indian thoughts on childhood and children. This volume is also about you and for you, and for all of us who live in this complex and interesting country.

S. Anandalakshmy

Founder,
Department of Human Development and Childhood Studies
Former Director, Lady Irwin College

Introduction

This book is an outcome of students' desire to encounter portrayals of Indian childhood in the texts prescribed for their courses on Human Development. In this book, a focused attempt has been made to provide glimpses into children's lives in different contexts of India, and understand the rhythms, routines and aspirations set in the contexts of diversity and familiarity. Orient BlackSwan initially approached us to revise a hugely popular textbook for school students. However, at an initial point itself, it was decided to shelve that project and work on an entirely new text for undergraduate students.

Creating a text aimed at college students is often not an acceptable proposition, as higher education needs to stoke the imagination to discover and build ideas. With the universalisation of education, higher education has now become more accessible, and a socio-cultural diversity now exists in the profile of students, who come from both affluent and deprived backgrounds. Not all students have easy and frequent access to reading materials, and hence a consolidated text would help a wide range of students to understand curricular demands, besides the narratives that describe socio-cultural realities.

The book captures the universals in the human lifecycle, along with nuanced descriptions of cultural rituals and practices in different regions of India. The different chapters follow a stage and age-related approach in dealing with issues and understandings of human development.
The unique features of the book are:

- The text refers to universals in development in simple language, which will be understood even by students who may not be proficient in English.
- The text weaves in socio-cultural practices and rituals related to children from the womb, till the time individuals are socially independent.
- The book recognises regional variations and other special features of growing in India that specially influence lifecycle processes.
- The chapters contain exercises that will help students to use simple ways to explore the lives of children and families in their environments, thereby building a stronger understanding of children, childhood and families.

I would like to thank all the authors who readily participated in this exercise to make Human Development accessible to a larger number of students. I appreciate their teamwork in meeting deadlines, responding to queries, and providing the required references. I would like to acknowledge the contribution of Ms Ridhi Sethi, who gave a thorough reading, and organised and updated, the text of Chapter 4. I am grateful to the social media site Facebook, which, by putting material in public view, helped us to acquire photographs of many activities involving children. We thank the Rajkumari Amrit Kaur Child Study Centre for letting us use the pictures of children from their collection. Acknowledgements are also due to Dimple Rangila, Bhrigupati and Prerna Singh, for allowing us to use pictures of their children.

My thanks to the OBS team for their patient association in making this book a reality.

Asha Singh
New Delhi

1

Basic Ideas in Human Development

HIGHLIGHTS

- Definition of the concept of human development.
- Study of Human Development and Childhood Studies within the discipline of Home Science.
- The significance of studying human development, and the universals in the development of individuals.
- Different domains as well as stages of development.
- The principles of development are also outlined.
- Methods of studying and researching children.

INTRODUCTION TO HUMAN DEVELOPMENT

Human development is the study of humans from conception to death. It develops an understanding of the many influences on development, as well as the age-related changes from the womb to the tomb. Most books have described human development as the study of the growth and changes occurring in our lives, in our bodies, our feelings, our ways of thinking, and our relationships. Human development also emphasises the different roles that individuals play at different points in their lives (Berk 2009; Rice 1995). It is important to understand that human growth and development contains both universal aspects of change due to maturation, and variations in developmental responses, due to environmental diversities.

Understanding the different changes throughout the lifespan leads us to the branch of psychology, where a systematic attempt is made to study cognitive, physical-motor, psycho-physiological, and psycho-social functioning. This scientific study of human beings focused on children in the late nineteenth and early twentieth centuries, and is also known as developmental psychology. In the 1950s, research in some parts of the world focused on the relationship between child-rearing and adult personality, and also examined adolescence in its own right. By the late twentieth century, the interest had extended to all aspects of development and change over the entire lifespan.

Research also generated a growing awareness and recognition of the significance of cultural contexts and the many pathways to development. The notion of many children with many forms of childhood began receiving wider acceptance. 'Cultural contexts' implies the influence of several features of the social environment, physical living conditions, economic capacity, and family systems on human development. Anthropological inquiry, especially the research conducted by Margaret Mead (2001 [1928]), brought into focus the role of culture in shaping human beings; personality was no longer believed to be determined only by biology and genes. Mead's work, however, was viewed with scepticism as her results and findings leaned heavily on observation.

Till the last quarter of the twentieth century, child-rearing practices were the primary sources of deriving information about children. The work of theorists from diverse fields—for instance, Piaget, Vygotsky, George Herbert Mead, and John Dewey—led to the realisation that children are not always passive recipients of knowledge, but create their own understanding as they grow amidst social groups. In Indian epics and literature, the socio-cultural understanding of children and childhood largely highlight innocence, curiosity and playfulness as dominant features.

How does a baby grow up slowly and learn to crawl, sit, stand, walk, talk, and recognise objects and people? The child grows into a social being and forges an identity as an adult, in turn creating a family and nurturing her/his young, and moves towards middle adulthood to old age. This cycle of human development has generated an interest to understand the different aspects of human development.

Box 1.1 Children of the Forest

Rudyard Kipling's *Jungle Book*, and its film adaptation, is very popular with both children and adults. The story of a child raised in a jungle, and the descriptions of his encounters evoke interest in a very unique experience of childhood. The main protagonist is the child Mowgli, who is brought up by animals in the absence of the usual human parents. The child grows up with animal-like skills and develops an affinity and bond with non-human species.

The story is inspired by many cited cases of wild children in different parts of the world. Textbooks by Euro-American authors mention the Wild Boy of Aveyron in France in 1800. He emerged from the jungle naked, and came begging for food near the hamlet of Aveyron. People had spotted him running fast on all fours. Word about this strange 'beast' had spread, and interested a French doctor, who attempted to rehabilitate him. After many attempts to teach language to this boy, the doctor understood that an absence of language in critical periods of childhood makes it almost impossible to acquire communication skills.

Indian records of two girls, Kamala and Amla, who had been raised by wolves, were maintained by Reverend Singh in Midnapore in 1920. The journal entries concerning the girls' behaviour find resonance in the descriptions of the animal-like behaviour and absence of language reported in the case of Victor of Aveyron. Feral children can be socialised and domesticated enough to learn to wear clothes and sleep on a bed, but language skills do not develop after a lack of exposure to human sounds in the early periods of life. Most children raised by animals reportedly showed an affinity to the behaviour patterns of animals, rather than human beings.

At different points in time, kings have isolated children, allowing them no contact with human sounds to understand how children learn to speak. Such an experiment was also attempted by the Mughal King Akbar. Being interested in the origins of language, he had infants isolated, with no exposure to verbal exchanges. These infants were raised by mute caregivers in *Goong mahal* (House of the Mute). Records captured in a book on Akbar (National Book Trust) state that these children grew up with no verbal skills, but communicated through gestures, imitating the 'speech' patterns of their caregivers.

Such historical instances, despite the unsophisticated and rudimentary tools of research available then, convey a dynamic relation between biological structures and the nature of interactions. These descriptions suggest how the environment shapes maturational processes.

Source: Asha Singh.

SOCIETY AND CHILDHOOD

Most societies organise processes and ways to care for the young. Books and writings on child development provide information about human interactions, and the changes that take place in individuals as they progress through the human lifecycle. Each culture has a reservoir of folklore, stories, and songs that familiarise children with the socio-cultural diversities, as well as depict the roles and responsibilities that culture expects from individuals at different points in their lives.

In India, too, interest in societal dynamics and children's developing competencies have been captured in poetry, stories, mythology, and more recently, in films. Contemporary writings in regional languages have also fleshed out child protagonists. Such portrayals mirror the status and position of children in society. For example, a story might have a child helper in a tea shop, who is accused of stealing. This conveys not only suspicion about children, but mistrust and assumptions about people struggling with economic limitations. An abundance of resources often reduces societal empathy and increases the dominance of the power of money in certain sections. There are stories of optimism that convey notions of resilience. Human development and societal dynamics are embedded in what we do, what we read, and what we see, and these sources can in turn help us to learn and reflect on the norms of society.

In different societies, the study of human development is mostly located within the social sciences or departments of education, or in the evolving discipline of childhood studies.

Changing Notions of Childhood

All cultures have some understanding of children. There are several ways to understand notions of childhood, or reflect on how society views children. Through the depictions of children in paintings or photographs, scholars have understood how children are viewed in everyday rhythms. Paintings, artifacts, or pictures of families from earlier centuries in Indian museums show children dressed in adult-like clothes, making them look like miniature adults (Figure 1.1). Such clothes are now only popular during festivities and celebrations. The simple act of dressing children differently from adults provides them with a cultural orientation. In some parts of contemporary India, girls even now wear the traditional sari, while boys wear Western clothes. This traditional attire, however, does not deter girls from cycling or accessing technology. Thus, at any point in time there is a coexistence of several realities.

Figure 1.1: Families in the late nineteenth century

Source: pinterest.com

In Western thought, the work of Philip Aries (1962) opened up fresh interpretations of notions of childhood. His contention was that the notion of childhood was absent in medieval society, with children being looked upon as miniature adults. It was only during the seventeenth or eighteenth century that the world of adults began to be distinct from the world of children. The growth of industry and movement away from agriculture impacted family dynamics. In the nineteenth century, certain universals of childhood began to take shape, and the twentieth century provided a deep understanding about the functioning of children's minds, evoking a new interest in the understanding of children.

In contemporary thought, children have been moved out of the workforce, and there is a world-wide emphasis on schooling. Another development is a growing focus on child rights, engaging the state in allocating resources for the welfare of children.

An interplay of several factors creates attitudes and patterns in societies. There is a multiplicity of childhoods: some children go to affluent private schools while some study in state-run schools, and this decision is directly related to economic capacity and access. Despite the universalisation of schooling, social groups where children have to contribute to economic activity continue to exist.

Economic diversity creates a wide range of family configurations. Historically, children of the rich have had an easier time; private tutors were hired to educate them at home, while children in middle-class and poorer homes worked in the fields. Children from impoverished families were sometimes sent away to stay with relatives, or apprentices to employers. Children could therefore be both an economic asset and a liability. In India, the high levels of poverty and high population has led to the creation of state provisions to support children. Child labour continues to exist, as does the reality of children living with relatives in search of livelihoods or education.

Literature and academic writings on the history of childhood provide examples of the influences that change community dynamics. Industrialisation and the consequent urbanisation created new roles for children, who were employed in hazardous activities like mining from the early age of seven. Developed nations, with the growing presence of technology, soon put an end to child employment, and urban areas created new lives, and new ways to train children had to be evolved. Schools for common people formed the next step in shaping children's lives. Initially, schooling was viewed with suspicion as primitive communities could not think of children without family surveillance. However, schooling gained momentum, and soon there was international pressure to universalise education.

Schooling radically changed the everyday lives of children, and children and families were no longer occupied together. New issues and concerns about childhood began to develop as children spent large chunks of their time as part of a collective, often losing their individuality in the midst of a large collective. While a peer group is a attractive proposition, the high adult-child ratio may lead to unresolved conflicts and unanswered questions. In the most current understanding of children, there is a recognition of children as active social actors, who impact their own lives in various ways and yet gain from adult intervention and guidance.

HUMAN DEVELOPMENT AND INTERDISCIPLINARITY

Children are raised in families; and families live in different social contexts, embedded in diverse physical-social environments. The nature of care practices, facilities and opportunities provided by families comprise the elements of social ecology. The relation the young have with their physical surroundings (mountains, rural areas, or tribal hamlets), language and religion determine the everyday rhythms and family life. Family configurations—the number of people, number of earning members—determine its position and status. Sociological concepts, theory and research help to identify social influences and their relation to human development.

Sociology and anthropology provide knowledge and information about society and culture. Sociology enhances the knowledge of social structure, social groups and social interaction patterns, while anthropology provides information about culture, culture and the individual, and emerging and evolving cultural practices. A knowledge of social science theories and research provides insights into socio-cultural issues, creating a rich understanding of human development and behaviour.

It is within the social-cultural framework that individuals grow and develop. As discussed later, human beings, irrespective of social-cultural variations, are governed by universal principles of development. How—and why—do individuals respond in certain ways? Human development also draws from the discipline of psychology; psychology increases the understanding of the way the mind functions, patterns in human reactions, and responsiveness as prompted by conscious and unconscious influences. The focus of psychology, sociology and anthropology is to understand the individual, and the different collective forces shaping the individual. Each discipline supports and widens the understanding of how individuals grow in the midst of multiple influences. Hence, the study of human development is grounded in the understanding of children and individuals from multiple perspectives, rather viewing them through a single lens that provides an incomplete picture.

Human Development and Home Science

In India, Child Development or Human Development are subjects set within the larger domain of Home Science. The field of child development transformed into human development, and forms one of the strong pillars of Home Science. Home Science is an inherently interdisciplinary subject, encompassing the pure sciences, social sciences, fabric sciences, design and communication. Home Science is the study of factors related to the health, happiness and management of the home, and that of all members who comprise the family. Family members in a home are usually of different ages and genders, with different personalities, interests and desires, and are each at their own stage of development. Health and well-being depend on care, food and resources. Home science identifies and teaches communication skills, which influence relationships in accordance with larger societal norms and customs.

Earlier, Home Science was believed to teach students how to create effective and efficient environments within the home by imparting the art of running a home, skills in communication, the science of food and nutrition, and the consequent healthcare and well-being. However, as the discipline grew, the different elements of Home Science began providing specialised information and training in specific areas such as nutrition, human development, resource management and design, communication and extension. The strength of Home Science lies in the interdisciplinary exposure that students encounter in the course of the three-year degree programme. Each student learns the basics of nutrition, care and interdependence of the family, communication, as well as the efficient use of resources. Each individual area has evolved as a specialisation, with its own career options.

Elements of Home Science

Home Science covers identified areas of specialisation, all of which draw from natural and human sciences as well as the humanities to gain expertise in managing resources effectively, and provide for the multiple social and physical needs of the family. In 2013, 100 years of Home Science in India was celebrated; in these 100 years, the subject has changed in many ways. While the discipline is often considered to be limited to the teaching of simple household chores systematically, in higher education it is recognised as a professional course, and falls under the Faculty of Science (University of Delhi).

The content of study builds a thorough understanding; for example, the inclusion of sciences have relevance to the home and are centred round the unfolding of processes within household physics, with students being taught the functioning of the refrigerator, iron, electrical wiring, and other household gadgets. To develop this understanding, students are taught both theory and scientific information. Similarly, an important feature in resource management is principles of budgeting. Students are trained in basic economic theory, laws of demand and supply, etc. Experts from different disciplines have redesigned the parent discipline; for instance, India's leading sociologist, Professor M. N. Srinivas, began teaching sociology in a Home Science college to provide a basis in social structure and family dynamics. This societal imaging helps to build an understanding of the way children are socialised within both macro and micro contexts. Each domain of Home Science is now a specialised field, with each area complementing the others to make it an integrated area of knowledge.

The specialisations are:

Food and Nutrition
Resource Management and Design Application
Fabric and Apparel Sciences
Human Development
Development Communication and Extension

Interrelationships in Home Science: Positioning Human Development

To learn about the growth of individuals, it will be essential to know what foods are needed at different stages of the lifecycle for adequate nutrition. This will require a scientific study of the body, how the body needs nutrients to grow, and how food intake gets processed and digested to foster growth and development. Home Science is also the study of the efficient and effective use of resources, roles and responsibilities within families.

Human development informs and complements the other fields in Home Science with knowledge and information about people, and the children living in families and communities. Documentation of the cultural practices relating to the care of pregnant women, rituals and celebrations marking the birth, or dietary practices linked to dietary requirements are all aspects of human development. Feeding and weaning practices would need nutritional knowledge, which is facilitated by the inter-disciplinarity of Home Science. Spreading the best practices would require effective communication skills appropriate to different community settings. Children's behavioural features are often a function of their age. The influence of the weather on their activity would call for knowledge of fabric, and even the design of apparel conducive to play. It is important to note that each facet of Home Science works to build a holistic perspective of human development.

HOW INDIVIDUALS GROW AND LEARN

All societies and communities—and even different species—have ways to socialise their young. Human beings have always been curious about how children think, how they learn to talk, or how they adopt appropriate behaviours in different situations. At different times, individuals have reflected upon, and drawn interpretations about, the functioning of the human mind. This section will describe the varying views and perspectives on human development.

Theories of Child Development: A Brief Overview

Speculations about children's interpretation of the world abound. Philosophers and thinkers have propounded frames of reference for both typical human development and individual differences. Descriptions of abandoned children show that environmental influences at the correct stages of life are crucial for children to develop skills to progress and grow.

At different points in time, the understanding of human behaviour has been influenced by specific factors, which have also become radically altered. From an initial belief in the dominance of genetic influences in determining human personality, there was a shift to the importance of the environment in shaping personality. It is argued that an evolutionary perspective can unite the study of species-typical development and individual variation. Study and research into the lifespan and determinants of development from many perspectives support an evolutionary framework, in which both the organism and the environment combine to produce development. Species-specific genes that interplay with diverse environments can lead to individual variations, and this variability in maturation and learning affect the personality and social and intellectual development.

These domains are used as examples to integrate theories of average development and individual differences. The principles of development, described later in this chapter, will enhance our understanding of the multiple influences of development. Given the wide range of environmental opportunities and emotional supports, most children grow up to be different, based on their individual genotypes. Understanding the ways in which genes and environments work together helps paediatricians, child counsellors and professionals to identify children in need of intervention, and tailor assistive supports for their particular needs.

Child development was largely ignored throughout much of history. Children were often viewed simply as small versions of adults, who had to be trained to become fully functioning members of society. Thinkers like John Locke and Rousseau, in the seventeenth and eighteenth centuries, described, through their own distinct approaches, how adults should organise ways of teaching and learning, creating a rudimentary understanding of the effective exchanges for human development. Locke proposed a more instructive approach that could lead to evolving minds, while Rousseau emphasised the importance of changing strategies of dialogue with age. Little attention was paid to the agency of individuals, the many advances in cognitive abilities, language usage and physical growth, and how individuals could be different.

In the nineteenth century, Pestallozi was searching for ways to understand the diversities of the human mind. Froebel, who was greatly influenced by Pestallozi, dwelt on ways to allow the freedom of exploration and expression in children. Interest in the field of child development began early in the twentieth century with the emergence of schools, which could test skills and talent. Freud's work searched for influences that prompted individuality; however, his work tended to focus on abnormal behaviour. Piaget, working in a testing laboratory, made the startling observation that certain items were beyond the comprehension of specific age groups. The systematic nature of errors led Piaget to pursue a developmental order, building an understanding of a young child's mind, which has qualitative features specific to age. Vygotsky's work around the same time also indicated the importance of adults in guiding and mediating children's interpretations.

Psychoanalytic Child Development Theories

Sigmund Freud is a central figure in raising awareness about the significance of early years, which is now supported by neuroscience research and the study of early brain development. His theories proposed the importance of childhood events and experiences, but almost exclusively focused on mental disorders rather than normal functioning. However, no criticism can undermine the massive influence of psychoanalytic thought, not only on the understanding of human development, but also on literature and in generating interest in people's narratives. According to Freud, child development goes through a series of 'psychosexual stages'. In *Three Essays on The Theory of Sexuality* (1905), Freud outlined these stages as oral, anal, phallic, latency, and genital. Each stage involves the satisfaction of a libidinal desire, and can later play a role in the adult personality.

Based on Freud's work, several theories emerged to extend the understanding of how children grow. Erik Erikson (1950) proposed a stage theory of development, focusing more on social inputs that move beyond the satisfaction provided by the bodily drives of Freudian Id and Ego. Erikson's theory also encompassed development throughout the human lifespan. He followed the psychoanalytic tradition that believed that each stage of development was focused on overcoming a conflict. Success or failure in dealing with conflicts can impact the overall functioning.

Attachment theories, grounded in Freudian thought, are very significant in understanding the magnitude of very early experiences and their consequences for later life adjustment. The work of Mary Ainsworth and John Bowlby will be of interest to students who want to discover the wonder of infancy and comprehend the vast competencies that babies can display.

Cognitive Child Development Theories

Just when theorists were exploring children's early experience, certain researchers were discovering how children make meanings of the world around them. Jean Piaget played a significant role in raising consciousness about the active agency of the child as meaning-maker. His work has deliberated on how children think, and he was the one to suggest that children think differently from adults and propose a stage theory of cognitive development. He also noted that children play an active role in gaining knowledge about the world.

The Russian theorist Vygotsky recognised children as active agents of their own environment, as well as ones who need a social network of significant adults to assist their discovery of the world. The presence of more experienced others guided and mediated processes of meaning-making by young minds. Thus, research and philosophy has opened the world of children and childhood in many ways. We can benefit from the many understandings and develop our own understanding of childhood according to cultural influences and ethnic beliefs.

Constructivist Approach

Following the theories of Piaget and Vygotsky, children are now viewed as more than receptacles for given knowledge; they are also able to participate in the process of learning. A paradigm shift that now views children as active learners is significant in the process of education. Educators need to devise engaging and interactive methods that recognise children as social actors, with their unique social experiences.

Behavioural Child Development Theories

Along with the belief in the reality of children's perceptions, there is a line of thought that understands children as passive recipients of what society provides. Such thoughts focus on the dominance of environmental inputs. We know that the role of the environment on children cannot be totally ignored, and behavioural theories of child development focus on how environmental interaction influences behaviour, following the work of theorists such as John B. Watson, B. F. Skinner, and the founder of experimental psychology, Ivan Pavlov. We have all heard of Pavlov's dogs salivating when a bell rang, irrespective of any visual or aroma of food. We can recall incidents of our own conditioned responses, which Pavlov's reaction also symbolises. However, we do not like to see ourselves as dependents with no inner reasoning. The conditioning reaction follows initial rewards and a continuity of behaviour. This thought was further developed by behaviourists. Behaviouristic theories deal only with observable behaviours. Development is considered a reaction to rewards, punishments, stimuli, and reinforcement.

ELEMENTS AND FORCES SHAPING DEVELOPMENT

Theories that provide insights into social or biological behaviour attempt to enhance understandings of human behaviour. Let us understand the elements of development and the forces that shape the processes of development.

Indian ethno-theories about children and childhood provide a wide range of perspectives, from innocence (child is an *avatar* of God) to socialising children with the *samskara* of good moral living. Modern Indian thought has also stressed the education of children, as reflected in the philosophies of Sri Aurobindo, Rabindranath Tagore and Mahatma Gandhi. Their views provided an integrated approach to dealing with young minds. Tagore stressed on the role of the arts and proximity to nature, while Sri Aurobindo emphasised holistic growth, which would address spiritual needs along with the other domains of development. Gandhi's views were an amalgamation of both Tagore and Aurobindo, with an additional perspective—that of inculcating in children the dignity of labour by promoting learning through work. Recent Western theories outline the developmental stages of children, and identify the typical ages at which these growth milestones occur.

Child in Indian Thought

Descriptions of childhood have been provided in Sanskrit and Tamil texts. *Manusmriti* and the Grahya Sutras propose a certain *samskara*, or heritage or way of life and upbringing. The rituals are age-related and mark the entry or the end of a particular stage of life across the lifespan. Each stage prescribes tasks to be mastered, fostering an understanding of the behaviour and psychological needs of individuals (the later chapters will describe many of the age-related rituals practised in different Indian regions).

India is a plural society with many ethnic systems and rites. In his seminal work on Indian childhood, *Inner World* (1980), Sudhir Kakar provides a psychoanalytic perspective of the Hindu child in India, and some of the rituals commonly practised in families. These rituals and ceremonies convey a developmental pattern to the evolving needs of individuals.

Namakaran: Naming ceremony, which initiates a social identity.
Annaprasana: Weaning, or the eating of the first solid food.
Vidyarambha: Beginning of student life.
Upanayanam: Initiation into adult life, denoted as a transition from youth to adulthood.
Samavartana: Marking the end of training in the *gurukula*.
Vivaha: Beginning a family.

Through ceremonies and festivities, cultures display not only community support, but also provide direction to the young. Indeed, all cultures organise developmentally appropriate and culturally-guided systems to socialise their young, and strive to create responsible and committed citizens.

Study of Development in Contexts

Most contemporary readings in human development address the unique experiences of people's lives in their particular contexts. We have come a long way from the time that Margaret Mead visited Samoa and learnt that not all babies bathe in a 'bathtub', or other anthropologists' discovery that people may not readily send their children to school, fearing an 'absence of family surveillance'. It is now commonly agreed that adolescence is a universal stage in an individual's development, but it presents itself in accordance with social norms. The notion that each group has its own code of cultural literacy and ecologically-driven skills has gained acceptance, igniting people's interest and curiosity in different cultures. Children of construction labourers often carry small objects on their heads when following their mothers. They learn to walk with care, avoiding the piled-up concrete,

Figure 1.2: Childhood in different spaces

Source: Galli Galli Sim Sim

and play joyfully with sand. Children can seek their own challenges within their own habitats.

The 3-year-old son of a trained classical dancer could differentiate between forms of dance and label the pictures. He could sing and recite *slokas*. In a group of storytellers, 6-year-old children had acquired the competence to narrate stories, using visual materials as cues. These are examples of varied contexts, in which children grow and imbibe their family competencies. Such observations indicate the variability of human behaviour, and necessitate expanding our notions about childhood competence and reframing milestones in certain domains.

The Relevance of Human Development

Human development familiarises you with predictable behavioural changes, expected age norms, age-related competencies, as well as the evolving needs of individuals. Courses in human development sometimes have an added dimension—'Family Studies'. This focus on the family builds on the significance of contexts for development, and the multiple influences of language, religion, region, or economic status and education.

Human Development and Childhood Studies also supports an emphasis on the specific experiences of childhood, in relation with the development patterns of caregivers in the family. A lifespan approach underscores the interactions between any growing individual and others in their own developmental niche. Individuals also gain an understanding of their own transitions and become aware of their own challenges ahead. In different cultures and situations, childhood unfolds through different pathways. Schooling and universal compulsory attendance have radically altered the lives of children, and they negotiate substantial parts of their daily rhythms away from the family. In contexts where schooling is absent, children spend time on their own, eking out a living or learning skills for future independence. While the emphasis may vary, what is common is that people are part of socio-cultural contexts, and their lives are interdependent and influenced by multiple factors.

The main aims of studying multiple dimensions of development during a lifespan are building an understanding of the self, developing meaningful relationships with others, and reflecting on the trials and triumphs of everyday experiences. One of the personal goals of students of lifespan development is self-assessment, for the purpose of self-improvement and self-enhancement (Heckhausen and Krueger 1993). Human development informs and enables parents and teachers to develop the appropriate skills and expertise to reach out to children.

A growing body of research indicates that the changing fabric of society—different kinds of families, differences in ability, different occupations—often lead people to seek advice, and counsellors can benefit from a systematic study of the features of human development. Understanding developmental patterns and what makes people different can help to create appropriate media content and other learning materials. Therapists, community workers and programme managers in international and national NGOs prefer to hire people with knowledge of developmental issues. The study of Human Development thus provides many professional opportunities.

The goal of familiarity with, and systematic study of, lifespan developmental patterns is to foster meaningful relationships and enable productive lives. A growing understanding of behavioural changes and evolving interests can help us to be positive and regulate our actions and communications, as it enables an understanding of the many influences on an individual's growth at different stages of development.

Figure 1.3: Teamwork resource for social development

Source: Rajkumari Amrit Kaur Child Study Centre collection

Stages of Development

Development is a lifelong process, and each feature of or influence upon a person contributes to create an integrated personality. At different ages, individuals pass through unique phases as biological and physiological functioning differs and matures with time. The many changes a human being goes through are clustered together and referred to as stages of development. The lifespan is divided into two broad areas—Childhood and Adulthood—and these are further divided into Child Development and Adult Development.

Child Development

Prenatal period: From conception to birth
Infancy: From birth to two years
Early Childhood: Three to six years
Middle Childhood: Six to 11 years
Adolescence: 11 to 19 years

Adult Development

Early Adulthood: 20 to 40 years
Middle Adulthood: 40 to 60
Late Adulthood: 60 years and above

DEVELOPMENTAL PERIODS AND SPECIFIC FEATURES

Each stage of life is unique. Understanding each stage helps us to predict behaviour and respond to the needs of individuals. Each period has certain milestones to be achieved; these are physical, such as ability to support one's own neck as babies, and later, to roll over. Crawling, sitting up, holding on to support and standing are all examples of physical milestones. Social smiles or interactions with strangers are social milestones. Milestones are crucial developmental events that enable children to develop the skills of mobility, interaction and social independence (discussed in later chapters).

Prenatal Period (Conception to Birth)

This is when the unborn baby is in the womb. It begins when the female ovum unites with the male sperm to form a viable zygote, which transforms from a single fertilised cell to millions of cells. This period has three sub-stages called trimesters, and development is influenced by both heredity and environment. Most cultures recognise the significance of pregnancy and have norms and practices pertaining to the care of the pregnant woman and the foetus (the unborn child). The growing organism is vulnerable to environmental influences and needs care.

Infancy

Infancy is the earliest period in an individual's life. It is then that the infant builds a basic blueprint of her/his surrounding physical-social world through the senses. In this period, it is of great help if babies are in supportive environments with nurturing sensory care, such as touch and social interactions rich in talk and movement. Recent neuroscience research indicates that this is the most rapid period of development, and that sensory-deprived environments can have detrimental effects. Human infancy, unlike other species, is the long period of dependency with the fastest pace of development, and hence babies need a responsive environment. Early attachment, consistency and continuity of care have been focal

Figure 1.4: Developing fine motor skills

Source: Rajkumari Amrit Kaur Child Study Centre collection

to child development research, which stresses the importance of early years and early learning.

Early Childhood

Babies enter this stage with basic mobility, which further matures to negotiating stairs or simple climbing. Physical mobility is the first simple step to self-directed exploration and experimenting with physical space. In these preschool years, children need to be watched as they can fall into precarious situations. Children learn to care for themselves and acquire a rudimentary sense of the self and gender roles. Play is very significant at this stage as it forms a natural pathway to learning, especially the social aspects of learning. Children also become interested in playing with other children. Parent-child relationships are crucial, and the nature of socialisation influences children's behaviour and attitudes.

Box 1.2 Early Childhood Development: Care and Education (ECCE)

In most parts of the world, for matters of policy and social action, the period from birth to the age of six is referred to as Early Childhood or Young Children. In September 2013, the Government of India passed a policy on Early Childhood Care and Education. Programmes include care of the pregnant woman, as the health and well-being of the mother is crucial for the unborn child. The very name—ECCE—signifies that the element of care takes prominence. In the early years, babies absorb reactions from the world through the responsiveness they experience in their environments. Along with adequate nutrition and healthcare, babies need physical proximity and a nurturing and responsive environment rich in adult-child interactions. Culturally, the recognition of care of babies is indicated by the presence of special rattles, mobiles or other stuffed objects, which meet the visual, tactile and auditory needs of infants.

Source: Asha Singh.

Figure 1.5: Exploring and asking questions

Source: Rajkumari Amrit Kaur Child Study Centre collection

Middle Childhood

This is often called the school-age period as during this time, children in primary school experience formal learning for the first time. This period is also relatively inactive physically, unlike early childhood or the pubertal period. Middle childhood is also called the period of consolidation, as in each domain children work out complexities in their basic skills; for instance, walking and climbing transform into climbing trees or scaling a wall. Secret languages or sharing of jokes begin during this stage. Children form long-lasting friendships during this stage. Parents and family relationships continue to be significant, but total dependence changes to interdependence. Physical maturity and social independence lead children into situations of play and exploration that render them vulnerable to accidents.

Figure 1.6: Outdoor play: Opportunity for physical development

Source: Rajkumari Amrit Kaur Child Study Centre collection

Adolescence

This is a much researched stage of development. The period unfolds in many ways, with the universal element being the stage of 'transition from childhood to adolescence'. As a biological phenomenon, adolescence begins in physiological processes, leading to physical changes in both male and female children. During this period, individuals across cultures or time are engaged in a self-search for roles and responsibilities, and seek training and means to be independent. Sexual maturity and the search for a positive identity foster increasing autonomy, weakening parental control and increasing belonging and companionship with peers.

Early Adulthood

During early adulthood, individuals are mostly autonomous and striving to seek intimacy, attempting to work on vocational choices, and are keen to attain success. Moving into adulthood also entails marriage, becoming parents, and setting up a family. With new relationships come new roles and responsibilities, and the developmental tasks of adulthood demand adjustments and a balance between work and family for both males and females.

Middle Adulthood

By this time, most people are masters in their professions, and may take leadership positions. In their personal lives, too, individuals provide direction to children, who are now moving towards independence and need emotional support. This period often coincide with feelings of separation, as children leave their homes. In the Indian context, couples also have to care for ageing parents. At times, individuals may be caught between intergenerational relationships, either of contestation or solace and companionship.

Late Adulthood

Individuals adjust to decreasing physical strength and remodel their lives with the onset of retirement. Contemporary social norms also confer senior citizen status to individuals, with some benefits in public spaces, rules and facilities. However, with increasing longevity and good health, most individuals continue to work and be a part of the economic workforce.

Box 1.3 Ageing

In recent times, life expectancy has increased due to changes in lifestyle and advancements in healthcare. Longevity (*dhirghaayu* in Hindi) is synonymous with life expectancy, that is, the average age that people live up to in a particular community. In India, there has been a considerable leap in life expectancy since independence, from 35 years to 65.5 years in 2011. Life expectancy depends not so much on genes as on environmental factors. In pre-industrial times, there were more infant deaths and more people died from accidents, disease and malnutrition. Before the twentieth century, healthcare was not very advanced.

It was common to hear of deaths from tuberculosis, which is almost fully treatable now. More women died in childbirth. The positive changes in health and well-being have increased the number of active working years for men and women. Sixty is now the age for senior citizens, and the retirement age in many professions has been raised.

Source: Asha Singh.

DEVELOPMENTAL TASKS: SIGNIFICANCE AND MASTERY

The idea of developmental expectations is crucial for guiding parents and teachers. An absence of expected behaviours can signal a need to probe further and assist the child. Developmental tasks have been listed in detail by Havighurst (1948) and Gessel and Ilg (1948). Each period has certain socially expected behaviours in relation to biological maturity.

The importance of developmental tasks is three-fold. First, it guides caregivers with a pattern of what children should be doing at particular ages. Second, developmental tasks set the goals to be achieved, and serve to motivate children to reach that potential. Third, the tasks predict the behaviours that need to be promoted in the future. It should be remembered that individual children will have their own pace; however, certain universal norms will facilitate societal expectations.

It is also important to ensure that age-related behaviours occur as expected, as the child can then move to the next level. For example, if the child has mastered bowel control or has moved on to solid food, the entry to early childhood programmes is easy. In the case of delayed adjustment, caregivers need to facilitate development through appropriate interventions.

Box 1.4 A. Havighurst's Developmental Task Theory

Robert Havighurst emphasised that learning is basic, and continues throughout the lifespan. Growth and development occurs in six stages.

Developmental Tasks of Infancy and Early Childhood:

1. Learning to walk.
2. Learning to take solid foods
3. Learning to talk
4. Learning to control the elimination of bodily wastes
5. Learning sex differences and sexual modesty
6. Forming concepts and learning language to describe social and physical reality
7. Getting ready to read.

Middle Childhood:

1. Learning the physical skills necessary for ordinary games.
2. Building wholesome attitudes towards oneself as a growing organism
3. Learning to get along with age-mates
4. Learning an appropriate masculine or feminine social role
5. Developing fundamental skills in reading, writing and calculating
6. Developing concepts necessary for everyday living
7. Developing a conscience, morality, and a scale of values
8. Achieving personal independence
9. Developing attitudes towards social groups and institutions

Developmental Tasks of Adolescence:

1. Achieving new and more mature relations with age-mates of both sexes
2. Achieving a masculine or feminine social role
3. Accepting one's physique and using the body effectively
4. Achieving emotional independence from parents and other adults
5. Preparing for marriage and family life
6. Preparing for an economic career
7. Acquiring a set of values and an ethical system as a guide to behaviour; developing an ideology
8. Desiring and achieving socially responsible behaviour.

Developmental Tasks of Early Adulthood

1. Selecting a mate
2. Achieving a masculine or feminine social role
3. Learning to live with a marriage partner
4. Starting a family
5. Rearing children
6. Managing a home
7. Getting started in an occupation
8. Taking on civic responsibility
9. Finding a congenial social group.

Box 1.4 contd.

Box 1.4 contd.

Developmental Tasks of Middle Age

1. Achieving adult civic and social responsibility
2. Establishing and maintaining an economic standard of living
3. Assisting teenaged children to become responsible and happy adults
4. Developing adult leisure-time activities
5. Relating oneself to one's spouse as a person
6. Accepting and adjusting to the physiological changes of middle age
7. Adjusting to aging parents.

Developmental Tasks of Later Maturity

1. Adjusting to decreasing physical strength and health
2. Adjusting to retirement and reduced income
3. Adjusting to the death of a spouse
4. Establishing an explicit affiliation with one's age group
5. Meeting social and civil obligations
6. Establishing satisfactory physical living arrangements.

Source: http://faculty.mdc.edu.

INTERVENTIONS FOR OPTIMAL DEVELOPMENT

There is a range for development in each stage. For example, all children may not begin to walk at one specific age, but it should happen between nine months to 14 months. In case the child does not attempt movement, s/he can be helped through assistance with activities and objects. Similarly, if the child does not communicate, efforts can be made to enhance participation. Research indicates that early detection and intervention is useful for reversing the impact of developmental delays. Being alert to children's actions and responses is a primary feature of a responsive environment, which can foster optimal development.

Basic Principles of Development

There is a pattern in the way competencies, such as physical skills, language, or even thinking, are acquired. While all babies might look alike, people become different as they grow and mature. Research has shed light on the varying aspects of developmental interrelationships. Let us try and understand the focal issues.

Development is Multidimensional and Integrated

Children develop physically from a supine to a prone position, learn to crawl, and finally learn to stand and walk. At the same time, they learn and absorb information about the world, and communicate distress and express satisfaction. They develop social attachment and relationships. As human babies develop mobility skills through physical development, their senses teach them about sounds and visuals, helping them to develop cognitive skills. With advancing mobility, their access to the physical world enlarges, and they are able to move towards sounds and objects and communicate through basic language.

As they acquire more language, they strengthen their memory and cognitive maps, which are impacted by their physical independence. They initially express discomfort by crying, but soon learn to use words to convey emotions. Attachment initiates social development, and it is in the context of different social interactions that children and individuals develop the appropriate sociality and communication skills.

There are many domains of development; development is multi-disciplinary as well as interdependent.

Heredity and Environment

The debate between nature (genes) and nurture (social experiences and features of the environment) has persisted for long. However, if genes solely shaped behaviour, it would be difficult to explain how rich children become thieves or delinquents. If only experience guided development, it might be hard to explain why certain children excel in academics or the arts. Studies on identical twins reared apart with control and experimental inputs have been inconclusive in isolating nature or nurture factors. Contemporary belief supports the fact that human beings have certain innate capacities—language, thought, building relationships—and must be allowed the optimal exposure to develop these potentials.

The consequences of the interplay between what one inherits and how processes of maturation can be enhanced or slowed are many. A baby born with a perfectly standard physical constitution might become malnourished and have her/his growth retarded, due to a poor diet emerging from poverty, ill health, and/or lack of proper healthcare. On the other hand, a baby with a low birth weight will become healthy with adequate nutrition, physical care and stimulation. The critical factor is how heredity and environment interact, and how they can be regulated for optimal development.

Box 1.5 Society Mirrors Theoretical Issues

Bollywood has popularised the theme of *mele mein kho gaye*—twins or siblings separated in huge fairs. Invariably, the separated children find themselves in two different social contexts, which lead to these siblings emerging as the symbols of hero and anti-hero. The films do not focus on the nature-nurture debate, but indicate the role of environmental factors on development and personality. Traces of genetic material function to remould personality into a socially accepted direction.

Source: Asha Singh.

Development is Continuous and Discontinuous

There are different theoretical perspectives with regard to patterns in development. One view holds that growth is continuous, with slow and gradual changes. The continuous progress in physical skills and language does indicate gradual change. However, the stages of development also bring in certain discontinuities in form and pace, such as during periods of adolescence and puberty. Many psychologists now recognise the role of both aspects, and how the stages predict behaviour and assist in providing optimal environmental responses.

Development is Cumulative

Individual experiences and developmental issues at different points have a cumulative effect. Neglect in early years can impact how people form relationships in later life. Longitudinal research has shown that interventions during early childhood impacted academic performance, and showed lower figures on divorce and employment patterns. While the importance of a happy childhood is supported by theory and research, people denied one can be helped to overcome their difficulties by identifying the roots of their distress.

Box 1.6 Fear of Light: Lingering Memory of Pain

One boy reported a fear of light. He was unable to explain why no other form of light except for a torch-like beam evoked pain and fear, and described it to his mother. After many dialogues on the nature of the fear, the mother recalled that as a baby, the boy had had a long surgery. The light was associated with pain, and perhaps with the denial of human touch over a length of time. After this talk with his mother, the boy was able to overcome his fear.

Source: Asha Singh.

Development is Variable

Growth is multi-dimensional; growth is also uneven, in that not all dimensions develop at the same pace. One individual may have an edge in physical development, with language skills developing at another pace. It is quite common to see mobility in infants before they begin to express themselves verbally.

Development Regulates Individual Differences

Just as growth and development have their own trajectory, each individual has her/his own pace and path of development. Two-year-olds may present varying statuses in development. There may also be gender differences, which become visible during middle childhood as pre-pubertal characteristics. There is a range in development often termed 'averages', which serve as a reference point to check behaviour traits. One has to exercise caution while stating averages, as there can be a wide range in individual development. Therapists, on their part, make a note of milestones to identify any developmental delays.

Development is Influenced by Culture

Children in different communities develop varying skills, depending on what is valued. Communities differ in the way they organise childcare at different ages, the behaviours they consider appropriate, and in their disciplinary practices. For example, there are different sleeping patterns for infants. In most Indian families, babies sleep with their mothers, while in Western cultures babies sleep in different rooms. The notion of the *palna* or crib is not new in Indian culture, but the crib is always placed in close proximity to adult caregivers.

Stability and Change

Development fosters change, which may follow the cycles of stability followed by a new growth cycle. This is highlighted by the rapid pace of learning and change in early childhood, which transforms to slow changes during middle childhood. Adolescence again fosters a growth spurt.

METHODS OF RESEARCH IN HUMAN DEVELOPMENT

The human mind has been curious about the way children develop different, complex skills, especially since no other species has such a long period of dependency. In the context of India, Tulsidas and Surdas have written poetic descriptions of the childhoods of mythological figures like Rama and Krishna. Such generalised narratives resonate with more specific accounts of childhood in other parts of the world. Charles Darwin, working on a detailed study of biological diversity and inter-linkages, captured in his theory of evolution, wrote detailed observations of his children in the form of Baby Biographies.

Some theoretical descriptions have provided glimpses into the understandings of human behaviour, based on the testing of assumptions through observation and other measures. Theories investigated the influences on children or relationships in the context of childhood. Swiss psychologist Jean Piaget prompted a focus on the agency of the child, and her/his unique mental processes during childhood. Piaget improved on the idea of baby biographies and presented a systematic and more scientific procedure to recording childhood actions. The following section will discuss some of the ways of studying behaviour, and the applicability of specific techniques to research questions.

Research and the Study of Human Development

The human mind is curious about events and phenomena, especially those that are surprising and unfamiliar, people's interaction patterns, or changes in behaviour. Parents often feel that children are not reading enough, or teachers observe that parents are not taking enough interest. Such observations would remain speculations till a systematic examination could be built as evidence in support. A conclusion can only be arrived at after collecting information, or data. These facts, collected from a sample, would be categorised and analysed, and a conclusion arrived at. This process of investigation and deriving inference from a body of facts and figures comprises research. Research can be of many kinds, with several methods of collecting data, referred to as techniques of studying human behaviour.

Types of Research Design

A study is conducted on a group of people based on the research questions. Participants are selected from sections of social groups, depending on the nature of the problem.

Cross-sectional Research

This is conducted at a particular time to study a specific variable with people of different ages, who are matched for all features such as socio-economic status, educational background and ethnicity. The differences can be attributed to age, as the groups are matched on all other factors. This type of research is quick, as the data is gathered at one point in time.

Longitudinal Research

This is a study of variables over time, conducted on a set of people. Data is gathered at the beginning, and the sample followed over time. Data continues to be collected from the same set of participants at different points. Although such studies are expensive and difficult to sustain, they provide in-depth information about changes over time.

Case Study

An in-depth study of individuals, groups or institutions using multiple methods is referred to as the Case Study approach. This approach can use standardised as well as other techniques of study.

Experimental Design

Research can also be conducted in controlled situations, somewhat like a laboratory. This design notes the reaction or response to specific stimuli, such as watching children's movements, and verbal and non-verbal responses to a television show. In experimental design, there sometimes can be a comparison between two or more groups, where each group may get different treatment under similar conditions. The groups are classified according to the specific variables introduced (or not introduced). For example, there may be two groups; one group is the control group that does not receive the intervention, while the other group does, and is called the experimental group.

Techniques of Study

Once the design of the study is decided, it is important to identify the methods or techniques of gathering data. Human beings can be studied in many different ways. These methods have been derived from ordinary, everyday experiences, such as talking and watching other people. However, the difference in scientific study is that we use systematic, reliable, standardised, and valid methods of studying people.

Systematic study: The methods of data collection need to be scientific and appropriate to the questions under investigation.

Reliability: Implies that on repeated use, methods should give consistent or stable results. Therefore, when we conclude something from a method, it is not because of the lack of stability in the tool.

Validity: The tool should assess or measure what it is supposed to measure and not something else. A test of intelligence should be meaningful for intelligence as a concept, and not for some other quality.

Standardisation: This is the procedure of testing a tool on several individuals before using it in any study.

Selecting a Tool

Once the basic design is decided, the next step is to understand and identify the method of data collection. The technique of study would be determined by the age, educational background, and nature of the research problem. For example, infant studies would rely more on observation, while a large-scale investigation of educational practices can receive substantial information through a questionnaire. The interview method is critical to understanding relationships, as the nuances of interactions cannot be gathered through written methods. Similarly, the attitudes and choices of illiterate populations can only be gathered through interviews.

Interview is a technique that uses face-to-face conversation to gather data. It entails in-depth conversation guided by certain objectives. One person (interviewer) questions the other (interviewee) on certain issues, and then draws conclusions from these conversations. Interviews can be structured (questions are pre-determined) or unstructured (flexible), or semi-structured (in-between). The 'interview schedule' is the list of questions used for interviewing, and 'interview guide' is the term given to the list of areas used for an unstructured interview.

The steps in constructing and conducting an interview are:

1. Decide on an issue that you want to study and look for a suitable title.
2. List out the important areas on this issue that need investigation.
3. Write out questions and word them carefully and simply, in the order of simple to more complex.
4. Prepare an introductory passage for the respondent to explain your purpose.
5. Try out the questions before conducting the final interview to ensure that the wording is valid. Try to use a conversational approach.
6. Take some time to make the respondent feel comfortable in your presence. This is also called rapport-formation.
7. Conduct the interview in a cordial manner.
8. Thank the respondent, and wind up the interview politely.
9. The interview can be audio-recorded or noted. Audio-recordings are more accurate and need to be transcribed. Transcription is the procedure of playing back the tape and writing out the responses. When not using a recording device, care should be taken to keep accurate notes. It is advisable in such cases to write out the detailed interview responses as soon as the interview is finished.
10. Analyse the interview responses.
11. Draw conclusions from the interview/s.

Types of Interview

Structured: In its simplest form, a structured interview involves one person asking another person a list of pre-determined questions with a predefined set of answers about a carefully selected topic.

Semi-structured interviews are conducted with a fairly open framework, which allows for focused, conversational, two-way communication. They can be used to both give and receive information. It contains a set flexible questions that can be used as a guide.

Unstructured: An informal discussion that has no strict guidelines, allowing the discussion to be open and not necessarily concise in its nature.

Advantages:

1. Interview is a powerful technique for studying in-depth issues.
2. Questions can be re-worded or repeated in case they are not understood correctly.
3. The interviewer and interviewee can proceed at their own speed.
4. Doubts can be clarified and further questioning can proceed in case the need arises.

Disadvantages:

1. Requires intensive training.
2. Sometimes, writing and recording can make a person feel conscious.
3. Sometimes, the face-to-face conversation can make a person uncomfortable, especially when questions are intimate in nature.

Precautions:

1. The questions should be carefully constructed.
2. The interview should not be too long.
3. Care should be taken to establish rapport, to make the person feel comfortable.
4. Ensure that you have informed the interviewee of the confidentiality of her/his answers.

Questionnaire

The questionnaire is a technique that also uses questioning as a strategy to gather opinions; however, these are always in written form. A method used for collecting data, the questionnaire is a set of written questions that calls for responses on the part of individual(s) or the subject(s), and may be self-administered or group-administered. The questionnaire is a very concise, pre-planned set of questions to elicit information about feelings, beliefs, experiences, perceptions, or attitudes on a selected topic.

Steps in conducting a questionnaire:

1. Since it is a written form, in addition to the formulation of questions, we need to provide a written introduction and instructions to the respondent.
2. The sequence of questions and the wording has to be done carefully.
3. The rest of the steps are the same as the interview.

4. Can use both closed-ended (limited choice or multiple-choice answers) or open-ended questions.

Advantages:

1. Less-time intensive: Expenses for travel and the time taken to train interviewers and send them for interviews are reduced by using questionnaires.
2. Information can be collected from a large number of individuals.
3. Uniformity of questions: Each respondent receives the same set of questions, phrased in exactly the same way. Questionnaires may therefore yield data that is more comparable than information obtained through an interview.
4. Standardisation: If the questions are highly structured and the conditions under which they are answered controlled, then the questionnaire could become standardised.
5. The questionnaire is quick to conduct.
6. A lot of data can be gathered in a relatively short period of time.

Disadvantages:

1. Can only be conducted with literate respondents.
2. No scope for clarifying meanings or provide explanations.
3. No scope for follow-up questions.
4. Interpretation requires training, and can sometimes misrepresent people's views.
5. Low return rates.
6. Informant may not answer questions.

Precautions:

1. The wording, sequence of questions, and instructions have to be carefully prepared.
2. Confidentiality must be ensured.
3. Pre-testing must be done.
4. Blank spaces must be provided.

Table 1.1. Differences between Questionnaire and Interview

	Interview	**Questionnaire**
1	Takes place in a face-to-face situation	Administered through a printed form
2	Except for infants and young children, can be used with everybody	Can only be used with a literate population
3	It is a time-consuming method	Easy to administer, but the return rate may be low
4	Since it is time-consuming, it is useful only with a selected population	Can be administered to a large section
5	The analyses of responses is complex	Relatively easy to analyse, and responses are received in pre-defined categories
6	The meaning of questions can be clarified to the interviewee in a face-to-face situation	The subjects make their own interpretation since they cannot clarify doubts
7	It is possible to have an in-depth understanding about the subject	Questionnaire limits the responses of the subjects, since it is close-ended
8	The subjects may give only socially desirable responses	The anonymity while answering questionnaires allows subjects to be more honest
9.	Constructing an interview schedule is relatively easy	Construction of close-ended question is time-consuming and complex

Source: Adapted from Students' Record Books.

Observation

Observation is a useful technique in studying young children, and can also be used as a supplement to other techniques. It refers to the systematic watching of the activities of the person being observed. In observations, it is important to plan the procedure beforehand to ensure good results. Observations can be of various types, which can include time-sampling, event-sampling or specimen description. Observation is a technique that involves directly observing behaviour with the purpose of describing it. To observe means to examine an object, an individual, a group of people, or an event, with all the senses. The recording of observations may take many forms, from simple and casual to exact and sophisticated. Some examples of the methods of recording include:

Time-sampling: This requires taking short, uniform time periods to observe and note down children's behaviour. A checklist can also be used to guide observations.

Event sampling: Observation of a specific behaviour, such as aggression or language or social interaction.

Specimen description: Narrative about a single event or situation, with details of all behaviours.

Checklist: A list against which the teacher (or parent or any other adult) checks the behaviours or traits observed during the period of observation. An observer may observe an activity or an event and then complete a checklist on whether key behaviours have taken place.

Specimen description: Detailed notes on an identified situation, recorded while the behaviour is occurring. It is often aided by video or audio recordings, and is used to discover cause-and-effect relationships in individual children's behaviour, to analyse classroom management, etc. When using specimen description, the observer records the student's behaviour and all events antecedent and subsequent to that behaviour. The observer might also write notes on everything that happens in her/his presence. More sophisticated recording may involve audio-visual devices.

Participant and non-participant observation: Participant observation takes place when an observer participates with the people and in the events s/he is observing. Non-participant observation occurs when an observer observes events without interacting with the person(s) being observed.

Structured or unstructured observations: Non-participant observation may be further classified as structured or unstructured.

The aim of unstructured observation is to observe and record behaviour in a holistic manner, without the use of a pre-determined guide. Structured observation, on the other hand, refers to a technique in which an observer observes events using a guide that has been planned in advance. Events in structured observation are recorded according to an observation guide. The observer is not involved in the activities being observed, but records them as inconspicuously as possible.

Advantages of the observation method:

1. Provides direct information about the behaviour of individuals and groups.
2. You know the situation is real and not artificially set up.
3. Can observe things that may cause the behaviour, which is not possible in a lab.
4. Observation allows for watching behaviour, actions and reactions in natural settings.
5. Generally, can develop a holistic perspective.

Disadvantages

1. Expensive and time-consuming.
2. Selective perception of observer may distort data.
3. Investigator has little control over the situation.
4. Behaviour or set of behaviours observed may be atypical/not normal.
5. Results can change if the subject becomes aware of being observed.
6. The observer may not be able to note all the behaviours that occur.

Factors to be kept in mind while observing:

1. Note down the duration, date and place of observation, and information about the subject.
2. Note as many details as possible by recording the subject's behaviour as well as context.
3. Record behaviours as they occur.
4. Do not write interpretations.

5. Respect the person being observed, and do not disturb her/him or disrupt their activities.

Autobiography

An autobiography, from the Greek *auton*, 'self', *bios*, 'life' and *graphein*, 'write', is a biography, or life story, written by the subject. One of the more innovative ways of working with children and adults can be using this technique of self-description. These self-reports or auto sketches can be categorised within sub-themes for analysis. Participants can be given simple instructions.

An autobiography is information about one's own life written by that one person. When writing your own autobiography, use interesting facts to explain as much about yourself as you can.

A person writing an autobiography can use a variety of documents and viewpoints; or an autobiography may be based entirely on the writer's memory.

Who are you in life?
The best way to start an autobiography is to state your name. When writing this paragraph, you usually explain the type of person you are. Use facts about yourself such as: Have you won any awards? What type of awards have you won? Did you finish school? Do you plan on going to college? Who are the members of your family?

What does life mean to you?
This is now your second paragraph. Here, you should state how you see life—that is, what life means to you. Are you happy or sad? Do you have a lot of friends, or just a few? How do you make your school days go by? What are your favourite places?

What is your outlook on the future?
In this paragraph, you should explain what you think your future will be like. Pick a year, and explain how it will be through your eyes. Where will you be? How will you be living? Will you be married? Who are the people who have inspired you?

Conclusion
The conclusion is the last, and important, paragraph of your autobiography. In the conclusion, you reflect on the experience of writing an autobiography.

Drawings as a Method of Research

Children's drawings develop from scribbles to images of objects, people and events. Children can be asked to draw on themes like the family, market, my pet, or simple situations from their everyday lives. The researcher or teacher can simply ask the child to describe their drawings and make a note of their verbatims as they talk.

Uses / Advantages

1. Children gain confidence and develop proficiency in communication.
2. As they describe, they convey their feelings and perceptions of people, places and objects.
3. Like role play, there is freedom to express, rather than simply respond to specific questions.

Standardised Tests

A standardised test is reliable, valid and based on norms. It is a test administered and scored in a standard manner. The tests are designed in such a way that the questions, conditions for administering, scoring procedures, and interpretations are standardised.

Validity: All tests are designed to measure something. If the test measures what it is intended to measure, then we can say that the test is valid (or has validity). In psychology, tests are usually judged according to their validity and reliability. The accuracy, or usefulness, of a test is known as its validity.

Reliability: Reliability is the consistency of your measurement, or the degree to which an instrument measures the same way each time it is used under the same condition and with the same subjects. In short, it refers to the repeatability of your measurement. A measure is considered reliable if a person's score on the same test given twice is similar.

Transcription

Transcription may refer to the conversion of spoken words into written language. Every utterance is captured and recorded. That includes all uhms, ahs, false starts and stutters, repetitions, distracting speech patterns, ('you know', 'like'), and remarks such as 'right' and 'yeah'. Also included are pauses, laughter, crying, interruptions, personal comments, external noises; in short, everything we hear! Unclear speech is indicated in the transcription.

Role Play

In role play, different individuals (or professional actors) assume a role, playing themselves or another person in a given situation or scenario, based on the objectives. It is a method for exploring the issues involved in complex social situations.

Those involved in role play are expected to 'act out' the demands of the particular situation or role. Play situations may be reality-based or imaginative, and may range from simple to complex.

Application/use/advantages:

1. To gain new knowledge and appreciate different points of view and perspectives, based on the role(s) being played. Also, to know oneself.
2. Increases the development of empathy through substituted experience.
3. It may be used to train professionals. It helps to develop and practice new skills and behaviours, such as improving communication, and also to integrate knowledge in action by addressing problems, exploring alternatives, and seeking novel and creative solutions.
4. Role playing is the best way to develop the skills of initiative, communication, problem-solving, self-awareness, and working cooperatively in teams.
5. It helps in exploring solutions and resolving conflict.
6. Provides anticipatory preparation for emotionally challenging events.
7. Facilitates the identification of critical features of complex human interactions.
8. Quick, cheap, and easily available resource.

SUMMARY

- This chapter defined the concept of 'human development', and the various aspects to the study of Human Development and Childhood Studies, as encountered in higher education in India. Viewing childhood in a historical context, it discussed the changing notions of childhood across the world, before positioning the study of human development within the discipline of Home Science. The chapter also provided an overview of the various theories underlying Child Development—psychoanalytic, cognitive and behavioural—and provided a detailed discussion of the position of the child in an Indian context. The different stages of development, from conception to old age, are then discussed, followed by the research methodology used in the study of human development.

KEY TERMS

Stages of development – Age-related periods of growth

Domains of development – Different areas of development and learning

Contexts of development – Social influences and circumstances of individuals

Principles of development – Universal features for growth and development

Techniques of study – Different tools for studying behaviour

Milestones – Acquisition of skills in different domains with maturation

Developmental tasks – Basic skills to be mastered for further development, and expected by society.

EXERCISES

1. Identify local stories about children. Discuss the content for:
   The plot
   Characters and their roles
   Presentation of gender roles
2. Are children only raised to be obedient, or is there a recognition of their thoughts and points of view?
3. What is the view of children in India?
4. Interview three school teachers and three parents of college-going students, and three college-going students about Home Science.
5. What does the subject Home Science mean to you?
6. What is the relevance of Home Science in the technologically advanced modern world?
7. Do many students opt for Home Science?
8. Talk to a friend about parents, children and families.
9. What do parents talk about with their children?
   What kind of dialogues would be common?
   Is there a difference that comes in as children grow?
10. How would you analyse the responses to derive an understanding of what parents think of their children, and what children think of their parents?
11. Identify two families from different social groups—for example, a vegetable seller or a *dhobi*. Develop a set of questions to ask, and from what you see, describe details about 'A day in the life of the child in the family'. State if any behaviour is typical to the group, and those common to all children.
12. Does the lifecycle of a butterfly indicate discontinuity or continuity in development? Discuss.
13. Learn about care during pregnancy from a family elder. In your opinion, are families very strict with too many rules?
    Discuss your conversations.
14. Describe the age range for the following stages of development:
    Infancy: ____________________
    Preschool years: ____________________
    Middle childhood: ____________________
    Adolescence: ____________________
15. How would you relate infancy, preschool and early childhood years?

REFERENCES

Aries, P., *Centuries of Childhood: A Social History of Family Life*, New York: Vintage Books, 1962.

Berk, L. E., *Development through the Lifespan*, New Delhi: Pearson Education, 2009.

Corsaro, W. A., *The sociology of Childhood*, California: Sage Publications, 1997.

Erikson, E. H., *Childhood and Society*, New York: Norton, 1950. Available at www.simplypsychology.org/Erik-Erikson.html.

Freud, Sigmund, *Three Essays on the Theory of Sexuality*, Basic Books, 1975 [1905]. Available at Staferla.free.fr/Freud/%20complete%20works.pdf (accessed 10 December 2014).

Gesell, A. and Frances Ilg, *The Child from Five to Ten*, New York: Harper and Brothers, 1948.

Havighurst, R. J., *Developmental Tasks and Education*, Chicago: University of Chicago Press, 1948. Available at www.peoi.org/Courses/Coursesen/nursepractice/ch/ch6ahtml.

Heckhausen, J. and J. Krueger, 'Developmental expectations for the self and most other people: Age grading in three functions of social comparison', *Developmental Psychology*, 29, 1993, pp. 539–48.

Kakar, S., *The Inner World*, New Delhi: Oxford University Press, 1980.

Mead, M., *Coming of Age in Samoa*, New York: William Marrow & Co., 2001 [1928]. Available at http://www.biography.com/people/margaret-mead-9404056.

NCERT, 'Position Paper: National Focus Group on Early Childhood Education (3.6)', New Delhi: National Council of Educational Research and Training, 2006.

Rice, P., *Human Development: A Life Span Approach*, 2e, New Jersey: Prentice-Hall Inc., 1995.

Santrock, J. W., *Child Development*, 6e, Wisconsin: Brown and Benchmark Publishers, 1994.

Online sources

http://psychology.about.com/od/developmentalpsychology/a/devresearch.htm

http://lrrpublic.cli.det.nsw.edu.au/lrrSecure/Sites/LRRView/7401/documents/theories_outline.pdfReferences

2

Human Reproduction: Characteristics and Significance

HIGHLIGHTS

- The onset of human life, and steps and stages in human reproduction.
- The different stages in prenatal development and the need for care during pregnancy.
- Precautions to be taken during pregnancy, as well as cultural restrictions or taboos.
- Possible impact of external detrimental influences on the growing foetus.
- Care of the reproductive health of the woman, the role of the State, family and reproductive health of male partners.

WHAT IS HUMAN REPRODUCTION?

The study of human development begins with reproduction. Reproduction is significant as a process of procreation and preservation of the species. Human reproduction is embedded in the biological processes of maturation and perpetuation of the human species, and commonly establishes ties of belonging, significant for adults, children, and the larger society. Each child is an individual in her/his own right. The genetic make-up of the child interacts with the environment in distinctive ways to create a unique personality. Families, through their child-rearing practices and social customs, support the developmental process. Through this process of socialisation, the child's potential for physical, motor, language, cognition, and emotional development unfolds.

The birth of the newborn after 40 weeks in the womb is central to the process of human reproduction. As an individual, the child owes her/his identity to the continued developmental process that begins with the union of egg and sperm, and the sequence of embryonic and foetal stages within the womb and through life. At birth, the child gets a distinctive identity, defined by the fact of being human. The right to a name and nationality is provided to every child by the State, and the social location of the family, caste, class, and gender add features to being 'someone'. In the Indian and Hindu philosophical framework, the karma accrued from actions in one's previous life would also contribute to this identity.

The processes of human procreation take place entirely inside a woman's body; sometimes, though, it requires a little human intervention. The first 'outside the body' fertilisation of the human egg by human sperm in 1969 saw the beginnings of partial control in human hands. In-vitro fertilisation (IVF), popularly known as 'test tube babies' has been responsible for over a million births worldwide, and has made procreation possible for infertile couples. The initiation of a pregnancy in-vitro has allowed for the manipulation and alteration of procreation in many ways: (*i*) The early human embryo can be frozen and stored for later use; (*ii*) The early embryo can be disaggregated into its separate embryonic cells, and introduced into women other than the donor of the egg.

New knowledge and understanding of human development through research on human embryos has enhanced the appreciation of how nature works, as well as expanded the facilities that can help infertile couples have a child.

> **Box 2.1 Test Tube Babies/In-Vitro Fertilisation (IVF)**
>
> On 25 July 1978, Louise Joy Brown, the world's first successful 'test-tube' baby, was born in Great Britain. Before her birth, women with fallopian tube blockages had no hope of becoming pregnant. Dr Robert G. Edward and Dr Patrick Steptoe created history by performing the world's first in-vitro fertilisation (IVF). In July 1978, Dr Subhash Mukhopadhyay, a Kolkata-based doctor, performed a similar feat in India. Durga, alias Kanupriya Agarwal, India's first (and the world's second) test-tube baby was born on 3 October 1978, just two months after Louise Brown. This achievement is considered one of the most important medical advances of the past century. This path-breaking step to control infertility constituted a base for the development of the IVF segment in India and the world over.

NORMAL REPRODUCTION

The appropriate functioning of four components of a woman's body—the brain, the ovary, the fallopian tube, and the uterus—determine normal reproduction. Every month, the brain sends out a signal from the pituitary gland by releasing a hormone, called the follicle-stimulating hormone (FSH), which stimulates the follicles to grow. Under the influence of FSH, a group of follicles begins to grow, and by the fifth day of the reproductive cycle, a single dominant follicle has already been selected. This dominant follicle may be either on the right or the left ovary. As it grows, the follicle produces an important steroid hormone called estrogen. Estrogen causes the lining of the uterus—called the endometrium—to thicken in anticipation of the eventual implantation of an embryo.

By mid-cycle, this follicle has grown to a diameter of 20–22 mm. At this time, the brain releases a second hormone, called luteinising hormone (LH), from the pituitary gland, which induces ovulation to take place. Approximately 36 hours after the LH surge, the follicle releases the egg. The fallopian tube catches the egg. However, if the fallopian tube fails to catch the egg, pregnancy cannot occur. During intercourse, tens of millions of sperm are deposited in the woman's vagina when her male partner ejaculates. While the egg is safely held within the fallopian tube, these sperm swim from the vagina into the cervix, through the uterus, and up into the fallopian tube, where fertilisation occurs.

Fertilisation

Human life begins as a single cell, formed when sperm from the male fertilises the egg from the female. Fertilisation normally takes place in the mother's fallopian tube, which connects the uterus with the ovary. The uterus is the size and shape of a large pear; it is made of muscle, and stretches to allow the baby's growth throughout the months of pregnancy. A woman has two tubes and two ovaries, one each on each side of her uterus. Each month, an ovary releases an egg called ovum, which passes slowly along the tube towards the womb. If the egg is not fertilised within 12–24 hours or so of being released, it dies. If the woman has sexual intercourse during the days of her monthly ovulation cycle (when an egg has been released from the ovary), then the sperm cells released by the male may travel up to the fallopian tube, and one may fertilise the egg. When fertilisation is completed and the nuclei of egg and sperm have combined, a new being comes into existence, and is capable of further development.

STAGES OF PRENATAL DEVELOPMENT

The process of prenatal development occurs in three main stages.

1. Germinal Stage: Zero to two weeks after conception
2. Embryonic Stage: Third to eighth week
3. Foetal Stage: Ninth week until birth

The Germinal Stage

The germinal stage begins with conception, when the sperm and egg cell unite in one of the two fallopian tubes, and lasts for **two weeks** till implantation in the uterine wall. The fertilised egg, known as a **zygote**, then moves towards the uterus, a journey that can take up to a week to complete. Cell division begins approximately 24 to 36 hours after conception.

The zygote first divides into two cells, then into four, eight, sixteen, and so on. The zygote travels through the fallopian tubes to the uterus. When the eight-cell point has been reached, the cells begin to differentiate and take on certain characteristics. As the cells multiply, they also separate into two distinctive masses: the outer cells will eventually become the placenta, while the inner cells will form the embryo. Cell division continues at a rapid rate, and the cells then develop into what is known as a **blastocyst**. The blastocyst is made up of three layers:

1. The **ectoderm** (which will become the skin and nervous system)
2. The **endoderm** (which will become the digestive and respiratory systems)
3. The **mesoderm** (which will become the muscle and skeletal systems).

Finally, the blastocyst arrives at the uterus and gets attached to the uterine wall, a process known as **implantation**.

During implantation, the cells nestle into the uterine lining and rupture tiny blood vessels. The connective web of blood vessels and membranes that forms between them will provide nourishment to the developing being for the next nine months. When implantation is successful, hormonal changes stop a woman's normal menstrual cycle and cause several other physical changes.

The Embryonic Stage

The beginning of the **third week** after conception marks the start of the embryonic period. By this time the mass of cells have started becoming a distinct human being. The embryo begins to divide into three layers, each of which will become an important body system. The neural tube forms approximately 22 days after conception. This tube will later develop into the central nervous system, including the spinal cord and the brain.

Around the fourth week, the head begins to form, followed by the eyes, nose, ears, and mouth. The cardiovascular system is where the earliest activity begins, as the blood vessel that will become the heart start to pulse. During the fifth week, buds that will form the arms and legs appear.

The embryo has all of the basic organs and parts—except the sex organs—by the time the **eighth week of development** has been reached. The embryo weight is one gram and the length one inch by the end of the embryonic stage, which functions as the stage of organogenesis (the organs are formed).

The Foetal Stage

The foetal stage begins during the **ninth week and lasts until birth**. The early body systems and structures established in the embryonic stage continue to develop. The neural tube develops into the brain, and the spinal cord and neurons form. Sex organs begin to appear during the third month of gestation. The foetus continues to grow in both weight and length; at this point, the foetus weighs around 85.04 gms or 3 ozs.

The end of the third month also marks the end of the first trimester of pregnancy. During the second trimester, or months four through six, the heartbeat grows stronger and other body systems become further developed. Fingernails, hair, eyelashes, and toenails form. Perhaps most noticeably, the foetus increases quite dramatically in size—about six times. The brain and central nervous system also become responsive during the second trimester. Around 28 weeks, the brain starts to mature much faster, with activity that greatly resembles that of a sleeping newborn.

From seven months until birth, the foetus continues to develop, put on weight, and prepare for life outside the womb. The lungs begin to expand and contract, preparing the muscles for breathing. While prenatal development usually follows this normal pattern, there are times when problems or deviations occur. The process of birth and complications that may follow are discussed in Chapter 3.

REPRODUCTIVE HEALTH AND SOCIAL BEHAVIOUR

Reproductive health is concerned with physical, social and mental well-being in all matters relating to the reproductive system at all stages of life. All men and women need to be aware of the factors that ensure a safe and healthy reproductive life. They must have information regarding safe sex, and matters relating to health and hygiene, especially with regard to sexual life. Men's intimate participation in sex and reproduction cannot be disputed. Yet for much of its history, the field has focused almost exclusively on the fertility behaviour of women. Not much attention has been focused on men's roles and their implications for fertility and safe parenthood. Men's involvement has been in limited ways, often to ensure contraceptive continuation and acceptability, or to promote the diagnosis and treatment of sexually transmitted infections.

Research in reproductive health describes women's disadvantaged position without mentioning the role played by men. A growing body of ethnographic and anthropological qualitative research has been examining even more closely the impact of men—as individuals, as social gatekeepers, and as powerful family members who enforce cultural practices, often to the detriment of women's reproductive health. Gender inequities are widespread, and it is well-recognised that gender roles are strongly reinforced in cultural beliefs and practices. Notions of masculinity and femininity are outcomes of social construction, which shape sexuality, reproductive preferences and health practices. Ideas about manhood are deeply ingrained. From an early age, boys are often socialised into gender roles designed to keep men in a powerful and controlling position. Many believe that authoritarian behaviour towards girls and women is part of being a man.

Risk-taking and aggressive sexual behaviour on the part of young men are often commended by peers and condoned by society. These stereotypes harm both women and men, and corrode possibilities of establishing satisfying, mutually respectful relationships. Ideally, boys and young men should be encouraged to reflect upon and discuss issues surrounding masculinity, relationships and sexuality.

SIGNIFICANCE OF REPRODUCTIVE HEALTH

Reproductive Health of Adolescents in India

Adolescence is a period of increased risk-taking. Pubertal changes make adolescents physically different, and make teenagers socially and emotionally susceptible to the adult gaze, leading to self-consciousness. There is increased adult concern about reproductive health, which is accentuated in the absence of ways to impart reproductive information to pubertal youngsters. Compared to their male counterparts, female adolescents face disproportionate health concerns following puberty; foremost among these are early pregnancy and frequent childbearing. Male adolescents often lack a sense of shared responsibility for sexual and reproductive matters, and respect for reproductive choices. This keeps alive traditions in many developing countries that encourage early marriage, followed quickly by the birth of a child. Even where these influences are waning, lack of sexual and contraceptive knowledge, along with difficulty in obtaining contraceptives, result in continued early childbearing among adolescents.

Although adolescent males have as many health issues and concerns as adolescent females, they are much less likely to seek help from a parent, teacher, or a counsellor. This is likely related to both individual factors and to the system itself, which is not always encouraging; nor is it set up to provide comprehensive male healthcare.

The health of adolescent males and females is an important area. Although this is generally a physically and emotionally healthy group, there are significant healthcare issues, involving puberty, sexual health, risk behaviours, substance use, and mental health. These issues present challenges to parents, teachers and to the society at large, but also provide important opportunities to connect with young boys and girls, teach them about how their bodies work, reduce the incidence of risk-taking behaviours, and arrange for early intervention.

Reproductive Health

The World Health Organization (WHO) defines reproductive rights as follows:

> Reproductive rights rest on the recognition of the basic right of all couples and individuals to decide freely and responsibly the number, spacing and timing of their children and to have information to do so, and right to attain the highest standard of sexual and reproductive health. They also include the

right of all to make decisions concerning reproduction free of discrimination, coercion and violence.

Reproductive rights include some or all of the following rights:

1. Right to legal or safe abortion.
2. Right to control one's reproductive functions.
3. Right to access, in order to make reproductive choices free of coercion, discrimination and violence.
4. Right to access education about contraception and sexually transmitted diseases, and freedom from coerced sterilisation and contraception.
5. Right to protection from gender-based practices such as female and male genital mutilation.

Sound reproductive health is integral to the vision that every child is wanted, every birth is safe, every young person is free from HIV, and every girl and woman is treated with dignity. Implicit in this vision is the idea that men and women will be able to exercise their rights to information on, and access to, safe, affordable and acceptable methods of fertility regulation, as well as quality healthcare services. The latter will enable women to experience safe pregnancy and childbirth across the world.

Reproductive health programmes must place emphasis on improving the access to quality reproductive health services, delivered by gender-sensitive providers. The highest priority needs to be given to ensuring that women have access to skilled birth attendants, and that women who develop life-threatening complications during pregnancy, childbirth or post-partum can immediately access treatment at adequately-equipped facilities. Maternal deaths and disability can be reduced dramatically if every woman has access to health services throughout her lifecycle, especially during pregnancy and childbirth.

Socially Responsible Behaviour

Responsible behaviour towards reproductive health on the part of individuals is critical. In the changing social situation, young boys and girls often indulge in sexual activity with insufficient knowledge. Parents must talk to their children about the importance of reproductive healthcare. Social responsibility must be shared by other members of society, such as teachers, elders of the community, and doctors. Information about the dangers of irresponsible sex should be made available through public circulation, as well as greater dialogues. At the time of the first pregnancy, the history of the couple's reproductive health, including prior abortions, need to be placed before the doctor. Within a marriage, it is important to space children, keeping in mind the health of the woman.

The Importance of Family Planning

Inadequate reproductive healthcare for women results in high rates of unwanted pregnancy, unsafe abortions, and preventable death and injury as a result of pregnancy and childbirth. The involvement of men is an essential part of protecting women's reproductive health. Men, too, have reproductive health needs. The number of unwanted and closely spaced births can be drastically reduced by providing access to quality contraceptive services. It is vital that services be made available to women and men from lower-income groups, especially in rural areas, which are currently under-serviced. It also helps to protect them from health risks and facilitates their social participation, including employment.

Gender-sensitive programmes can address the dynamics of knowledge, power and decision-making in sexual relationships, between service providers and clients, and between community leaders and citizens. Reproductive healthcare should include the following components:

Family planning should have strong government support, and service providers who are well-trained, sensitive to cultural conditions, and friendly and sympathetic to the clients' needs. Services should be affordable and a choice of contraceptive methods should be made available. Counselling must ensure informed consent in contraceptive choice, privacy and confidentiality.

Abortion and Post-abortion Care. Abortion is an important public health issue. Family planning services ensure a reduction in unwanted pregnancies and prevent abortions. In circumstances where abortion is not against the law, quality health services should ensure safe abortion practices, and effective post-abortion care would significantly reduce maternal mortality rates.

Prevention and treatment of sexually transmitted diseases (STDs and HIV/AIDS). Both culture and biology predispose more women than men to STDs. The integration of family planning and STD/HIV/AIDS services within reproductive health services can reduce levels of STDs, including HIV/AIDS. Gender-based violence and its link to HIV transmission needs to be addressed.

Involvement of men in reproductive health programmes. Greater involvement of men in reproductive health decisions will give more power to women. Men can advance gender equality and improve their family's welfare by protecting their partners' health and supporting their choices (for example, adopting sexually responsible behaviour, communicating about sexual and reproductive health concerns and working together to solve problems, and considering adopting male methods of contraception); confronting their own reproductive health risks (learning how to prevent or treat sexually transmitted infections, impotence/infertility, sexual dysfunction, and violent or abusive tendencies); refraining from gender violence; practising responsible fatherhood; and promoting gender equality, health and education.

It becomes the responsibility of the governments to provide quality reproductive healthcare and protect individual reproductive rights, while being sensitive to local and cultural issues. There is an increased need for sensitisation of both the judiciary and the governments while protecting the reproductive rights of people with disabilities, especially in cases of mental illness.

Contraception

Not all contraceptive methods are appropriate for all situations, and the most appropriate method of birth control depends on a woman's overall health, age, frequency of sexual activity, number of sexual partners, desire to have children in the future, and family history of certain diseases. Individuals should consult their healthcare providers to determine which method of birth control is best for them.

Barrier Methods

Intended to prevent sperm from entering the uterus, the methods are removable and may be an option for women who cannot use hormonal methods of contraception. Types of barrier methods include:

Female condoms. These are thin, made of flexible plastic, and pouch-like. A portion of the condom is inserted into a woman's vagina before intercourse to prevent sperm from entering the uterus.

Diaphragms. This is a shallow, flexible cup made of latex or soft rubber, and is inserted into the vagina before intercourse, blocking sperm from entering the uterus. Spermicidal cream or jelly is used with a diaphragm.

Male condoms. This condom is a thin sheath that covers the penis and collects the sperm, preventing it from entering the woman's body.

Hormonal methods. Hormonal methods of birth control use hormones to regulate or stop ovulation, and prevent pregnancy. Depending on the types of hormones used, these pills can prevent ovulation, thicken the cervical mucus (which helps to block sperm from reaching the egg), or thin the lining of the uterus.

Combined oral contraceptives. Combined oral contraceptive pills (COCs) contain different combinations of the synthetic estrogens and progestins, and are given to interfere with ovulation. A woman takes one pill daily, preferably at the same time each day.

Emergency Contraceptive Pills (ECPs). ECPs are hormonal pills, taken either as a single dose or as two doses 12 hours apart, intended for use in the event of unprotected intercourse. If taken prior to ovulation, the pills can delay or inhibit ovulation for at least five days to allow the sperm to become inactive. Pregnancy can occur if the pills are taken after ovulation, or if there is subsequent semen exposure in the same cycle.

Intra-uterine Device (IUD). This is a small, T-shaped device that is inserted into the uterus to prevent pregnancy. An IUD can remain and function effectively for many years at a time.

A *copper IUD* releases a small amount of copper into the uterus, causing an inflammatory reaction that generally prevents sperm from reaching and fertilising the egg. If fertilisation of the egg does occur, the physical presence of the device prevents the fertilised egg from implanting into the lining of the uterus. Copper IUDs may remain in the body for 12 years.

Sterilisation is a permanent form of birth control that either prevents a woman from getting pregnant, or prevents a man from releasing sperm. The sterilisation procedure usually involves surgery, and these procedures are usually not reversible.

Vasectomy is a male surgical procedure that cuts, closes, or blocks the vas deferens. This procedure blocks the path between the testes and the urethra, and therefore the sperm cannot leave the testes and reach the egg. It can take as long as three months for the procedure to be fully effective. A back-up method of contraception is used until tests confirm that there is no sperm in the semen.

ENSURING SAFE MOTHERHOOD

Safe motherhood means ensuring that all women have access to the information and services they need to go safely through pregnancy and childbirth. However, this cannot be undertaken without the involvement of men, families and communities. It also means that women and men should have had good reproductive health from the onset of puberty. Safe sex, socially responsible behaviour, and the right to choose the timing of pregnancy are aspects of sound reproductive health. Discrimination and devaluing of women has had negative implications for women's health, reducing, for example, their timely access to health services during labour and delivery, their use of antiretroviral treatment to reduce mother-to-child transmission of HIV (because of fear of disclosure), or their ability to control the type and frequency of sexual practices, to initiate and refuse sex.

Gendered social expectations have many repercussions for women and men's reproductive health. Social norms favouring male children and promoting women's economic dependence on men, for example, contribute to high rates of fertility in many settings. An inability to negotiate sex, monogamy and condom use on equal terms results in women and girls globally being at high risk of unwanted pregnancy, illness and death from pregnancy-related causes, and sexually transmitted infections.

Combating sexually transmitted infections and the heterosexual spread of HIV is impossible without involving men. Efforts should be made to highlight men's shared responsibility and encourage their active participation in responsible parenthood, sexual and reproductive behaviour, including family planning; prenatal, maternal and child health; prevention of sexually transmitted diseases, including HIV; prevention of unwanted and high-risk pregnancies.

Let us describe facets of health before and during the reproductive cycle.

Maternal / Paternal Health before Conception

Sexual dysfunction refers to a problem during any phase of the sexual cycle that prevents the individual or the couple from experiencing satisfaction from sexual activity. Fortunately, most cases of sexual dysfunction are treatable.

Sexual dysfunction can be a result of a physical or a psychological problem.

- Physical causes: Many physical and/or medical conditions can cause problems with sexual function. These conditions include diabetes, heart and vascular (blood vessel) disease, neurological disorders, hormonal imbalances, chronic diseases such as kidney or liver failure, and alcoholism and drug abuse. In addition, the side effects of certain medicines, including some antidepressant medication, can affect sexual desire and function.
- Psychological causes: These include work-related stress and anxiety, concern about sexual performance, marital or relationship problems, depression, feelings of guilt, and the effects of a past sexual trauma.

Male infertility is caused by:

- Low sperm count or sperm quality
- Problems with the tubes carrying sperm
- Erection and ejaculation problems
- Inflamed testes
- Medical treatment, such as radiotherapy or surgery for a hernia, undescended testes or twisted testicles
- Working with chemicals or radiation
- Sexually transmitted infection
- Stress

- Age: Male fertility is thought to decline with age, although it is not known to what extent.

Common causes of *female infertility*:

1. Failure to Ovulate: The causes of failed ovulation can be categorised as follows:
   a. Hormonal problems
      - Failure to produce mature eggs
      - Malfunction of the hypothalamus
      - Malfunction of the pituitary gland
2. Scarred ovaries
3. Premature menopause
4. Follicle problems
5. Endometriosis
6. Behavioural factors
7. Diet and exercise
8. Smoking, alcohol, drugs
9. Environmental and occupational factors
10. Medical treatments and materials

Primary Risk Factors

Female Health Concerns

- Maternal age less than 20 years and over 35 years.
- Maternal under-nutrition, short stature, underweight (<40 kg)
  - o haemoglobin less than 8gms per 100ml
- Risk effects of chronic conditions such as diabetes mellitus
  - o hypothyroidism and thyrotoxicosis
- Inter-pregnancy interval of <24 months.
- Rhesus negative blood group
- Past obstetrical history of difficult deliveries, abortions, still births
  - o neonatal deaths, low birth weights or developmental defects

Prenatal Care and Counselling in High-Risk Pregnancies

Care During Pregnancy

Antenatal care refers to the regular medical checkups and health education given to a pregnant woman in order to make pregnancy safer, and reduce maternal morbidity and mortality. ANC is also necessary to screen signs of high-risk pregnancy and high-risk labour. The important components of antenatal care are outlined below.

Early registration: As soon as pregnancy is suspected, the first visit for the registration of a pregnant woman for Antenatal clinic (ANC) should take place. The first visit should take place in the first trimester (first three months of pregnancy). However, if a woman comes late in her pregnancy for registration, she should be registered, and care given to her according to the gestational age or stage of pregnancy.

The healthcare provider, with the help of various community-based functionaries such as Anganwadi worker (AWW), the Traditional Birth Attendant (TBA)/*Dai*, members of Mahila Mandals, self-help groups, the panchayat, and village health committees (who are likely to be aware of pregnant women in the village) should update the list and provide services.

Importance of early registration

- Assesses the health of the mother and obtains baseline information on blood pressure (BP), weight, etc.
- Helps the woman recall the date of her menstrual period.
- Screens for complications early and manage them appropriately by referral and where required.
- Helps the woman access facilities for an early and safe abortion if she does not want to continue with her pregnancy.

Weight: A pregnant woman's weight should be checked at each visit. Normally, a woman should gain 9–11 kg during her pregnancy. If the diet is not enough, and contains less than the required amount of calories, the woman might gain only 5–6 kg during her pregnancy.

An inadequate dietary intake can be suspected if the woman has gained less than 2 kg per month. She needs to be put on food supplementation. A low weight gain usually points towards intrauterine growth retardation, and results in a low birth-weight baby. She should be referred to the medical officer in this case.

Height: There is an association between maternal height and delivery outcome. In very short women, there is an increased risk due to a small pelvis. Hospital delivery is recommended for all women shorter than the average.

Respiratory Rate (RR): It is important to check RR, especially if the woman complains of breathlessness.

Blood pressure: Measuring the BP of a pregnant woman is important to rule out hypertensive disorders of pregnancy.

Examination of the abdomen: Abdominal examinations should be done to monitor the progress of pregnancy and foetal growth. It is important to know the foetal position and foetal presentation (whether head or bottom first) before a delivery.

Iron-folic acid (IFA) supplementation: Anaemia is common and dangerous during pregnancy. There is a need for increased requirements of iron during pregnancy. Women with severe anemia (hb<7g/dl), or those who have breathlessness and increased heart rate due to anaemia, should be started on a therapeutic dose of iron, and referred to a doctor.

Injection tetanus toxoid administration: Two doses of injection TT should be administered to a pregnant woman. This is important to prevent neonatal tetanus. The first dose of TT should be given after the first trimester, or as soon as the woman registers for ANC (whichever comes later). The TT injection is not to be given in the first trimester of pregnancy. The second dose is to be given one month after the first, but at least one month before the Expected Date of Delivery (EDD).

Promotion of Maternal Nutrition

The pregnant woman's diet should provide for the needs of (*i*) the foetus, (*ii*) the mother's health, (*iii*) physical strength required during labour, and (*iv*) successful lactation.

- Proteins are essential for the growth of the foetus. The pregnant woman should take plenty of milk, dal, eggs, fish, poultry, and meat. If vegetarian, she needs to increase her intake of different cereals, pulses and nuts.
- Iron is very important for making the baby's blood, and to reduce the incidence of anaemia. Calcium is necessary for making the baby's bones and teeth. The best source of calcium is milk. Calcium is also present in ragi and bajra.
- Vitamins are important for pregnant women. She should have plenty of vegetables, especially dark green leafy vegetables and fruits.

Hygiene, Exercise and Adequate Rest

Physically demanding work during pregnancy can contribute to problems, such as miscarriage, premature labour, or underweight infants, especially if a woman is not eating enough.

A pregnant woman should also get as much rest as possible. She should lie down for an hour or so during the day, and sleep between six and 10 hours every night.

Physical hygiene reduces the chances of infections or illnesses. It is especially important to take care of the breasts and the genital area by washing them often with clean water; harsh chemicals or detergents are not necessary, and can be harmful. Loose clothes made of light cotton are ideal during pregnancy.

Adequate Delivery Assistance

Birth Preparedness

- All pregnant women must be encouraged to opt for an institutional delivery. Any complication can develop during delivery, and present a risk to both mother and child.
- A health facility must have adequate staff, equipment, supplies, and drugs available to provide the best care.

Signs of labour: Advise the woman to go to the health facility or contact the TBA if she has any one of the following signs, which indicate the start of labour:

- A bloody sticky discharge
- Painful abdominal contractions every 20 minutes or less
- The bag of waters has broken, and she feels clear fluid coming out of her vagina.

Provisions for Obstetric Emergencies (Including Referral Services)

- Women need to be especially careful to avoid diseases and infections while pregnant. For example, they should use mosquito nets at night and avoid drinking contaminated water.

- Danger signs: The woman and her caretakers should be informed about the danger signs during pregnancy, delivery and the postpartum period. She must be told that if she has any of the following during pregnancy, delivery or postpartum/post-abortion, she should immediately visit a hospital or health centre without further delay.

Prenatal Environmental Risk Factors

Teratogens

A teratogen is any environmental agent that could potentially cause damage to the foetus during the prenatal period. Its impact depends on the following factors:

- Long exposure to teratogens over longer time periods usually has more negative effects.
- The effects of most teratogens vary with the organism's age at the time of exposure. For example, the embryonic period is when serious defects are most likely to occur, since the foundations for all body parts are being laid down.

A pregnant women needs to exercise caution during pregnancy. She needs to be careful of the following different forms of teratogens, such as:

Illegal Drugs

- Babies born to users of cocaine, heroin, or methadone are at risk of prematurity, low birth weight, physical defects, breathing problems, and death.
- Evidence suggests that prenatal exposure to cocaine has lasting effects. These include genital, urinary tract, kidney, and heart deformities, as well as brain seizures.
- Mixed findings have been documented regarding the links between marijuana use and low birth weight or prematurity.

Prescriptive and Non Prescriptive Drugs

- Thalidomide, a sedative used in the 1960s, caused severe limb deformations in embryos when taken by mothers between the fourth to the sixth week after conception.
- Heavy caffeine intake is associated with prematurity, miscarriage, and newborn withdrawal symptoms, such as irritability and vomiting.
- Repeated use of aspirin is linked to low birth weight, infant death around the time of birth, poorer motor development, and lower intelligence scores in early childhood.

Tobacco

- The effects of smoking during pregnancy include low birth weight and increased chances of prematurity, impaired breathing during sleep, miscarriage, and infant death.
- The nicotine in cigarettes causes the placenta to grow abnormally—the transfer of nutrients is reduced, and the foetus gains weight poorly.
- Smoking raises the concentration of carbon monoxide in the bloodstreams of both mother and foetus—carbon monoxide displaces oxygen from red blood cells.
- Passive smoking is also related to low birth weight, infant death, and possible long-term impairments.

Hormones

- If the quantity or timing of hormone release is off, defects of the genitals and other organs can occur.

Radiation

- Radiation exposure can cause miscarriage, slow physical growth, an underdeveloped brain, and malformations of the skeleton and eyes.
- Low-level radiation can increase the risk of childhood cancer.

Alcohol

- Foetal alcohol syndrome (FAS) is the set of defects that results when women consume large amounts of alcohol during most or all of pregnancy. The unborn foetus can be afflicted with mental retardation, slow physical growth, and facial abnormalities.

- Foetal alcohol effects (FAE) refers to the condition of children who display some, but not all, the defects of FAS.

Environmental Pollution

- Mercury exposure is linked to mental retardation, abnormal speech, difficulty in chewing and swallowing, and uncoordinated movements.
- High levels of lead exposure are linked to prematurity, low birth weight, brain damage, and a wide variety of physical defects.

Maternal Disease

Certain diseases during pregnancy can cause miscarriage and birth defects.

- Rubella (German measles) can cause a wide variety of abnormalities, especially when it occurs during the embryonic period.
- Acquired immune deficiency syndrome (AIDS), a disease that destroys the immune system, is infecting increasing numbers of newborn babies.

Rh Blood Incompatibility

- The Rh factor is a protein that, when present in the foetus's blood but not in the mother's, can cause the mother to build up antibodies which can return to the foetus's system and destroy red blood cells.
- Rh blood incompatibility can result in mental retardation, heart muscle damage, and infant death. The danger increases with each additional pregnancy.

Maternal Age and Previous Births

- Women who delay having children until their 30s or 40s face a greater risk of infertility, miscarriage, and babies born with chromosomal defects.

Prenatal Diagnosis

Prenatal diagnosis uses a variety of techniques to determine the health condition of an unborn foetus. The use of these could prevent an untoward outcome for the foetus or the mother, or for both. Here are some techniques that are used for diagnosis.

- **Ultrasonography**: This is a fairly recent technique, used to learn the health of the growing foetus. High frequency sound waves are used to create visible images from the pattern of echoes made by different tissues and organs, including the baby in the amniotic cavity. This procedure is non-invasive, that is, it is harmless to both the foetus and the mother.

  The developing embryo can first be visualised at about six weeks gestation. Recognition of the major internal organs and extremities to determine if any are abnormal can best be accomplished between 16–20 weeks gestation. Although an ultrasound examination can be quite useful to determine the size and position of the foetus, the size and position of the placenta, the amount of amniotic fluid, and the appearance of foetal anatomy, there are limitations to this procedure. Minor abnormalities may not be detected until later in pregnancy.
- **Amniocentesis:** This is a procedure in which a needle is passed through the mother's lower abdomen into the amniotic cavity inside the uterus, and fluid is removed for testing. Within the amniotic fluid are foetal cells (mostly derived from foetal skin) which can be grown in culture for chromosome analysis, biochemical analysis, and molecular biologic analysis. The amniotic fluid is enough for this to be accomplished starting at about 14 weeks gestation. For prenatal diagnosis, most amniocenteses are performed between 14–20 weeks gestation. However, an ultrasound examination always precedes amniocentesis in order to determine gestational age, the position of the foetus and placenta, and determine if enough amniotic fluid is present.
- **Chorionic villus sampling (CVS)**: In this procedure, a catheter is passed via the vagina through the cervix and into the uterus to the developing placenta under ultrasound guidance. The introduction of the catheter allows the sampling of cells from the placental chorionic villi. These cells can then be analysed by a variety of techniques. CVS can be safely

performed between 9.5 and 12.5 weeks gestation. It has the disadvantage of being an invasive procedure, and has a small, but significant, rate of morbidity for the foetus.

- **Maternal blood sampling:** This technique makes use of the occurrence of foetal blood cells gaining entry to maternal circulation through the placental villi. The foetal cells can be sorted out and analysed by a variety of techniques to look for particular DNA sequences. It can be used to identify particular chromosomes of the foetal cells recovered from maternal blood, and diagnose conditions such as the trisomies and monosomy X.

Factors Facilitating Good Health During Pregnancy

Exercise is essential for pregnant women, as healthy, physically fit women who get regular exercise are known to give birth to babies with high birth weight. Exercise also helps with other problems that pregnant women might have. Since the growing foetus places some strain on the back, abdominal, pelvic, and thigh muscles, exercises that strengthen these areas are particularly helpful.

Maternal Health. To provide maternal health, one must ensure that pregnant women receive care, so that they remain safe and healthy throughout pregnancy and childbirth. Safe motherhood encompasses social and cultural factors, and addresses health systems and health policy. Most of our healthcare practices have their origins in traditions based on knowledge and wisdom passed down from one generation to another. These practices are promoted by village healers, midwives, practitioners of Indian system of medicine (Ayurveda, Siddhi and Unani), and elders in the family.

Nutrition and Diet. Prenatal malnutrition can damage the immune system and the structure of organs, including the pancreas, liver and blood vessels. Autopsies of malnourished babies who died at or shortly after birth reveal that these children had fewer brain cells, a lower brain weight, and abnormal brain organisation.

Emotional Stress. Severe stress during pregnancy is associated with a higher miscarriage rate, prematurity, low birth weight, respiratory illness, and physical defects. When a mother experiences fear and anxiety, blood supply to the brain, heart, and limbs increases, resulting in decreased blood supply to the uterus. Stress hormones also cross the placenta. Risks are greatly reduced when mothers have supportive significant others, whom they can turn to for emotional support.

CULTURAL BELIEFS RELATED TO PREGNANCY

Every family and community has certain understandings related to pregnancy, which are often considered the myths prevalent in society. First and foremost, the disclosure of pregnancy is not announced till after the first trimester. Many people feel that the news of getting pregnant should not be disclosed for the first three months, relating this taboo to the 'evil eye'. It is a matter of personal belief and should not interfere with the required medical assistance for the care of the pregnant woman.

Several myths are also related to the sex of the child. Many people claim to give or prescribe certain medicines that will help a woman have a child of the desired sex. In many parts, several restrictions and prohibitions are related to food and food habits as well. For example, a pregnant woman is always told to eat for two, to eat food rich in *ghee* from the eighth month onwards, not to eat papaya, wear specific charms to prevent the evil eye, not cross a river or a stream, etc. It is important to understand that what is needed is adequate rest and exercise in balanced proportions.

Myths are also related to the negative impact of solar and lunar eclipses, and many pregnant women do not use knives during an eclipse.

Birth

Women are isolated during labour due to birth-related pollution beliefs. Profuse bleeding after delivery is viewed as a good sign, as it is linked to the purification of the uterus.

After Birth

Confinement: The mother and the child are usually isolated immediately after delivery, due to beliefs about the pollution and impurity linked to the delivery process. The period of seclusion and confinement of post-partum women varies across regions. In many regions, the confinement period is 40 days. This is practised to protect mother and infant from exposure to disease and evil spirits. Cold baths or showers are avoided. Post-partum practices are usually upheld and enforced by the mothers-in-law, aunts, and other elderly female relatives.

Diet: Some women may be required to follow a diet of puffed rice, tea and hot water for the first three days after delivery. The consumption of milk, butter, ghee, and some types of fish is encouraged, due to the belief that these foods will increase the quantity and quality of breast milk. Post-partum women may consume a large quantity of garlic, to aid in the contraction of the uterus or to 'dry the womb'. Common foods traditionally avoided by post-partum women include certain varieties of green leafy vegetables, fibrous vegetables, melons, pumpkin, papaya, eggplant, shell fish, eggs (in certain castes and communities), certain varieties of fish, lemons, limes, oranges, grapes, chillies, bell peppers, spices, bananas, yoghurt, and oily food.

The placenta may be disposed of by burying it under the floor of the room where the birth occurred, or in the courtyard of the house. The placenta is buried to prevent an enemy or evil spirit from seizing it and influencing the well-being and longevity of the child. Health professionals should offer the placenta to a post-partum woman.

Ceremonies: In India, the arrival of a new family member is celebrated in diverse ways. The main aim is to shower the parents-to-be with love and blessings. Most cultures the world over have ceremonies/celebrations before a baby is born. India, being a vast and diverse country, has many different customs and celebrations—*Godh Bharai* (north Indian Hindus), *Valakaappu* (Tamil Hindus) and *Seemandham* (south Indian Hindus), to name a few. Maharashtra, Gujarat, Bengal, and other states have their own versions of these ceremonies. According to a tradition in many north Indian families, it is considered inauspicious to buy any clothes or items for the baby before her/his birth. In fact, when the baby is born, s/he is made to wear the old clothes of some other member of the family. This is because of the softness of the material, as well as to enable positive family vibes and values to be passed on to the baby. Ceremonies practised in different parts of the country are described in Chapter 3.

GENETIC FOUNDATIONS OF INDIVIDUALS

Genetic code. Each of us is made of cells and inside every cell is a control centre called the nucleus, which contains rod-like structures called chromosomes. Chromosomes are made up of a chemical substance called **deoxyribonucleic acid** or DNA, which store and transmit genetic information. It is a long, double-stranded molecule that looks like a twisted ladder. Each rung of the ladder consists of a specific pair of chemical substances, called bases. It is this sequence of bases that provides genetic instructions. A gene is a segment of DNA along the length of the chromosome. A unique feature of DNA is that it can duplicate itself through a process called mitosis. This ability permits the one-celled fertilised ovum to develop into a complex human being, composed of a great many cells.

Sex cells. Individuals are created when two cells called gametes or sex cells—the sperm and the ovum—combine. A gamete contains 23 chromosomes, half as many as a regular body cell. Gametes are formed through a cell division process called meiosis, which ensures that a constant quantity of genetic material is transmitted from one generation to the next. When sperm and ovum unite at conception, the cell that results is called a zygote. This will again have 46 chromosomes.

Patterns of genetic inheritance. Twenty-two of the 23 pairs of chromosomes are matching pairs, called autosomes. The 23rd pair consists of sex chromosomes. In females, this pair is called XX, and in males, it is called XY. Chromosomes come in corresponding pairs, except for the XY pair in males. Two forms of each gene occur at the same place on the autosomes, one inherited from the mother and one inherited from the father. If the genes from both parents are alike, the child is homozygous and will display the inherited trait. If the genes are different, the child is heterozygous, and in this case, the relationships between the genes determine the trait that will appear.

Dominant recessive inheritance. In many heterozygous pairings, dominant recessive inheritance occurs, that is, only one gene affects the child's characteristics. It is called dominant; the second gene, which has no effect, is called recessive. Many disabilities and diseases are the products of recessive genes. One of the most frequently occurring recessive disorders is phenylketonuria or PKU. This condition affects the way the body breaks down proteins contained in many foods. In dominant recessive inheritance, if the genetic make-up of the parents is known, the percentage of children in a family who are likely to display or carry a trait can be predicted.

ABNORMALITIES OF SEX CHROMOSOMES

Down Syndrome

Children with Down Syndrome have one extra chromosome. The physical characteristics of children with Down Syndrome include a protruding tongue, thick lips, flat nose, short neck, wide gaps between the toes, short fingers, and risks of heart problems and hearing loss. Such children often have good visual discrimination skills and may be better at understanding verbal language than producing it. Mental retardation can range from mild to severe.

Klinefelter's Syndrome

This is a condition that occurs in men who have an extra X chromosome in most of their cells. The syndrome can affect different stages of physical, language and social development. Some males often do not make as much of the male hormone testosterone as other boys. Teenagers with Klinefelter's Syndrome may have less facial and body hair, and may be less muscular than other boys. The most common symptom is infertility. They may have trouble using language to express themselves, and some speech and language delays.

Turner Syndrome

This is related to the X chromosome (one of the two sex chromosomes). Turner Syndrome results when one normal X chromosome is present in a female's cells, while the other sex chromosome is missing or structurally altered. The missing genetic material affects development both before and after birth. It is a chromosomal condition that affects development in females. The most common feature of Turner Syndrome is short stature, which becomes evident by about age five. An early loss of ovarian function is also very common. The ovaries develop normally at first, but egg cells usually die prematurely, and most ovarian tissue degenerates before birth. Many affected girls do not undergo puberty unless they receive hormone therapy, and most are unable to conceive.

Sickle Cell Disease

This disease causes the red blood cells to grow rigid, and the passage of blood through small vessels causes pain. Children with this recessive-gene defect develop problems with blood circulation. They may experience many serious conditions, including strokes, infections, tissue damage, and fatigue. Symptoms become obvious during the first or second year of life.

Tay-Sachs Disease

Infants with this disorder typically appear normal until the age of three to six months, when their development slows and the muscles used for movement weaken. Affected infants lose motor skills, such as turning over, sitting and crawling. They also develop an exaggerated startled reaction to loud noises. As the disease progresses, children with Tay-Sachs experience seizures, vision and hearing loss, intellectual disability, and paralysis. An eye abnormality called a cherry-red spot, which can be identified with an eye examination, is a characteristic of this disorder. Children with a severe infantile form of Tay-Sachs disease usually live only into early childhood. Tay-Sachs disease is a rare inherited disorder that progressively destroys nerve cells (neurons) in the brain and the spinal cord.

MODERN METHODS OF HUMAN REPRODUCTION

Infertility leads to grief and inadequacy in a couple who wish to have a child. The family and society are not particularly kind in accepting the inability of a woman to give birth. She is marginalised, called unkind names such as *banj* ('barren field'), and is often held solely responsible for the situation. Before medical assistance, religious rites are performed and the help of Godmen sought. Medical intervention is expensive, and available only in metropolitan cities. Some of the assisted conception treatments include:

- Intrauterine insemination: In this technique, sperms are inserted directly into the uterus at the time of ovulation.
- In-vitro fertilisation: Eggs are gathered from ovaries and combined with the sperms of the male partner in a laboratory dish. The resulting embryos are transplanted into the woman's uterus.
- Donated sperms: If a male has a low sperm count, or produces no sperm at all, donor sperm may be used for donor insemination or IVF. There are sperm banks that collect and store these donated sperms.
- Donated eggs or embryos: If a woman is unable to conceive using her own eggs, an egg donated by another woman can be combined with her partner's sperm. The resulting embryo is then implanted in her uterus.
- Surrogacy: In this practice, another woman carries a couple's baby, or a baby from a donor embryo, to term. She then entrusts the couple with the baby's care after the birth. There is a lot of ongoing debate on this issue, as surrogacy is now becoming a business for many people, and the practice is being misused.

There are two types of surrogacy—traditional and gestational. In **traditional surrogacy**, a surrogate mother is artificially inseminated, either by the intended father or an anonymous donor, and carries the baby to term. The child is thereby genetically related to both the surrogate mother, who provides the egg, and the intended father or anonymous donor.

In **gestational surrogacy**, an egg is removed from the intended mother or an anonymous donor, and fertilised with the sperm of the intended father or anonymous donor. The fertilised egg, or embryo, is then transferred to a surrogate, who carries the baby to term. The child is thereby related to the woman who donated the egg and the intended father or sperm donor, but not the surrogate.

ADOPTION

When medical intervention also fails to provide a child to a family, child adoption is one alternative available to couples. The negativity that exists vis-à-vis infertility leads to adoption practices that draw the least attention. The traditional and well-accepted practice of adopting from within the family may still be the preferred mode of adoption. However, this cannot be substantiated, as figures for such adoptions are unavailable. Traditional notions concerning bloodline, caste and class are well-entrenched in the minds of people and are reflected in the adoption practices in the country, more so in the less progressive states of India.

In India, the mythological stories of Krishna, Karna, Andal, Sita, and many others have adoption as an important element. Several other tales in Hindu mythology suggest that the concept of raising a stranger's child has always existed. Children were brought up by sages or *rishis*; girl children were brought up and given in marriage to princes and kings, indicating a child-centredness in adoption. The myth of Shakuntala and Andal assume importance as examples of female adoptions. They were both considered goddess Earth's gifts to their respective parents.

SUMMARY

- This chapter focused on the steps and stages in human reproduction, the precautions that need to be taken during pregnancy, and the various cultural restrictions and taboos prevalent in different regions of India. It also contained a detailed exposition of reproductive health and its significance, as well as reproductive rights, as defined by the WHO. The importance of family planning and the inclusion of men in matters relating to reproductive health are dealt with, as is the issue of infertility (both male and female), and the common causes of male and female infertility. Factors facilitating good health during pregnancy, care of the foetus, and the various genetic disorders that might affect the unborn child are discussed. The chapter closed with a discussion of the various fertility aids available now, thanks to the advances made in modern science, medicine and technology.

KEY TERMS

Reproduction – The process of producing offspring

Fertilisation – The union of the egg and the sperm

Prenatal Development – Growth of the unborn foetus

Antenatal care – Care of the pregnant woman

Child birth process – When a woman is ready to deliver the baby

Ensuring safe motherhood – Precautions during pregnancy

Indian traditional birth practices – Non-hospital practices and positions for delivering the baby

Reproductive health – Taking care of the body from the onset of puberty and protection from disease

Contraception – Birth control measures

Fertility – Body's ability to conceive.

EXERCISES

1. Why is the period of the embryo regarded as the most dramatic prenatal phase?
2. Describe through diagrams the embryonic stage.
3. List teratogens and other maternal factors that affect brain development during the prenatal period.
4. Remi, pregnant for the first time, has heard about the harmful effects of alcohol and tobacco. Nevertheless, she believes that a few cigarettes a day will not be harmful. Provide her with the research-based reasons for not smoking and drinking.
5. Identify any three pregnant women from different regional or religious groups and inquire about the cultural practices related to pregnancy. You could focus on announcement, any ritual celebrations, or precautions that they are told to observe.
6. A woman over the age of 35, who has just learned that she is pregnant, wants to find out whether her embryo has a genetic defect. She also wants to minimise injury to the developing organism. What prenatal diagnostic method is she likely to choose?
7. List factors that increase the chances that an infant will be born underweight. How many of these factors could be prevented by better health care for expectant women?
8. Discuss the miracle of human intervention in reproduction and its boon for childless couples.
9. What are some of the current trends in couples having children? Discuss the process of surrogacy.
10. What is reproductive health? Discuss the implications for male sexual behaviour.
11. What are some of the attitudes that render female sexuality vulnerable?
12. List some precautions to be followed by women during pregnancy. What is the role of the father and the family in the care and well-being of a pregnant woman?

REFERENCES

Berk, L., *Child Development*, New York: Allyn & Bacon, 2006.

Bhargava, V., *Adoption in India: Policy and Experiences*, New Delhi: Sage Publications, 2005.

Santrock, *Child Development*, New York: McGraw-Hill, 2006.

Singh, M., *Care of the Newborn*, 6e, New Delhi: Sagar Publications, 2004.

3

Birth and The Newborn

HIGHLIGHTS

- Practices, rituals and taboos related with the care of pregnant women.
- Community systems and rituals that celebrate and share the joy of the couple.
- The process of birth, signs to recognise the beginning of delivery, the birth process, and assistive processes for birth.
- Capacities of the newborn.
- State programmes that address the issues of pregnant women.

BIRTH AND THE NEWBORN CHILD

In Chapter 2, we discussed the needs of pregnant women and the growing foetus. For individuals, the journey to becoming a parent is a life-changing event, marked by the birth of the newborn. Bringing a new baby home is one of the most exciting experiences, and is a time for celebration. Families and communities come together to honour and welcome the new child. Rituals and ceremonies are common the world over to mark a child's birth and survival. These rituals not only celebrate and acknowledge the child, but are also important ways for families to solidify their connection to the community, and their heritage and culture. By felicitating the parents, the primary caregivers, the rituals provide them with a new sense of identity.

These festivities also serve as markers of social inclusion, helping children to grow and develop their own sense of identity. Parents re-tell stories of the rituals to their children as they grow, giving them a path on which to connect with the larger social group. Every community in India has its own unique customs for making the expectant mother feel special. The third trimester is particularly eventful for the first-time mother, as close family and friends gather together to wish her well for the impending delivery.

LIFECYCLE RITUALS IN INDIAN FAMILIES

A detailed series of lifecycle rituals mark the major transitions in the life of an individual. Hindu rites are complex and often differ between regions and castes. In the Hindu way of life, certain *samskara* (customs and rituals) are performed as group celebrations to mark the turning points in an individual's lifecycle (pregnancy, childbirth, education, marriage, and death). The festivity and celebration provides a positive energy and inclusion within the cultural fold. These rituals become societal ways to nurture the young couple and the new member.

Ceremonies are also performed during pregnancy to ensure the health of the mother and the growing child. The origins and performance of rituals vary with religion, and sometimes within the same religion. Some customs have been described to illustrate the regional and religious diversity in practices pertaining to pregnancy and childbirth.

Indian scriptures (such as the Rigveda) describe rituals related to conception, recognition or public announcement of birth, as well as ceremonies that socially celebrate the newborn. These *samskaras* are largely followed by Hindus and religions closely aligned with Hinduism, such as Jainism and some schools of thought in Buddhism. In the

Grhya Sutras, the number of major *samskaras* is accepted as 16. We will discuss a few that occur during pregnancy, infancy and childhood.

PREGNANCY AND RITUALS RELATED TO THE NEWBORN

Garbhadhana

It was believed that couples needed pre-conception counselling as the emotions experienced by the prospective mother impacted the child-to-be. This ceremony is performed before the actual conception. *Garbadhana* (literally, implanting in the womb) symbolises the consummation of marriage and involves special prayers to aid in fulfilling one's parental duties to perpetuate the human race.

Punsavana

This ritual is performed during the third/fourth month of pregnancy. The term *Punsavana* literally denotes engendering a male child; the 'deity' governing the sex of the foetus is sought to be appeased by prayer, and a male child conceived. The male child carries the family name and performs the obligatory last rites of his parents, and hence is much desired.

Simantonnayana

This sacrament literally means 'parting the hair', and is performed in the fourth or fifth month of the first pregnancy. This *samskara* aims to protect the mother and the unborn child from demons and spirits, and ensure good health, success and prosperity for the unborn child. In some parts of India, it is known as *Valaiakappu*. The pregnant woman wears red or green glass bangles, which are a sign of prosperity; however, it is also believed that the sound of these bangles will reach the womb and comfort the foetus. The mother is allowed to fulfill any of her wishes as she is believed to be entering a hazardous period. Therefore, any cravings for certain foods are fulfilled. The woman is now expected to rest as much as possible and remain in the company of learned and sacred people. She should also avoid extremes of emotion.

Jatakarmaia

This ceremony welcomes the child into the family and is aimed at the development of the child's intellect. The father touches and smells the newborn, and whispers religious *mantras* (verses) into her/his ears. A small 'dot', often in the shape of an '*Om*', is drawn behind the baby's ear with *kajal*, to ward off evil. Symbolically, a female member of the family washes a nursing mother's breasts before breast-feeding commences.

Namakarana

Namakarana, or the naming ceremony, takes place on the 10th or 12th day after birth, when the mother is considered 'clean' and allowed to carry out normal household chores, such as cooking. The name is selected so the child can be inspired to follow a righteous path. There are several ways of naming a baby: the commonest is according to the *Nakshatra* or the sign of the Zodiac at the time of birth. The first letter of the name is obtained from the *Nakshatra*—for example, if the letter is 'P', the name could be Pooja (for a girl). The paternal aunt plays an important role in the choice.

Nishkramana

Literally the first outing, this takes place on the fourth month after birth, when the child is taken out into the open for the first time.

Annaprāśana

This ceremony marks the transition to semi-solid foods from exclusive breast-feeding. The ritual, which takes place when a child is six months old, is when the child first eats solid food, usually rice. A few grains of rice mixed with *ghee* are fed to the infant. Different parts of India have region-specific weaning foods, depending on the cereal that grows locally.

Chudakarana

Also known as *choulam* or *mundana* (literally, tonsure), this ceremony is when the child's hair is cut for the first time. In the child's third or fifth year, the head is shaved, leaving behind a small tuft of hair. This ceremony can be performed at any stage, depending on family tradition.

Karnavedha

This refers to the ear-piercing ceremony. The ears are pierced with a particular thorn, and butter applied to the wound. Traditionally, both male and female children had their ears pierced. It was usually carried out after the age of three. In some families, the father will not look upon the baby's face till certain rituals have been performed, including ear piercing. A goldsmith performs this ritual for both sexes.

Vidyarambha or Akshararambha

This literally means to begin one's education. The ceremony initiates a young child into the stage of learning at the age of either three or five. Impressions of some *aksharas* are made on the child's tongue, or 'Hari Sri Ganapataye Namah Avegnamastu' chanted. The child is made to write the letters from the 'Hari Sri' chant with her/his index finger on raw rice in a bell-metal vessel, and each word uttered as it is written. Either the father or an eminent teacher officiates at this ritual.

In some families, the sixth day after birth is considered the most auspicious in a person's life. A thin white cotton thread is ceremoniously tied around the wrist, ankle or neck, and a pen and blank piece of paper are placed in the baby's cot, as it is believed that on this day the goddess of learning charts the baby's future. The mother may observe a fast on this day.

Upanayanam

The tenth sacrament is the ceremony of wearing the sacred thread. This is held for a male child when he reaches the age of eight. Children who die before this stage do not need purification by fire, as they are classed as being 'without sin'. It is also an initiation into formal education for a male child.

The remaining six *samskaras* are performed to mark the entry into various stages in the journey onwards: *Keshanta* (cutting of hair), *Vivaha* (marriage), *vanaprasta* (retirement and transfer of responsibility), *sanyas* (detachment), and finally, *anteyshthi* or death.

ETHNIC DIVERSITY AND CELEBRATIONS

India is defined by the coexistence of multiple religions, regional variations and geographical differences in terrain and accessibility. There are festivals and places of worship of many religious persuasions—Muslim, Christians, Sikhs, Parsi, Jains, Buddhists—as well as social groups with their own linguistic identity, customs and traditions. Tribal groups living in interior regions have their own ways to welcome a newborn into their particular belief system. Certain religiously prescribed ways of socialising children and families are given below.

Muslim Rituals at Birth

Islam does not prescribe any specific birth-related rituals, and so what families observe are derived from local practices. Muslims believe that the first words a child should hear are the words of God. Hence the *Azaan* is spoken into the newborn's right ear, and the *iqamat* into the left ear. Smoke is used to clean the labour room. The juice of palm dates chewed by a Muslim priest is applied to the upper jaw of the child. Only after this is the child allowed to feed on the mother's milk. On the seventh day following delivery, the mother is bathed in warm water. The midwife is given clothes and money by the relatives.

Circumcision

In India, the custom of circumcision varies from region to region. First, the child is bathed and then dressed in clothes brought by his maternal uncle. He is then taken to the mosque to offer ***namaz.***

A barber is usually called home to conduct the ceremony. These days, a doctor or a surgeon does the circumcision. A cloth screen is erected on all sides and the child sits in the lap of his maternal uncle. Women are not allowed to watch the rite. With a sharp razor or surgical blade, the doctor cuts off the foreskin of the penis. Antiseptics are then applied to prevent bleeding. The child is then given something to drink.

Christian Rituals at Birth

There are no special rituals concerned with the birth of a child among Christians. When a woman is about to deliver a baby, the priest of the congregation is called, and he prays for a safe delivery. After 40 days, the mother takes her newborn to the church for Thanksgiving. There, she gives an offering to the Lord. The first birthday is usually celebrated elaborately, with the parents arranging a special feast for the guests, all of whom give gifts to the child. The child cuts a special birthday cake, which is shared between the guests.

Baptism

This is an important ritual in the life of a Christian. A child is admitted to the church congregation only through baptism. According to Christian belief, a child is born tainted with the sin passed on to him from the great sin of Adam and Eve. At baptism, the child is relieved of this sin, and he becomes a child of God and a member of the church. Baptism is usually done before the first birthday. The child is given white clothes, shoes and a cap by her/his parents, and relatives give her/him gifts. Parents then organise a celebratory feast.

Zoroastrian Rituals

The Parsis follow rituals to protect the newborn from infection and disease. After the birth, the new mother is normally confined to the house for 40 days, to safeguard her and her child from disease. A lamp is lit on the day of birth and kept in the room for about 40 days to ward off any evil elements.

Some families observe *Pachori* on the fifth day after birth, while some observe *Dasori* on the tenth day. On the morning of the fifth day in the maternal house, five kinds of vegetables are cooked with small round *chapatis* or cakes, and sweet preparations of dry ginger and wheat. These are laid by the mother's bed in the dishes in which they were cooked. Betel, dry dates, rice and red powder are dropped into the mother's hand. Relatives throw incense into a fire urn and declare the *Pachori* ceremony over. Large quantities of cooked food are sent to the husband's home by the mother's parents. The new mother is bathed from head to foot.

If the *Pachori* ceremony is not performed on the fifth day, it takes place on the 10th day after birth, and is called Dasori. On the 40th day, the new mother is given a ceremonial bath with consecrated water, administered by the head priest. This is supposed to cleanse her, so she can interact with other people.

Para Haoma

The ceremony of giving the first drink to the newborn is called *Para Haoma*. Consecrated Haoma juice, which is supposed to make the child healthy, is given to the baby. These days, though, a sweet drink made of molasses or sugar is also administered.

Navjote

The formal admission of a child into the Zoroastrian fold is called *Navjote*. This is done between the seventh and the 11th year. The child takes a special bath called *Nahn*, and is then given a purifying drink. S/he stands on a raised platform while his mother performs the *Achoo Michoo* ceremony, where certain items are rotated over the head of the child seven times. This is to invoke the blessings of the seven *Amesha Spentas*. Certain prescribed texts are read, and the Kushti tied round the child's waist. A long prayer is then held, where the child declares that s/he will be a true Zoroastrian and follow the rules and regulations. Both Parsi boys and girls are given this privilege. Finally, the priest recites the *Doa Tandorosoti Prayer*, which calls for the well-being of the child, his parents, and the community (Kapoor 2002).

BELIEFS AND CUSTOMS RELATED TO PREGNANCY IN INDIA

Each socio-religious group in India has its own way to celebrate and prepare for the safe arrival of the newborn. Some of the practices and customs clearly show that communities have their own understanding of the needs and requirements of women going through the process of childbearing. There are similarities among various Hindu customs across regions, even though they are called by different names. The seventh to ninth months are particularly marked by ceremonies that involve gifting, the fulfilment of cravings, and preparing for the arrival of the baby, underlining the fact that childbirth involves risks, and needs the prayers and blessings of elders.

Box 3.1 Birth Practices and the Impact of Technology

It has become increasingly common for young couples to learn the sex of their unborn child. This process of knowing the gender, especially in Euro-American contexts, has influenced the discourse around the growing foetus and the arrival of the newborn. Couples name the unborn child and referring to any activity of the foetus by that given name.

A lady living in New York was expecting her first child. When asked whether she wanted to learn her child's gender, she said that they had decided to ask their gynecologist to provide them the information in a sealed envelope, which they would open in the presence of family and close friends. She wanted to make a little ceremony of this first identity-building of their child-to-be. Modern interventions influence the social fabric in different ways.

In India, given the cultural penchant for a male child, there is reported misuse of sex determination procedures. There has been a proliferation of sex determination clinics; however, regulations have been put in place to prevent prospective parents and their families learning the gender of the unborn baby, and then opting for sex-selective abortions.

(Interview)

Tamil Tradition

In Tamil Nadu, a traditional ceremony called the ***Seemandam*** is held during the fifth, seventh, or ninth month of pregnancy. Only married women, close relatives and friends are invited to the ceremony, which is hosted by the husband's parents. The pregnant woman is gifted a new sari by her parents and in-laws. A few drops of a special herbal juice are squeezed into the nostrils of the expectant mother, and mantras chanted to protect the baby.

Another colourful ceremony called the ***Valakaapu*** (*vala*: bangles, and *kaapu*: security) is also performed with the *Seemandam*, when the expectant mother is presented with glass bangles—an even number of bangles on one arm, and an odd number on the other. Five married women decorate her arms with glass bangles in three auspicious colours. Soft music is played, and this, together with the sound of the bangles, is believed to be good for the baby's developing ears.

Kerala Customs

In Kerala, ***Puli-Kuti***, or 'drinking tamarind juice', is a pregnancy ceremony of the Nair community. It is performed at a time fixed by the local astrologer on a particular day in the ninth month. The pregnant woman is seated facing eastwards in the courtyard (*natu-muttam*) of the Tharavaad (ancestral family house), after having bathed and dressed in the proper clothes. The maternal uncle's wife and the pregnant woman's brother conduct this ceremony.

Among the other Malayalee communities, the pregnancy ritual is fairly simple. During the seventh month, the pregnant woman is taken back to her maternal home by her parents and relatives. They bring traditional sweets and are offered a traditional meal.

Maharashtrian Ceremony

A grand function called the '***Dohal Jevan***' is held in Marathi homes during the seventh and ninth months of pregnancy. 'Dohal' means a craving for certain foods. This ceremony originated as a means to satisfy the food cravings of the expectant mother. Flower garlands are draped around her wrists, neck, waist, and head. Nutritious food and a variety of sweets are made and kept covered for the mother-to-be to choose from. When she does, these are announced to all present there. There is speculation about the gender of the unborn baby, depending on the selected item.

In Marathi, each food item is referred to by a gender. For example, *bhat* (rice) is masculine and *poli* (chapati) is feminine. Similarly, among the sweetmeats *pedhas* are masculine and *barfis* feminine.

Gujarati Godh Bharai

Godh Bharna (*godh*: the woman's lap, and *bharna*: fill) is the most important pregnancy ritual. During this ceremony, the expectant mother is dressed in finery presented by her own mother. Her maternal relatives bring five colourfully decorated metal *thalis* (round plates), and the ceremony begins with the mother-to-be's entrance through the front door of her in-laws' house. The women sing traditional songs. With each step the expectant mother takes, a piece of coloured silk is placed under her feet along with a little *supari* (betel nut), a one-rupee coin and a quarter-rupee coin, till she reaches the place where the puja will be performed. She is made to sit on a low, four-legged wooden seat, and a small red dot put on her forehead for good luck. Both her mother and mother-in-law fill her *godh* (lap) and the *palav* of her saree with gifts and jewellery. The elders bless the mother and her unborn child, to the accompaniment of traditional festive tunes.

Punjabi Godhbharai

The Punjabi ceremony is quite similar to the Gujarati tradition, and is called ***Godhbharai***. All close relatives are invited during the seventh month for a special puja. The expectant mother sits on the floor, and after the puja, her mother-in-law wraps coconuts and fruits in a red dupatta and places it in her lap. The other women place gifts in her lap, and a small child or doll is placed in her lap too.

Bengali Shaad

The Bengali ***Shaad*** (taste or longing) is held in the ninth month of pregnancy. This ritual originated in an age when childbirth was a potentially dangerous process, with no certainty of the mother's survival. It was a way of ensuring that the pregnant woman had no unfulfilled wish for food, clothes or jewellery before going into labour; it was also a way of making sure that she was well-fed and strengthened for childbirth.

The expectant mother is dressed elaborately in a new sari and jewellery. Specially prescribed food—including a cooked fish head and five types of fried food—is set out in front of her on a huge silver platter. The first mouthful that she takes has to include a pinch of everything on the *thali*, and the conch shells blow, alerting the Gods that the *shaad* has begun, and a future mother is now under their care. The mother's meal ends with *payesh/kheer*.

Goan Baby Shower

Baby showers are fun-filled events. During the seventh month of pregnancy, the woman is taken to her mother's house, and dressed beautifully. Special sweets called dodal and cakes are prepared. The expectant mother is given gifts ranging from clothes to jewellery; however, no material goods are brought for the baby before birth.

In Muslim homes, a ceremony called ***Satvasa*** is held during the seventh month of pregnancy. Seven varieties of fruit and a green saree set are presented to the mother-to-be, while the husband is garlanded as a gesture of honour. Parents and relatives are then served a special meal. There is no compulsion to give gifts, although sweets and eatables are acceptable.

Box 3.2 Understanding the Birth Process

As Riya's due date drew closer, she became increasingly excited about the arrival of her first child. A few days prior to her due date, she felt slight discomfort and when she went to relieve herself, she noticed a little blood. She spoke about this with her doctor and learnt that she had a 'show'—she had lost her mucous plug (as it is called in technical terms). At night, she felt a few slight contractions which were 15–20 minutes apart. Since the nursing home was nearby, she was told to time her contractions, and arrive when they become strong, or recurred after every five minutes. At 3:30 AM, she felt the contractions were very strong and closely spaced, and so asked her husband to take her to the nursing home. The essentials for herself and the baby were already packed in two separate labelled bags.

Box 3.2 contd.

Box 3.2 contd.

Upon reaching the nursing home, she was told that the process of dilation of the cervix had started. Labour pain was then induced to speed up the process. She experienced strong contractions. Through all this, her husband was by her side. Her water bag burst after a while, and at 9:30 AM, she was taken to the delivery room, where she insisted on walking herself. In the next 15 minutes, she felt the urge to push the baby out. And finally, the baby was delivered. In the final stage, the placenta came out.

As she held her baby in her arms, tears rolled out of her eyes. This was the best moment of her life.

Source: Dimple Rangila.

BIRTH

In this section, we will learn about the signs that signal that the baby is ready to enter the world. We will also refer to the different ways of giving birth, and to some of the modern interventions.

The birth of a child changes the lives of people dramatically. The birth itself can take many forms. Various medical conditions or circumstances, as well as the mother's preference, can affect the way a child is born and determine the delivery method.

Prenatal Period refers to the time between conception and birth. This period lasts for 40 weeks, or roughly nine months. It is divided into three trimesters, with each trimester lasting approximately three months. During this time, the embryo develops into a foetus, and then into a viable human baby. Many changes take place in both mother and child during the prenatal period, including weight gain and physical and hormonal changes in both.

Perinatal Period pertains to the time immediately before, during and after birth. This period is defined in diverse ways. Depending on the definition, it starts at the 20th to the 28th week of gestation, and ends one to four weeks after birth.

The **Post-natal Period** begins from birth, and ends when the baby is six weeks of age.

Preparing for Childbirth

Preparations for the birth of a child are made on the advice of doctors, older relatives and experienced friends. There are choices related to the issues and concerns associated with the birth of a child. The first choice is to do with whether the birth will take place at home or in the hospital. In India, the presence of midwives or *dais*, who assist in delivering babies, is common. They were trained by their elders and learnt the several procedures by being apprenticed to local practitioners. In contemporary times, even if a woman opts for delivery at home, it is advised that a hospital be within a 2-km radius.

The young couple also needs to be aware of many other significant factors. It is important to know, for instance, about the intake of drugs during labour and delivery that may or may not be prescribed by a doctor. Families also take decisions regarding who will be present during the time of delivery. When deliveries took place at home, there was sufficient emotional support for the couple. Among Indian families, it is preferred that only females be present during delivery. With hospital deliveries gaining ground, the mother is often isolated in the labour room, away from the husband and family members (unlike in the West, where the husband is often allowed to remain present during delivery). With changes in the family configuration, new dynamics have emerged to assist and provide care for young mothers, and address and alleviate birth-related anxiety in both parents.

In the 1960s, many women preferred the 'natural' or prepared approaches to delivering a child. These approaches help women to view labour and delivery as life events to be celebrated, and not as medical procedures to be endured (Kail 2001). Doctors have devised certain exercises that facilitate the journey of the foetus from the womb through the birth canal. Couples are helped to learn ways—through breathing exercises, for instance—to help the foetus on its outward journey. Prepared approaches means attending pre-natal classes to learn the basic facts of pregnancy and childbirth. These approaches vary worldwide, across cultures. Currently, there are a few modern methods that could help couples learn some basic techniques to ease the birth process.

Box 3.3 Group Learning about Child Birth: Prenatal Classes

In many developed countries, urbanisation and new configurations in families has led to little transfer of information or knowledge from elders to the next generation. In such situations, new social groups emerge to provide assistance and support to young pregnant women. Gynecologists or hospitals may organise a series of sessions where they help the couple with exercises, incorporating them in their daily rhythms till the arrival of the baby.

Prenatal classes are typically held in the last six to eight weeks before birth. Among other things, women are told about the ways in which prospective fathers can be of help. They also learn that it is essential to prepare for the hospital by keeping a bag packed and ready, with clothes for the newborn and the mother, feeding bottle, diapers, and small sheets and blankets. Such groups become a natural support, as all the women there are in a similar state of expectancy. Their conversations and the available counsel of an expert reduce individual anxiety.

Source: Asha Singh.

Assisting in the Processes of Birth

Fernand Lamaze was an obstetrician who visited the Soviet Union in 1951 and was much impressed by the childbirth method used there. He published a book called *Painless Childbirth* in France in 1956, and the English translation was published in 1958. The psychoprophylactic method is another term for the Lamaze method of childbirth, which includes education about the physical aspect of childbirth. Based largely on breathing and relaxation, the technique is taught to the pregnant woman and her husband; the latter is taught to be her coach during labour and also provide emotional support. This method provides a comfort zone for the pregnant woman—while the pain may not be drastically reduced, it certainly makes the woman feel more in control and gain positive experiences of childbirth. No drug is used in this practice. Women who chose this method reported reduced use of painkillers and also a decrease in the incidences of birth complications.

Fredrick Leboyer, a French obstetrician, pioneered the concept of 'gentle birth'. He focused on the environment introduced to the newborn during delivery, and considered it needlessly cruel and frightening for a newborn to have to emerge from a world of warmth and darkness into a cold, noisy room with bright lights. After the delivery, the newborn is held upside down and even slapped sometimes (to aid breathing), and the umbilical cord cut at once so that the baby can breathe independently.

Leboyer proposed a womb-like environment with soft music. A newborn should be welcomed into the world with gentleness and compassion. He focused on a friendly environment, where the room is dimly lit and noise kept to a minimum. After delivery, the child is placed on the mother's abdomen and the umbilical cord is not cut until the blood vessels in it have ceased to beat. Lastly, the newborn is placed in a warm water bath.

CHILDBIRTH

Stages of Childbirth

A pregnant woman is told many details of how to recognise the *beginning of labour*, that is, the initiation of the foetus' journey from inside the womb to the outside world. Terms like 'her water bag burst', or 'contractions' are common when women recount their delivery processes. The labour and/or delivery for the first baby can be difficult and long, and as the body gets used to the process, the delivery becomes smooth. To reduce pain during labour, some traditional practices are recommended by families. Herbal potions, deep breathing, chanting of shlokas, and physical exercise during pregnancy are some of the practices. Some *dais* in Rajasthan recommend drinking plenty of ghee / oil in the last month to aid an easy delivery.

The impending birth of the baby is visible through several indicators. A series of hormones initiates the labour process. About two weeks before birth, the cervix thins and begins to open. The baby's head drops low into the uterus, an event called lightening. There is a reddish discharge when the cervix widens, often called 'show of blood'.

Stage 1: Dilation and Effacement of the Cervix

This is the longest stage of labour, and with a first baby, lasts on an average for 12–14 hours, and four to six hours in later births. Dilation and effacement refers to the widening and thinning of the cervix, resulting in a clear pathway from the uterus into the birth canal. Uterine contractions are forceful and regular. Gradually, they become closer and more powerful. Transition is reached when the frequency and strength of contractions are at their peak, and the cervix opens completely.

Stage 2: Delivery of the Baby

This stage lasts approximately 50 minutes for a first baby and 20 minutes in subsequent births. The mother squeezes and pushes with her abdominal muscles and forces the baby down and out. In the first delivery, an episiotomy (a small incision) is made to increase the size of the vaginal opening, which permits the baby to pass without damaging the mother's tissues. The baby's head crowns when the vagina opening stretches around the entire head.

Stage 3: Birth of the Placenta

The final stage lasts about five to 10 minutes if it is a vertex presentation (head down), and longer in any other presentation (breech). The final contractions and pushes cause the placenta to separate from the uterine wall and be delivered. If the cord is wrapped tightly around the baby's neck, it needs to be cut immediately. The cord is normally just long enough for a woman to hold her baby with the cord still attached, to both the baby and the placenta, which is still inside the mother. The doctor or midwife will clamp the umbilical cord about 3–4 cm (1½–2 inches) from the baby's navel with a plastic clip, and place another clamp at the other end, near the placenta. The cord will then be cut between the two clamps, leaving a stump about 2–3 cm (1–1½ inches) long on the baby's navel.

There are no nerves in the cord, so cutting it is not painful for either the mother or the baby. Skin-to-skin contact between mother and baby results in rising levels of oxytocin, the hormone that encourages affection, bonding and contentment. This hormone also helps to release milk when the baby breastfeeds, and causes the uterus to contract.

Traditionally, in Indian home deliveries, the placenta is buried under the floor of the room where the birth has occurred, or in the courtyard of the house. This is done to keep an enemy or evil spirit from seizing it and influencing the well-being and longevity of the child. Health professionals should offer the placenta to a postpartum woman. Cold baths or showers are avoided. In the hospital, a postpartum woman may accept a warm bath, but may be reluctant to have a warm shower.

The date and time of birth is extremely important for Indian families. A horoscope provides a picture of the planets during the birth of any person, which differs from person to person due to the continuous movement of the planets. Astrological analysis of a person begins with the preparation of a horoscope, which requires the exact date, time and place of birth. A child's horoscope (birth chart) is created based on that information. This allows for future predictions, and plays a role in the choice of marriage partners.

The Baby's Adaptation to Labour and Delivery

The force of the contractions causes the infant to produce high levels of stress hormones. Stress hormones send extra blood to the brain and the heart, and help prepare the lungs to breathe and arouse the infant into alertness at birth.

There are many reasons why a normal delivery may not take place, giving rise to a need for a caesarean delivery. Some caesareans occur in critical situations, some are used to prevent critical situations, and some are elective.

Caesarian Section

Caesarian birth happens through an incision in the abdominal wall and uterus, rather than through the vagina.

Emergency Caesarian Section: If a baby at or near full term is found to have a slow or irregular heart rate, it signals distress, called **Foetal distress**. The baby may also send SOS signals by **passing meconium** (black stools), which becomes evident when the amniotic fluid leaks out. This could happen due to a separation of the placenta and bleeding, or other problematic situations affecting the mother. Likewise, if the umbilical cord slips out during labour, blood supply to the baby could be hampered. This results in an emergency, and if the baby is not delivered immediately at this point, s/he could die in the womb.

Maternal distress may sometimes subject the mother to life-threatening conditions during or before labour, like excess bleeding or a surge in blood pressure. In such cases, an emergency caesarean has to be done to save the mother's life. The mother's birth passage being too narrow, or the baby being oversized for the mother's birth canal, or failure of the contractions to progress can endanger the baby's life, necessitating a caesarean section.

Elective Caesarian Section: Under certain conditions, caesarian birth is advised, and women choose this over natural birth. A **previous caesarian** section quite often becomes an indication to deliver the next child by a caesarean section as well. Concerns about previous scars on the uterus giving way during normal labour often leads to this decision. Other conditions that necessitate an elective caesarean are:

- **Placenta praevia grade 4** means 'placenta first', and is a rare condition that occurs in around 0.5 per cent of pregnancies. Instead of implanting on the uterine wall, the placenta implants partly or wholly over the cervix—which can block the baby's descent into the vagina for birth.
- Abnormal position of the baby, such as **breech presentation,** in which the baby exits the pelvis buttocks or feet first (as opposed to the normal head-first) or **transverse,** where the baby lies across the mother's womb. Tumors within the mother's pelvic cavity or large ovarian cysts could also necessitate a C-section.
- **Genital herpes in the mother.** If the mother, on a rare chance, develops this condition, caesarian section can prevent the mother's infection from passing to the baby during its journey through the mother's birth canal.
- Medical problems in the mother, like high blood pressure and diabetes, are also dealt with by caesarean deliveries.
- **Triplets** or more number of babies.
- **HIV** infection in the mother is another instance where caesarean section is done, to prevent the transmission of the infection to the baby.

Assisted Deliveries

When a baby needs help to be born (through the use of instruments that are attached to her head), it is referred to as an assisted birth. About one birth in eight is assisted. A doctor may recommend an assisted birth if:

- The baby is not making any progress through the pelvis or is distressed during the pushing stage of labour.
- A mother is exhausted and cannot push any more due to a medical reason, such as extremely high blood pressure, certain heart conditions, pulmonary hypertension, or a history of stroke. These can cause serious complications during the second stage of labour. Neuromuscular disorders can cause weakness or paralysis, and make effective pushing impossible.
- To rotate or turn the baby's head into a more favourable position so s/he is facing the right way to be born.

Forceps

Forceps are a reliable and effective way to assist a delivery, but have to be used with care by a properly trained doctor. The forceps are placed so that they hold the sides of the baby's head near the ears and the cheeks. The doctor then gently pulls the baby's head downward while the mother pushes during a contraction, and then guides the baby out of the birth canal.

Pros and cons of forceps: There are several advantages of forceps: they work well even if the contractions are weak, or if the mother is finding it hard to push due to exhaustion. They are seen to have a low failure rate. If the doctor can get the forceps around the baby's head easily, vaginal birth may be done without resorting to a caesarean. The disadvantage of forceps is that there are higher chances of vaginal or perineal damage (than, say, with a vacuum).

Vacuum Extractor

The vacuum extractor consists of a cup attached to a tube, which connects to a suction pump. The cup—either plastic or metal—is placed on top of the baby's head and held in place, while the suction creates a vacuum that helps the cup adhere to the baby's scalp. The doctor pulls downward while the mother pushes during a contraction. Vacuum births are known to be very safe as long as the expectant mother is least 34 weeks pregnant. Before that, the baby's head may be too fragile to deal with the suction.

Pros and cons of vacuum: The vacuum is often a little easier to apply and may be less uncomfortable. However, vacuum fails in up to 20 per cent of cases, and is especially likely to fail if the baby is not in an ideal position for birth. A caesarean section sometimes has to be performed if the vacuum fails.

Box 3.4 Natural Childbirth

Natural childbirth programmes typically consist of: classes that educate parents about the anatomy and physiology of labour and delivery; and relaxation and breathing techniques used by the mother to counter the pain of the contractions. This approach is designed to reduce pain and medical intervention, and make childbirth a rewarding experience for parents.

Research findings favour the sitting position. Labour is shortened because pushing is easier and more effective. The baby also benefits from a richer supply of oxygen because placental blood flow is increased. Studies suggest that there are many benefits to natural childbirth. Mothers have more positive attitudes towards labour and delivery, and report feeling less pain. As a result, they require less medication. Research also indicates that social support plays an important part in the success of natural childbirth.

THE NEWBORN

Appearance of the Newborn

Newborn babies appear very different from the way they are visualised in the media—as either cute or pretty. They have an 'oversized' head (one-fourth their entire length), a narrow chest, large round abdomen, and short, bowed legs. The baby is wet and slippery, coated with **vernixcaseosa**—the white creamy substance that protects the skin before birth. A newborn's nose is often flat and usually covered with **milia**. These are little pimple-like bumps, and are immature oil glands that will go away without treatment. A downy fuzz of fine hair, called **lanugo,** covers the newborn's body, and gradually wears off. Regardless of whether babies are born with a thick mop of hair or a fuzz, this is replaced by the permanent hair. The baby's head is likely to be elongated and rather pointed at the back, due to being 'moulded' during the passage through the birth canal. The newborn has certain capacities that help in her/his survival in the world, and outside their mother's body (Berk 2013).

THE NEWBORN BABY'S CAPACITIES

Newborn Reflexes

A reflex is an inborn, automatic muscle reaction / response to a particular form of stimulation. Some reflexes have survival value. For example, the rooting reflex helps a breast-fed baby find the mother's nipple. Sucking helps in the feeding process of the newborn. Some reflexes may have had significance in our evolutionary past, but no longer serve a special purpose (for example, the Moro reflex).

What reflexes should be present in a newborn?

Some reflexes occur only in specific periods of development. Reflexes help to identify normal brain and nerve activity. Table 3.1 shows some of the normal reflexes seen in newborn babies.

Table 3.1: Reflexes Seen in Newborn Babies

Reflex	Stimulation	Response	Duration
Babinski	Sole of foot stroked	Fans out toes and twists foot in	Disappears at nine months to a year
Blinking	Flash of light or puff of air	Closes eyes	Permanent
Grasping	Palms touched	Grasps tightly	Weakens at three months; disappears at a year
Moro	Sudden move; loud noise	Startles; throws out arms and legs and then pulls them towards body	Disappears at three to four months
Rooting	Cheek stroked or side of mouth touched	Turns toward source, opens mouth and sucks	Disappears at three to four months
Stepping	Infant held upright with feet touching ground	Moves feet as if to walk	Disappears at three to four months
Sucking	Mouth touched by object	Sucks on object	Disappears at three to four months
Swimming	Placed face down in water	Makes coordinated swimming movements	Disappears at six to seven months
Tonic neck	Placed on back	Makes fists and turns head to the right	Disappears at two months

Source: Adapted from Santrock 1994.

Box 3.5 Babies in Families

In many Indian families, the baby is held by many adults, such as grandmothers or aunts. We are all familiar with the presence of *Dadis* (paternal grandmother) or *Nanis* (maternal grandmother), and the way they play with the baby. They often examine each toe and finger, stoke the sole of the foot, make gurgling sounds, and expect the baby to respond. True to human interaction theories, the baby responds; lack of response often leads to anxiety and may promote further interactions. Such sensory-rich interaction is significant for the babies' growth and well-being. The adult caregivers' intuitive responses to babies become natural ways to check their basic reflexes.

Grandmothers, who traditionally spend a lot of time with babies, ensure that the baby's needs are met, and may also facilitate early detection and early intervention. A mother reported that her mother-in-law was concerned about the way the baby was breast-feeding. She noticed a pattern in the way the baby gasped for air. The baby's actions were playful as the mother fed on demand, and this particular action may have gone unnoticed. However, the mother heeded the observation of the grandmother, who had brought up children and grandchildren, and spoke to the paediatrician. Medical probe identified a condition called 'hole in the heart', which prompted the baby to assist her process of breathing while sucking.

Keen and careful observations bond us with babies, and in some contexts help in capturing strengths and weaknesses. Quick and appropriately timed responses help babies to blossom.

Source: Asha Singh.

The Importance of Assessing Newborn Reflexes

An evaluation of neonatal reflexes is performed during examinations. Reflexes provide a way of assessing the health of the baby's nervous system.

The abnormal **presence** of infantile reflexes in an older child can be discovered during a neurological examination. **Assessment** of neonatal reflexes is a screening tool for children with neurological difficulties. Primary reflexes may persist for certain children beyond their normal time span, causing a disruption in subsequent development. Children with neurological damage will have a common denominator of prolonged neonatal reflexes. Since recent studies have demonstrated that repetition of these reflexes seems to eventually inhibit them, parents can work with the infant by assisting with the repetition of persistent reflexes.

Sensory Capacities

Babies can see, hear and respond to interesting sights, sounds, and other sensory stimuli at a much earlier age than was originally believed.

- At birth, the dermal or touch system is the most mature of all the sensory capacities. The skin sends a multitude of sensory messages to the brain. The skin is the most extensive and basic of all sensory systems, and contains receptors for temperature, contact and pain. Sensitivity to touch, pain and temperature change is present at birth. Touch helps to stimulate physical and emotional development. Body contact plays a major role in the establishment of relationships. During the first few hours and immediately after birth, the mother's extreme sensitivity to her infant facilitates and favours the development of emotional ties. Direct skin-to-skin contact is advised immediately after birth.
- Smell: Newborns are extremely sensitive, and respond differently, to smells, as indicated by the different facial expressions apparent immediately after birth. The infant is able to distinguish the mother's breast milk within the first week of life. A newborn infant is attracted to the odour of her own mother's lactating breast. This helps her to find a food source and identify her own mother. In addition to body contact, which is inseparably linked with movement, smell plays an important role in the establishment of emotional ties.

  Through smell, infants are able to elicit and maintain contact with their environment. Infants are attracted to what is familiar, and express this comfort through bodily movements and facial expressions. The infant's calm and quiet response is highly satisfying to the mother. She is reassured that her care has been effective, and is encouraged to engage in a series of affectionate mutual exchanges. While communication through touch and smell is subtle, it occupies a critically important place in the development of emotional ties, and sets the stage for more complex mother-infant communication.
- Taste: Clearly differentiated facial expressions indicate that infants can discriminate between sweet, sour, salty, and bitter tastes. There seems a preference for sweet liquids. They are born with the ability to communicate their taste preferences.
- Hearing: Hearing is a complex inborn ability, and this system is fully established at birth. The foetus can respond to noise in the uterus. One striking characteristic is the newborn's preference for the human voice, particularly the high-pitched and expressive female voice. There are some sounds in languages that children may not be able to distinguish in the early years, for example 'ang' (the dot over 'aa' in Hindi). Research indicates that infants stop sucking briefly in response to a noise, and then resume sucking immediately. In response to the human voice, however, sucking is interrupted and then resumed in active sequences, supported by regular pauses, as if in anticipation of repeated vocalisations.

  Their ability to perceive speech sounds outside their language is more precise than an adult's. Observations of infants in the earliest days of life reveal that they react in specific ways to the mother's voice. Babies suck longer and more vigorously when they hear the mother's voice. This is indicative of the fact that the infant is programmed to respond specifically to the individual who feeds him. They have an inborn reflex to coordinate eye movements with sound, and this enables them to turn towards the source of a sound. In a couple of months, this association between sight and sound becomes a skilled action, enabling an infant to choose where to focus attention.

By two months, an infant is able to detect subtle distinctions between similar sounds as 'pa and ba', or 'ma and na'. Thus, the auditory perception of a 2-month-old is identical to that of an adult. The perception of verbal sound is influenced by the child's environment, and becomes functional only through appropriate stimulation. From perceiving sound to using meaningful language, however, is a long journey. The ability to hear is only the first step; in order to formulate a response, a child must be able to receive and process information.

- Vision: This is the least mature of the newborn baby's senses. They cannot focus their eyes very well and their visual acuity, or fineness of discrimination, is limited. At birth, infants are equipped to focus on and follow the well-shaped form of a human face. During the first few hours of life, an infant will attend to and follow with the eyes and head a picture of the human face. Newborns can see things only within a distance of 30 cm, but these visual capacities increase dramatically within the first two months.

With the maturation of the nervous system and adequate sensory stimulation, the infant's attention span increases, and they remain in the awake state for longer periods. This in turn allows for more complex modes of early communication. These early expressions of emotional ties pave the way for later cognitive and socio-emotional development. Infants will begin to withdraw from their environment in the absence of human contact and appropriate environmental responses. They see equally unclearly across a wide range of distances, and prefer coloured rather than gray stimuli.

Newborn States

The infant's state (or level) of arousal is important to consider in attempting to understand their capacities and behaviours. States of arousal refer to different degrees of sleep and wakefulness; infants move in and out of these states throughout the day and night. These states of arousal range along a continuum, from deep sleep to active crying. Each is characterised by a specific repertoire of behaviours that are often performed together, rather than independently, and are strongly associated with biological changes. The infant 'state' is important to address when considering the degree and quality of interaction, as it constitutes a system through which important information is transmitted and received.

During the quiet, alert and wakeful state, which usually follows feeding, the infant is most receptive to external stimulation. The duration and quality of this state increases during the first month of life, and varies tremendously from infant to infant. The frequency and duration of the wakeful state is affected both by maternal caregiving behaviour, and by the infant's capacity to regulate her/his own state of wakefulness. For example, newborns are equipped with a capacity known as **habituation**, which helps to shut out disturbing stimulation.

Crying is the first way that babies communicate their physical needs. Various methods can be used to calm a crying infant. The cries of brain-damaged babies and those who have experienced prenatal and birth complications are often shrill and piercing.

Sleep: REM sleep accounts for 50 per cent of the newborn's sleep time. During irregular rapid-eye-movement (REM) sleep, the brain and parts of the body are active. The eyes dart beneath the lids and heart rate, blood pressure, and breathing are uneven. The body is quiet, and heart rate, breathing, and brain-wave activity are slow and regular during regular non-rapid-eye-movement (NREM) sleep.

Neonatal Assessment

Each newborn baby should be carefully checked at birth for signs of problems or complications. A complete physical assessment includes every body system.

APGAR Score

The APGAR score is assigned in the first few minutes after birth to help identify babies at high risk. It is one of the first checks of a neonate's health. The baby is checked at one minute and five minutes after birth for heart and respiratory rates, muscle tone, reflexes, and colour.

Each area is given a score of zero, one, or two. This adds up to a maximum of 10 points. A total score of 10 means a baby is in the best possible condition. Nearly all babies score between eight and 10, with one or two points less for blue hands and feet because of immature circulation. If a baby has a difficult time during delivery, this can lower the oxygen levels in the blood, which in turn can lower the APGAR score. APGAR scores of three or less often mean a baby needs immediate attention and care. However, only 1.4 per cent of babies have APGAR scores less than seven at five minutes after birth.

A quick way to know the health of the newborn is to look at:

Appearance: What is the colour of the baby? A score of 0 is given if the body is blue all over; a score of 1 is given if the body is pink, but the hands are blue; and the baby gets a 2 if s/he is pink all over. The child is also scored on the nature of her/his cry, which could range from no response to weak or strong crying. Crying indicates the reflexes. The neonate's heartbeat is also noted at birth at two five-minute intervals, and scored from 0–2, depending from absent, to below 100, to above 100 per minute. The respiratory effort is also scored similarly, between 0–2 depending on whether it is absent (0), or weak and gasping at intervals (1), while 2 is given for regular and strong breathing. The movement of the newborn is also observed by the flexion of the arms and legs, referred to as muscle tone.

APGAR is often used as an acronym for easy memory for parents, expanded as:

Appearance: colour
Pulse: heart rate
Grimace: reflex—irritability
Activity: muscle tone
Respiration: breathing effort

Birth Weight and Measurements

The average weight for term babies in India (born between 37 and 41 weeks gestation) is about 2.8–3.2 kg. In general, small and very large babies are at greater risk of problems. Babies are weighed daily in the nursery to assess growth, and fluid and nutrition needs. Newborn babies may lose as much as 10 per cent of their birth weight. Premature and sick babies may not begin to gain weight right away (Ghosh 1998).

Physical Examination

A complete physical examination is an important part of newborn care. Each body system is carefully examined for signs of health and normal function. The paediatrician also looks for any signs of illness or birth defects. Physical examination of a newborn often includes an assessment of the following:

- General appearance: physical activity, tone, posture, and level of consciousness
- Skin: colour, texture, nails, presence of rashes
- Vital signs:
    - breathing rate—normally 30–60 breaths per minute
    - temperature—able to maintain a stable body temperature of 98.6° F (37° C) in normal room environment
    - pulse—normally 120–160 beats per minute
- Head and neck:
    - fontanels (the open 'soft spots' between the bones of the baby's skull)
    - appearance, shape, presence of moulding (shaping of the head from passage through the birth canal)
    - clavicles (bones across the upper chest)
- Genitals and anus: for open passage of urine and stool
- Arms and legs: movement and development

Gestational Assessment

Assessing a baby's physical maturity is an important part of care. Maturity assessment is helpful in meeting a baby's needs if the dates of a pregnancy are uncertain. For example, a very small baby may actually be more mature than it appears by size, and may need different care than a premature baby.

An examination called the Dubowitz/Ballard Examination for Gestational Age is often used. A baby's gestational age can often be closely estimated using this examination. It evaluates a baby's appearance, skin texture, motor function, and reflexes. The physical maturity part of the examination is done in the first two hours of birth. The neuromuscular maturity examination is completed within 24 hours after delivery. Information often used to help estimate babies' physical and neuromuscular maturity are given below.

Physical Maturity

The physical assessment part of the Dubowitz/Ballard Examination looks at physical characteristics that look different at different stages of a baby's gestational maturity. Babies who are physically mature usually have higher scores than premature babies.

Points are given for each area of assessment, with a low of –1 or –2 for extreme immaturity, to as much as 4 or 5 for post-maturity. Areas of assessment include:

- skin textures (that is, sticky, smooth, peeling).
- lanugo (the soft downy hair on a baby's body): this is absent in immature babies, then appears with maturity, and disappears again with post-maturity.
- plantar creases: these creases on the soles of the feet range from absent to covering the entire foot, depending on the maturity.
- eyes and ears: eyes fused or open, and amount of cartilage and stiffness of the ear tissue.
- breast: the thickness and size of breast tissue and areola (the darkened ring around each nipple) are assessed.
- genitals, female: appearance and size of the clitoris and the labia.
- genitals, male: presence of testes and appearance of scrotum, from smooth to wrinkled.

Neuromuscular Maturity

- Six evaluations of the baby's neuromuscular system are performed. These include:
    - how the baby holds her/his arms and legs—posture
    - how far the baby's hands can be flexed towards the wrist—square window
    - how far the baby's arms 'spring back' to a flexed position—arm recoil
    - how far the baby's knees extend—popliteal angle
    - how far the elbows can be moved across the baby's chest—scarf sign
    - how close the baby's feet can be moved to the ears—heel to ear

A score is assigned to each assessment area. Typically, the more neurologically mature the baby, the higher the score. When the physical assessment score and the neuromuscular score are added together, the gestational age can be estimated. Scores range from very low for immature babies (less than 26 to 28 weeks), to very high scores for mature and post-mature babies.

The Neonatal Behavioural Assessment Scale (NBAS) is a test developed by T. Berry Brazelton to assess the baby's reflexes, state changes, responsiveness to stimuli, and other reactions. Newborn behaviour and parenting styles combine to shape development. Thus, changes in NBAS scores over the first week or two of life provide the best estimate of a baby's ability to recover from the stress of birth.

PRETERM AND LOW BIRTH-WEIGHT INFANTS

Preterm is defined as babies born alive before 37 weeks of pregnancy are completed. There are sub-categories of preterm birth, based on gestational age:

- extremely preterm (<28 weeks)
- very preterm (28 to <32 weeks)
- moderate to late preterm (32 to <37 weeks) (WHO)

Small-for-date babies are below their expected weight when the length of the pregnancy is taken into account. Small-for-date infants usually have more serious problems than preterm infants.

An estimated 15 million babies are born preterm. Almost one million children die each year due to complications of preterm birth. Children who do survive face a lifetime of disability, including learning disabilities and visual and hearing problems. Inequalities in survival rates around the world are stark. Half of the babies born at 32 weeks (two months early) die due to a lack of feasible, cost-effective care, such as warmth, breast-feeding support, and basic care for infections and breathing difficulties in low-income settings. In high-income countries, almost all of these babies survive (WHO 2014).

Characteristics of Preterm Infants and Consequences for Caregiving

Preterm infants are tiny, sleepy, unresponsive, awake sporadically, and irritable. They appear very small with very thin skin, which is red, wrinkled and translucent, with easily visible veins. There is little subcutaneous fat. The appearance and behaviour of preterm babies can lead parents to be less sensitive and responsive in caring for them. Preterm infants as a group are at risk of child abuse. They need to be protected from infection and aided in temperature regulation. Physical needs that are normally met by close human contact are met by medical devices in preterm babies. Special infant stimulation is needed: this includes stimulation involving motion, touch, or audio awareness to promote growth and alertness. Oxygenation of the baby's body may be increased by skin-to-skin contact with the mother. This also improves temperature regulation and feeding, and overall infant survival.

Post-term infants: Since the normal length of pregnancy is 38 weeks, infants born after 42 weeks are post-term. About 10 per cent fall into this category. The possibility of oxygen deprivation and head injuries are increased in post-term births. Doctors usually induce labour in post-term pregnancies, since the likelihood of birth complications and infant death increases as the pregnancy continues.

Figure 3.1 Imitating at the age of three months

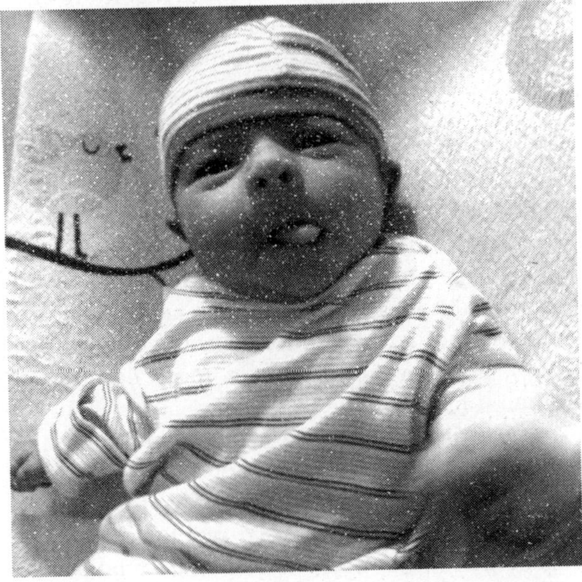

Source: Prerna Singh

Figure 3.2 Understanding parents at four weeks

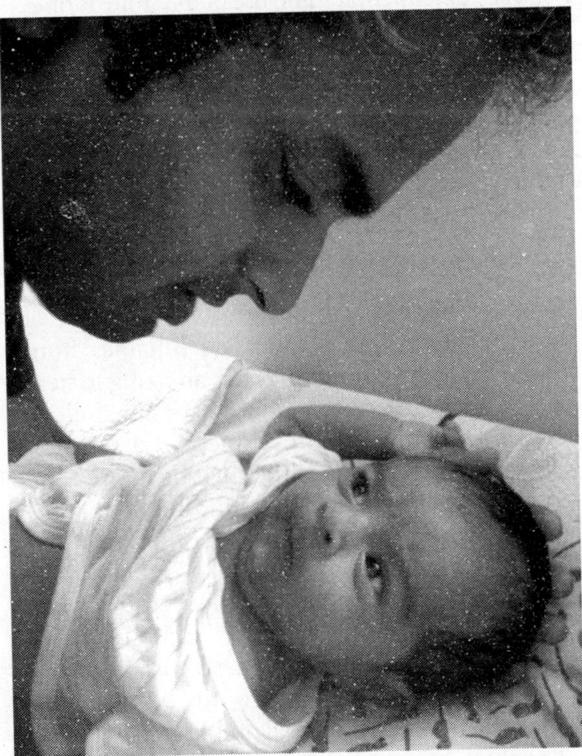

Source: Prerna Singh

BIRTH COMPLICATIONS

1. Cerebral palsy is a general term for a variety of problems, all involving muscle coordination resulting from brain damage before, during, or just after birth.
2. Anoxia refers to an inadequate supply of oxygen. It may be caused by the squeezing of the umbilical cord or placenta previa, which is the premature separation of the placenta.
3. Respiratory distress syndrome is a disorder in which the lungs are so immature that the air sacs collapse, causing the serious breathing difficulties often found in preterm infants.

Understanding Birth Complications

Research on infants who experienced birth complications indicates that, as long as the birth injuries are not overwhelming, a supportive home environment can restore children's growth. When negative factors outweigh positive ones, even sturdy newborns can have lifelong problems.

Early Mother–Infant Interaction

Infants are equipped with a complex repertoire of communication skills, including smiles, gestures and vocalisations. For example, newborns in the early days of life have a facial expression suggesting a smile, which lasts for the first few months. Although the early smile seems to be reflexive, parents react to this expression as if it were an attempt to communicate. At approximately two to two-and-a-half months, the unexplained smile turns into a social smile, which appears regularly at the sight of a face. This facial expression becomes a tool and a means of communication, and paves the way for more complex human interaction.

The maternal response to the smile plays a major role in the development of social communication. By the age of three months, the smile is well-established and is used systematically to engage in communication. The smile establishes the infant's capacity and need for interaction within the first few months. The infant's smile reassures the mother that her child can distinguish her from other people. The use of the smile is one of the first means of intentional communication. Through repeated smiles and exchanges, the infant begins and maintains interactions. It is only through interaction that the child's smiles and other modes of communication become recognised and interpreted as signals.

Box 3.6 Infant Rhymes and Games

In the Children' Museum in Chicago, one of the interactive machines plays lullabies from different parts of the world. It is amazing to hear and experience the similarity in the melody and the simplicity in the tunes. In a research study of infant rhymes, the investigation of the content indicated that they mostly comprised of similar-sounding words, describing relationships and how precious the baby is. Such tools of sociality can be found in most cultures and communities as they are easy cultural ways to interact with babies, whose vocalisations are very basic. Through simple words, such rhymes meet the social, emotional and linguistic needs of babies, and provide new mothers with ready ways to interact and become responsible and responsive caregivers.

Similarly, infant games are physical gestures and playful interactions, and the actions stimulate their muscles with the sense of touch.

Source: Arora 1989.

Feeding and Infant Care Practices

Much of mother-infant interaction is focused on feeding during the first four to six months of life. Feeding provides an opportunity to observe the infant's increasingly complex set of capacities, and helps the baby to forge a bond with the mother. Mother-child interaction with respect to feeding is a dynamic process that changes continuously over time, and is affected by factors intrinsic to both the mother and infant, as well as extrinsic factors imposed by the social and cultural environment.

Many Hindus believe that certain foods have either a 'cooling' or a 'heating' effect on the functions of various organs, and affects mood, personality and physical well-being. For example, if a baby has a cold, a breast-feeding mother may avoid 'cold' foods, while she might take those same foods when the baby is running a temperature. This concept is removed from the actual temperature of food, or the intensity of spices. High-protein, acidic, and salty foods are considered 'hot', whereas 'cold foods' are often sweet. Lentils, millet and grapes are examples of 'hot' foods, and cereals, potatoes, milk, and white sugar are examples of 'cold' foods.

In the earliest days of life, the mother-infant relationship rests on the satisfaction of the physiological need of hunger. This harmonious relationship develops in the first four to five days, during which time the infant coordinates the sucking pattern to match that of the mother. Through rapid early maturation, the infant becomes more alert and utilises his rapidly developing sensory systems to interact with both people and objects in the environment. The infant learns to recognise the smell and taste of milk, discovers the mother's gaze, and recognises her speech. Gradually, feeding is associated with a feeling of pleasure and intense social stimulation. The establishment of an optimal feeding pattern is dependent on the interplay of infant, maternal and environmental factors.

This adaptability of human infant behaviour is more dramatic when viewed under stressful environmental conditions, combined with maternal risk factors that would seemingly jeopardise the development of the infant. It is recognised that the human infant is well-equipped to adapt to the stress of a harsh environment and develop according to a predetermined path of optimal development. This ability is particularly apparent in the rapid catch-up growth exhibited by low birth-weight infants. It is argued that although the biological capacity for catch-up growth is inherent in the species, it is dependent on appropriate maternal feeding and caregiving behaviours.

Transition to Parenthood

The transition to parenthood signifies an increase in emotional ties and marks an entry into a new role. For women, especially, becoming a parent is a more life-changing transition, in terms of work hours, childcare, leisure, and housework, as well as in terms of their relationship with their husbands and others. Kaitz and Katzir (2004) show that men are just as affected by the transition to parenthood as women. Today, men are more involved in the care of their child during the first couple of months.

CHANGING SOCIAL PRACTICES AND STATE SUPPORT

Childbirth practices vary around the world. Before the 1800s, childbirth in Western nations usually took place at home, and was a family-centred event. It moved to the hospital during the nineteenth-century Industrial Revolution. The routine use of medical procedures during labour and delivery was questioned by many, and the natural childbirth movement arose during the 1950s and 1960s. A small but growing number of women are choosing to have their babies at home. In home deliveries, women often give birth in the upright, sitting position rather than lying flat on their backs with their feet in stirrups. In Europe, women are encouraged to give birth on their sides to reduce the need for an episiotomy.

There are advantages and disadvantages to having a baby either at a hospital or at home. These should be considered carefully before deciding where to give birth. Hospitals have rigid rules that grant mothers little control over birth, but are better equipped to handle complications. Health centres are less likely than traditional hospitals to use unnecessary medical procedures, and encourage early mother-newborn contact. They, however, are more expensive than home deliveries. Home births take place in a familiar environment that is optimally suited for early parent-child contact. Training of birth attendants is not uniform, though, and routine medical procedures are usually not available.

In India, there is a continuum of skilled attendants—a formal midwifery cadre, including auxiliary nurse midwives (ANM), lady health visitors (LHV), staff nurses, and doctors. The National Rural Health Mission (NRHM), launched in 2005, declared that safe delivery services should be available at the community level; this, however, is still not widely available, and neither are primary and referral facilities. India's safe delivery rates have been increasing, with a reported 71.8 per cent of rural deliveries taking place with a skilled birth attendant, both in institutions and at home (CES 2009). Sixty-eight per cent of rural deliveries occurred in institutions, and of these, 70 per cent were in public facilities.

With the increase in institutional deliveries, there is growing awareness about safety and security measures regarding prenatal care. There is a swell in members seeking referral services, complicating post-natal care, emergency, or difficult cases.

A number of best practices have been implemented across the world to mitigate delays and increase the availability of skilled birth attendants in rural areas. These broadly include: (*a*) enhanced in-service training on skilled attendance; (*b*) creating new cadres of midwives; (*c*) mechanisms to make skilled attendants available at the community level, including incentives, rational placement, adequate facilities and supply chains, and other support; (*d*) improving care linkages between pregnancy, delivery, immediate postnatal/postpartum care, and continued postpartum/postnatal care; (*e*) improving referral transport;

and (*f*) community mobilisation towards institutional delivery.

Despite being amongst the top five countries in terms of absolute numbers of maternal and child deaths, India has made encouraging progress in reducing maternal and child mortality rates. In 2010, India's child mortality rate (59 per 1,000 live births) almost equalled the global average of 57. At the national level, maternal mortality ratio (MMR) declined from 254 (SRS 2005) to 212 (SRS 2007–09)—a decline of about 14 points per year on an 'All-India' basis. In terms of numbers, though, there are 56,000 maternal deaths each year. About two-thirds of maternal deaths occur in just a few states—Assam, Uttar Pradesh (including Uttarakhand), Rajasthan, Madhya Pradesh (including Chhattisgarh), Bihar (including Jharkhand), and Odisha.

The mortality rate in children below the age of five is 59 per 1,000 live births (SRS 2010), which translates into 15.8 lakh deaths in the country per year. Of these, 8.8 lakh (56 per cent) children die in the first month of life; and 12.5 lakh (79 per cent) children die in the first year, including the neonatal period. The neonatal mortality rate has remained stagnant, constituting an even larger proportion of the total child deaths (0–5 years) in 2010. A rural-urban differential in under-five mortality is evident and stands at 28 points; however, the encouraging trend is that the decline in rural child mortality has been faster than the urban.

There is also a gender differential of nine points in the under-five category (female: 64; male: 55), underlining the need to address social determinants of health, including the status of women and girl children, female literacy, and women's economic and social empowerment.

Considering the large number of maternal and child deaths in the country, it is important to understand why these deaths occur.

Maternal mortality results because of multiple reasons, which can broadly be classified into medical, socio-economic and health system-related factors. Medical causes can be direct or indirect. The most common direct medical causes of maternal death as per SRS (2001–03) are haemorrhage, mainly postpartum (37 per cent), sepsis caused by infection during pregnancy, labour and the postpartum period (11 per cent), and unsafe abortions (8 per cent). A significant proportion of maternal deaths are also attributed to 'indirect causes', the most common of which are anaemia and malaria.

Among children who die before their fifth birthday, almost one-third die of infectious causes, nearly all of which are preventable. As per WHO–CHERG 2012 estimates, the causes of child mortality in the age group 0–5 years in India are (*a*) neonatal causes (52 per cent); (*b*) pneumonia (15 per cent); (*c*) diarrhoeal disease (11 per cent); (*d*) measles (3 per cent); (*e*) injuries (4 per cent); and (*f*) others (15 per cent). The major causes of neonatal deaths are prematurity (18 per cent), infections (16 per cent) such as pneumonia and septicaemia, asphyxia (10 per cent; that is, inability to establish breathing immediately after birth), and congenital causes (5 per cent).

Preterm birth has emerged as the leading cause of neonatal death, underlying the need for a rapid scale-up of maternal health interventions in order to improve neonatal health outcomes (http://www.unicef.org/india/1._RMNCHAStrategy.pdf).

ETHICAL, SOCIAL AND LEGAL ISSUES IN PERINATAL DECISIONS

Ethics refers to the moral principles or a set of moral values which determine the code of conduct stipulated by a profession. In 1860, the foetus was recognised as a living being in the Indian Penal Code, and any person causing the wilful death of a foetus in the womb was to be held accountable. However, if a doctor believed that termination of pregnancy was in the best interests of the mother, it was legally permitted. The Medical Termination of Pregnancy Act (MTP) was enacted by the parliament in 1971. According to its provisions, if pregnancy is less than 12 weeks of gestation, it can be terminated on the advice of a registered medical practitioner. The advice of two doctors is mandatory before undertaking an abortion between 12–20 weeks of gestation.

However, sex-selective abortion of female foetuses by ante-natal sex determination is highly unethical, and has been banned throughout the country under the PC&PNDT Act 1994 (The Pre-conception and Prenatal Diagnostic Techniques [Regulation and Prevention of Misuse] Act). The express purpose of this Act was to prevent the misuse of prenatal diagnostic techniques for the purpose of prenatal sex determination, leading to female foeticide. It intended to regulate the use of prenatal diagnostic techniques to detect genetic/ metabolic disorders, or chromosomal abnormalities and sex-linked disorders.

The PNDT Act was amended in 2003 to prevent the use of new fertility technologies, which facilitate selection of the foetus' sex before conception. Key highlights of the law are:

- Prohibition of sex selection, before and after conception.
- Regulation of prenatal diagnostic techniques (for example, amniocentesis and ultrasonography) for the detection of genetic abnormalities, by restricting their use to registered institutions. The Act allows the use of these techniques only at a registered place for a specified purpose, and by a qualified person registered for this purpose.
- Prevention of the misuse of such techniques for sex selection before or after conception.
- Prohibition of the advertisement of any technique for sex selection, as well as sex-determination.
- Prohibition on the sale of ultrasound machines to persons not registered under this Act.

Any termination of a normal female foetus, amounting to female foeticide, shall be regarded as a professional misconduct on the part of the physician, leading to criminal proceedings as per the provisions of this Act (Clause 7.6). It is important to note that the penalty for sex determination and female foeticide includes striking off the name from the register, apart from criminal action.

SUMMARY

- This chapter, which focuses purely on the Indian context, dealt with the practices, rituals and taboos related with the care of pregnant women. It also discussed the various community systems and lifecycle rituals that celebrate pregnancy and birth in every regional and religious group in the country, from the north to the south, from Hindus and Muslims, to Christians and Parsis. It discussed the process of birth in great detail, with attention paid to the specific stage of childbirth and the various delivery options. The newborn baby, its capacities and reflexes are also discussed exhaustively as is the importance of neonatal assessment, with special reference to the APGAR score. Birth complications have also been dealt with, as have the various feeding and infant care practices. The state support offered during childbirth in various regions is also discussed, as is the PNDT Act and its significance in India.

KEY TERMS

Neonate – Newborn

Weaning foods – Semi-solid foods for infants, meant to slowly move the baby from breast milk to other foods

Competencies of the newborn – The capacity of the newborn to absorb stimulation from the environment

Lactation – Body's capacity to secrete milk.

EXERCISES

1. Talk to three families from different regions or religious backgrounds in your neighbourhood regarding the practices related to pregnancy and care of the pregnant woman.
2. Name and briefly describe the three stages of labour.
3. Interview five women with children to investigate their experiences of childbirth:

   Where did you deliver the baby?

   Did the family choose the place for delivery?

   Who helped in the delivery?

Were any members of the family present at the time of delivery?
Who gave you information about childbirth?
Did you attend any classes for childbirth?

4. Describe some Indian customs and rituals during pregnancy.
5. Define prenatal, perinatal and post-natal periods.
6. Briefly describe the normal birth process.
7. Briefly discuss the sensory and perceptual abilities of a newborn child.
8. Who is a premature baby? What are some of the characteristics of a premature child?
9. What do you understand by the term 'newborn states'?
10. Describe one method for evaluating/assessing a newborn child.
11. Define a reflex. Why are reflexes important for the newborn?
12. What are assisted deliveries? Discuss any one.

FILL IN THE BLANKS

1. The ____________ are a series of sacraments, sacrifices and rituals that serve as rites of passage.
2. The ____________ is based on five vital functions and provides a quick indication of a newborn's physical health.
3. Some reflexes help infants get necessary nutrients, other reflexes protect infants from danger, and still other reflexes ____________.
4. The ____________, launched in 2005 envisions that safe delivery services should be available at the community level.
5. Abnormal position of the baby, such as ____________, in which the baby exits the pelvis with the buttocks or feet first.
6. ____________ proposed a womb-like environment for the newborn with soft music.
7. The physical assessment part of the ____________ looks at physical characteristics that look different at different stages of a baby's gestational maturity.
8. The prenatal period lasts for ____________, which is roughly nine months.
9. The average weight for term babies in India (born between 37 and 41 weeks gestation) is about ____________ kg.
10. Newborns are equipped with a capacity known as ____________, which helps to shut out disturbing stimulation.

REFERENCES

Arora, K., 'Infant rhymes and games in five selected states of India', Unpublished Master's Dissertation in Child Development, New Delhi: University of Delhi, 1989.

Bee, H. and D. Boyd, *The Development Child*, New Delhi: Pearson Education, 2004.

Berk, L. E., *Child Development*, Boston: Pearson Education, 2013.

———, *Development through the Life Span*, New Delhi: Pearson Education, 2004.

Clarke-Stewart, A. and S. Friedman, *Child Development: Infancy through Adolescence*, New York: John Wiley & Sons, 1987.

Ghosh, S., *Know Your Child: A Handbook for Parents*, India: Jaypee Brothers Medical Publishers (P) Ltd, 1998.

Harris, J. R. and R. M. Liebert, *The Child: The Development from Birth through Adolescence*, New Jersey: Prentice-Hall, Inc., 1987.

Kail, R. V., *Children and Their Development*, Upper Saddle River: Prentice-Hall, Inc., 2001.

Kaitz, M. and D. Katzir, 'Temporal changes in the affective experience of new fathers and their spouses', *Infant Mental Health Journal*, 25(6), 2004, pp. 540–55.

Kapoor, S. (ed.), *Indian Encyclopaedia*, Vol. 1, New Delhi: Cosmo Publications, 2002.

Lightfoot, C., M. Cole, and S. R. Cole, *The Development Child*. New York: Worth Publisher, 2009.

Muzi, M. J., *Child Development*, Upper Saddle River: Prentice-Hall, Inc., 2000.

Santrock, J. W., *Child Development*, 6e, Wm. C. Brown Communications, Inc., 1994.

World Health Organization, *World Health Statistics*, Washington, D.C.: WHO, 2014.

Online sources:

http://www.who.int/mediacentre/factsheets/fs363/en/ (accessed 27 November 2014).

http://adc.bmj.com/content/89/12/1094.full (accessed 24 August 2013).

http://paa2010.princeton.edu/papers/101092 (accessed 24 August 2013).

http://www.lpch.org/DiseaseHealthInfo/HealthLibrary/hrnewborn/assess.html (accessed 24 August 2013).

http://www.nlm.nih.gov/medlineplus/ency/article/002395.htm (accessed 7 September 2013).

http://www.unicef.org/india/1._RMNCHAStrategy.pdf (accessed 27 November 2014).

4

Development in Early Childhood

HIGHLIGHTS

- Introduces key issues related to early childhood, childcare and preschool education.
- Discusses the significance of this period, and how best to work with young children to support optimal growth during this foundational phase.
- The importance of stimulation and interaction during the formative years.
- Discusses the child's environment—parents, extended families, extra-familial caregivers, teachers, along with home, preschool or daycare.
- Details of development in different domains during the early years.

THE INDIAN CONTEXT AND EARLY CHILDHOOD

The position of the young child in India is marked by contrasting beliefs. On the one hand, there is indulgence, and on the other, children are seen as burdens and as mouths to feed. The vastly varying economic contexts often compel people's choices and decisions. Traditionally, the early childhood years (from prenatal to the age of five) were considered to lay the foundation for the inculcation of basic values and social skills in children. The *ashrama* theory prescribes a set of rituals that fulfil individual need and herald the beginning of the next stage of development, such as *annaprashan*. At six months, the child is fed *kheer* (mashed rice cooked in milk), and from this point the child begins to eat semi-solid meals. Such a tradition conveys an awareness of growing bodily needs, with maturing biological systems.

It was believed that within the space of the family, young parents imbibe ways of child-rearing and family values as the *sanskaras*, and the scriptures advocate *lalan-palan* or *palan poshan*, translated as responsive care and nutrition. During the early years, the desirable mode of child-rearing is more about affect and indulgence. Much of the early care and education of the child was informal, confined within the family, and imparted largely through the wisdom of family elders. Care practices—besides basic feeding and physical care—included stories, lullabies and traditional infant games, learnt and passed down from one generation to the next. This repertoire of traditional childcare practices exists in different regions and in specific languages. While culturally rooted practices are significant for children's development, modern living has introduced modern provisions for children, keeping in mind changing social realities and polarised family configurations. Many regional and local practices need to be reviewed, revived, and perhaps remodified for contemporary contexts.

In India—as elsewhere—the changing family structure (from joint to nuclear) is leading to new ways of parenting, which is now the sole responsibility of the parents. Contemporary economic or individual demands are creating shifts in parenting responsibility, which is further reallocated. Wealthy families can hire paid help, creating surrogate caregivers, while in the lower socio-economic communities, the responsibility for childcare falls on the older siblings, depriving them of both their childhood and basic education. Changes in the demographic profile, such as migration and an increase in women's employment, have created a need for ensuring 'quality informal early care and education' for the young child within the home. Changing social contexts and the global realisation of the importance of the early years have energised societal discourse on the young child.

EARLY YEARS: THE BASIS FOR STRONG FOUNDATIONS

The early years constitute an important phase in an individual's life. The presence of infant games, rhymes and traditional toys conveys folk knowledge and an awareness of infants' alertness to environmental inputs. Most cultures display rudimentary responses to the needs of young children. However, growth and development are rapid in the first two years, and some of the most crucial attributes for learning take shape by the time children complete the first five years. Supportive and interactive environments enable the emergence of brain structures that allow for synaptic connections that promote learning and complex behaviour skills. Many theorists in the psychoanalytic tradition have also emphasised the importance of the early years.

Contemporary Research on Early Childhood

Neuroscience is the scientific study of the brain and its development. Studies in brain research indicate the negative impact of early deprivation. Low sensory input, such a poverty of words, touch or sociality, leads to underdevelopment of the brain.

Recent research in neuroscience shows that during the early childhood years, there are certain critical periods, also called **'sensitive periods'**, for the development of cognitive, linguistic, social, and psychomotor competencies, which are known to contribute to later success in life (Figure 4.1).

The sensitive periods in early childhood have been graphically presented by researchers McCain and Mustard (1999: 31). The notion of critical periods informs us that if babies do not receive adequate stimulation, they lose their advantage and may suffer long-term developmental delays. For example, the first two years are crucial for binocular vision, after which it starts waning. Babies also need experience in emotional control through tactile stimulation and a responsive environment in the first two years. Language learning is highest in the period between eight months to two years, while social relations with peers develops only after three years, and is critical between three to six years.

Neuroscience research has provided evidence of the evolving brain architecture, which functions effectively in response to care and sensory experiences. Development is also being studied through brain imaging, and EEGs of children in institutions or in adverse contexts to identify the nature of structures in relation to social interactions. Cognitive scientists and learning theorists are enhancing our understanding of social contexts and meaning-making. Early neglect can have long-term detrimental effects.

Neuroscience further reiterates that the development of complex skills is built over circuits and skills developed earlier. Basic neural connections occur in interactive contexts of play, and care amidst responsive adults. If we allow a slow start, we create a system that fails to provide early wiring. Several research studies have indicated a direct link between care in the early years and later attitudes. Early learning also impacts school enrolment, attendance, achievement, and retention in primary school. Early care and stimulation create a readiness for school tasks.

Economic Rationale Behind the Significance of Early Years

The criticality of early childhood is also derived from the economic rationale that strongly endorses that investment in early childhood programmes can give significant returns. A recent longitudinal study in the United States indicated that the return on every dollar invested in early childhood amounted to $7–17.07 saved in subsequent years (Schweinhart et al. 1993, 2005).

Research also indicates that early education programmes have the potential to prevent crime, and thus lead to an associated reduction in social costs (Heckman and Masterov 2004). Their argument is that early education affects labour force productivity and crime through its effect on cognitive and non-cognitive skills. The crucial importance of investing in these early childhood years to ensure an enabling environment for every child and thereby provide a sound foundation for life follows logically. This will also impact, in the long term, the quality of human capital available to a country like India, whose main asset in the years to come will be its 'youth power'.

Global Trends in Early Childhood Care and Education

Social contexts present a wide range of economic variations and social organisation in the ways that children are cared for. With the emphasis on the significance and critical sensitivity of meeting the developmental needs of young children has come a worldwide awareness of investing in early childhood care and education. There is growing awareness of the benefits of early childhood education. Concern for the young child's survival, protection, growth, and development has led to global debates on the issue, for instance the Convention on the Rights of the Young Child (CRC), 1989, and Education for All (EFA), 1990. While the former sought international commitment to the protection of children's right to survival, participation and development, the latter has postulated ECCE as the first goal to be achieved in the first step towards universal elementary education. India is a signatory to both Conventions and is thereby committed to advancing these issues through appropriate policies, programmes and budgetary allocations, and has been providing periodic progress reports on the same.

The recently held UNESCO World Conference on ECCE (Moscow 2010) also took note of the current ECCE situation across countries, and proposed a draft framework for action. According to the deliberations, there are at least 80 countries with some legislation relating to ECCE, and 30 countries with at least one year of compulsory pre-primary education.

Box 4.1 Early Childhood in India

Is India working towards energised early childhood programmes? Are there professionals with the motivation and enthusiasm to overcome the constraints of crowded classrooms? We are an emerging economy, and our teachers, parents and professionals must learn to operate with the bare essentials at low cost to provide every child her/his basic right, due morally and now constitutionally. In recent years, the 86th amendment to the constitution has made education, via Article 21A, a fundamental right for children between 6–14 years, paying little heed to children under six. However, Article 45 sustains 'state endeavors to provide free and compulsory care and education to children below six years'. India is one of the 108 countries who are signatories to the UN Convention for the Rights of the Child.

Can we generate certain curricular principles—akin to those in the NCERT National Curriculum Framework 2005—that are similar to the UNESCO brief on curricular universals? ECCE recommendations need to align with childhood propensities for wilful play, questioning and vigour. Pedagogical principles must employ art, play, mediation, exploration, experimentation, participation, and active involvement.

The approach paper of the Eleventh Five-Year Plan (2007–12) prepared by the Planning Commission emphatically stated that 'Development of the child is at the centre of the Eleventh Plan'. While continuing with the rights-based approach to child development, the plan recognises the importance of a holistic approach, focusing on outcomes and indicators for child development, as well as macro-perspective trends and governance issues. Early childhood development professionals touch the lives of children, and their agenda must be to become a cadre of experts who reach out to young citizens with informed practices, transacting curriculum based on informed choices.

THE DEVELOPMENTAL SIGNIFICANCE

The early years are a period of rapid growth; children acquire basic physical and motor skills, which permit them to expand their physical world and forge new relationships. Children learn to express themselves and listen, cope with fear and share pleasure, as well as discover oneself as distinct from others. During the early part of this period, growth and development are fostered through sensory experiences, and it is imperative for children to be with caring adults.

This has been elaborated by Swiss psychologist Jean Piaget. As children gain mobility and social skills, there is increased exploration and experimenting. Children become confident of their bodies, do things independently, and experiment with objects in the surrounding environment. There is enhanced curiosity about social and physical phenomena, with interest in noting what is going on around them. They enjoy the company of other children and seek to imitate adult behaviour. They learn to ask questions and assert themselves as individuals. They begin to negotiate with others, slowly acquiring self-control and discipline.

The formation of attitudes and values in later life, as well as the desire to learn, are also influenced by the environment and opportunities a child receives in these early years. An impoverished environment or emotional neglect can lead to negative consequences for a child's development, which may even be irreversible. There is growing evidence about the cumulative effect of disadvantages faced by children from poorer families, who become 'at risk' in terms of their life chances.

Developmentally appropriate practices are based on the belief that knowledge about child development should be the basis for making decisions about early childhood programmes and practices. It is very important for programme planners and teachers to have knowledge of how children develop, and what their needs and strengths during early childhood are. The early childhood programme should focus on varying abilities, the least restrictive environment, health, and nutrition, along with focusing on the four areas of development—physical-motor, cognitive, language, and socio-emotional development.

THEORETICAL PERSPECTIVE

How children learn, or how society needs to organise environments to assist in their learning, are questions that have fascinated thinkers. Such overviews are discussed over the chapters to spark young students to explore in-depth ideas about children and features of childhood.

Jean Jacques Rousseau (1712–78): Rousseau believed that children should be allowed to express themselves freely, and that in the early years, social and emotional adjustments were more important than the accumulation of information and skill. According to him, the teacher should be a guide who allows children to discover knowledge on their own by exploring different objects and situations, rather than teaching them through textbooks. Rousseau's philosophy also influenced Pestalozzi, Froebel, Dewey, and Piaget, as well as many other important theorists. It currently forms the backbone of early childhood theories and practices.

Johann Pestalozzi (1746–1827): Pestalozzi emphasised that education should be based on natural development, self-discovery, and on the child's own interest and experience. He believed that teaching methods should fit individual needs and that every person, irrespective of social class or ability, has a right to education.

Fredrich Froebel (1782–1852): Froebel emphasised group activities and social development during the early years in his book, *Education of Man*. He started the first kindergarten, or child's garden, where a curriculum based on 'gifts'—materials designed with a definite sequence, use and 'occupations', designed to develop certain skills—was followed. Another important contribution was the importance he placed on **play** in early childhood education. In Frobel's mind, play is central to knowing children's inner thoughts and social world.

John Dewey (1859–1952): Dewey introduced the term 'child-centred curriculum' and believed that the Frobelian philosophy was too rigid and teacher-dominated. He believed that the realities of everyday life should be the basis of all classroom activities, and should start with the child and not with an imitation of the teacher. He also placed importance on play activities that elicit problem-solving on the part of the child. According to him, the teacher's role was that of a facilitator, who encourages social skills by planning, organising, and providing opportunities for it. Dewey's philosophy has been criticised for giving too many choices to children, as a result of which children do not acquire the required knowledge on the subject matter.

Maria Montessori (1879–1952): Montessori, a medical doctor, became interested in early childhood education while working with children with special needs. While running her school *Casa dei Bambini*, she designed a system of 'didactic material' to provide practice in activities, which focused on concepts such as form, colour, texture, and quantity. Montessori activities were organised for individuals rather than a group, and children were allowed to choose how, and for how long, they wanted to use the material. Her method was perceived as too structured, with little opportunity for creativity and individual expression.

Jean Piaget (1896–1989): Piaget became interested in children's thinking in relation to wrong answers in intelligence tests. His training in cutting-edge biology was influential in the development of his ideas about learning, thinking, and his theory of intelligence. Piaget believed that children construct their own knowledge, and that they should be given the freedom to play, experiment, and participate in guided learning activities.

Lev S. Vygotsky (1896–1934): Vygotsky's belief that children learn best with the help of others, an application of his idea on the *zone of proximal distance*, has had an impact on how teachers are viewed in early childhood education.

Indian Thinkers

In India, the thinking about childhood is situated in ancient scriptures, or has to be derived from depictions of children in mythological texts and other literary sources. There have been Indian practitioners like Tarabai Modak, Gijubhai Badheka, or Krishnamurti, who conveyed their thoughts through their work. The position of the child was central, and there was recognition of her/his agency. Tarabai Modak realised the importance of a socio-cultural approach to the education of children, and created learning centres within spaces in the community. Gijubhai Badheka believed in interactive environments, and created a wealth of materials, such as *Mata Pita se Baathcheet*. Such texts created an awareness of the multiplicity of caregivers, who need to work together in the socialising of the young.

In recent times, Indian writers like Devi Prasad have created texts such as *Art as the basis of learning*, which emphasise the need for a child-related perspective, using art expression as a metaphor for children's communication. His writing conveys that children communicate their inner thoughts in diverse ways, and that we need to sensitively pick the cues and provide appropriate environments.

Rabindranath Tagore and Sri Aurobindo have also focused more on children's education than on development. Tagore believed in the value of nature in nurturing children. His story 'Tota', or 'The Parrot', is a commentary on what education should not be. Through this story, he unfolds the harm perpetuated by pressurising children and losing the joy in discovery and exploration. Sri Aurobindo emphasised the significance of value education and inner learning.

Box 4.2 Understanding Childhood Needs

Caregivers, parents and professionals need to understand that cognitive challenges and social skills are just as crucial as physical health and safety. We need extensive teacher and parent education, which is an essential feature, given the rapid social change and the emergence of new values. Young parents do not have adequate experience or the proximity of family elders to guide them. Reading materials and parenting sessions are useful measures to create sensitive caregiving competence. Practical knowledge of handling babies and an awareness of milestones are fundamental to comprehending the notion of early experience and early intervention. Parents need to understand that children grow best in watchful freedom and watchful regulation, neither of which is needed in disproportionate measure. Parents do well when they are involved, and have an interest in the child's learning and unfolding of social reality.

DEVELOPMENT IN EARLY CHILDHOOD

This section discusses the developmental patterns and sequences in growth. In each domain of development, there are strides of progress. The leaps in development during the first six years are at a pace that is not matched by normative changes at any other time. The child follows a biological series of milestones, and these abilities become observable at certain times, and can be flexible within a range. Sometimes the delay in milestones is due to deprivation and unresponsive environments. It is important to be aware of factors that influence development, such as nutrition, social stimulation and opportunity to explore in a safe environment. Physical milestones make the child active and present the first steps towards independence.

Physical and Motor Development

During early childhood, children show remarkable advances in physical and motor development. The newborn has little control and has to be supported at the neck with one hand, with the other hand providing support from under the hip. As a child grows, family members wait for important milestones, such as lifting the head with support when placed in a prone position (on their stomach; the supine position is when babies are on their back). Babies learn to crawl, sit with support, and stand with support, followed by walking, running, jumping, drawing, writing, cycling, etc. Each represents gross and fine motor development in early years.

Infancy

The first six months: The child gains **neck control** by six weeks, first by holding the head for 10 seconds or so when held on the parents' shoulder. The child soon learns to **roll from the back on to the stomach**. Slowly, children learn to **reach out for objects**. A significant milestone is the ability (learnt by six months) to **hold the hand away from the body**. Children also put out their hands and lift their chests. A common physical action is that of babies holding their toes and lifting their bodies in a playful manner. Physical skills can be enhanced during the first six months through good nutrition, play, and sensory inputs (playful noises, clapping, rocking, and providing objects to look at).

Six to 12 months: During this period, children begin to crawl and move about in their unique way, touching and exploring. They are able to sit and hold objects. Children like to put everything into their mouths. Babies can pass objects from one hand to the other, and slowly pull themselves up to a standing position with support. Children also practice using their hands and fingers. Some children can make walking motions and soon begin to walk holding on to furniture. By the end of the first year, children start walking, and can even sit down from a standing position.

Figure 4.1: Pulling to rest on hands

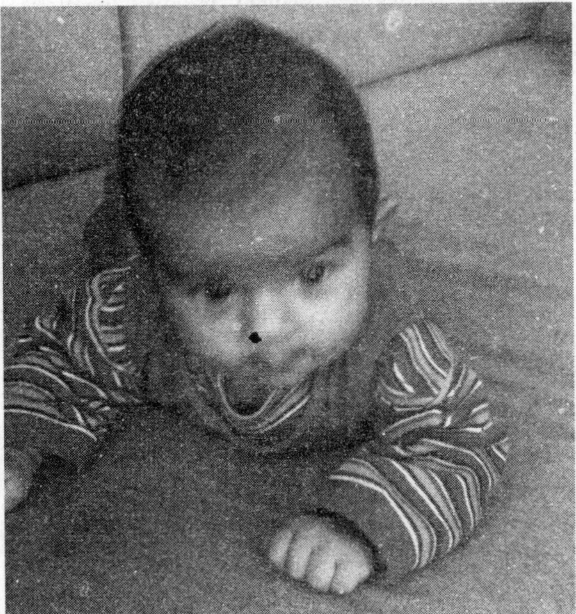

Source: Asha Singh

The Second Year

Growing motor skills enable children to see the world from many perspectives, and foster independent navigation. Between 11–13 months, most children have learnt to walk. They can also bend down and stand up again. They can climb furniture and also try to hold crayons. They can jump in one place, and by the age of two, they can bring both feet together and jump one step. They can kick a ball and throw it some distance with little force.

Three to Six Years: Physical Changes and Development

Although the growth of young children in early childhood slows down a bit as compared to infancy, three to six years is still a time of tremendous physical change. During this period, children's bodies change proportion as they begin to lose their 'baby fat', and develop sleeker, straighter bodies that resemble adults more than babies. Arms and legs stretch to catch up with and balance out the head and trunk, and children develop the muscles necessary for work and play. On an average, young children can expect to grow two to three inches in height per year.

Children's healthy growth is supported by healthy lifestyles. Children should get plenty of exercise and sleep, and eat a balanced diet in order to continue to develop strong muscles and bones and maintain a healthy weight. A family doctor usually checks the height and weight of children, comparing it with the normal range to make sure they are growing appropriately.

Figure 4.2: Trying new games: Building physical skills

Source: Rajkumari Amrit Kaur Child Study Centre collection

Motor Skill Development

In early childhood, motor skills develop rapidly with growth and maturity. Motor skills proceed from the centre of the body to the periphery, allowing children to crawl on their stomachs and later develop the skill to walk. A child may clasp a ball closely to the stomach, and only later, with the acquisition of fine motor skills, is able to take a catch.

Gross (or large) motor skills involve the larger muscles, including arms and legs. Examples of gross motor skills are walking, running, balance, and coordination. When studying gross motor skills, we look at strength, muscle tone, movement quality, and the range of movement. Young children should be given the opportunity to use their large muscles by being in spaces that allow movement (parks, or any safe outdoor space). Preschools should have outdoor spaces for children to run about, jump, or throw a ball. Families should also make the effort to take the child outdoors.

Fine (or small) motor skills involve the smaller muscles in the fingers. The actions that require fine motor skills tend to be more intricate, such as drawing, writing, or grasping objects. A lot of preschool activities are designed to facilitate fine motor skills, and provide important prewriting skills. Threading beads, drawing, and finger painting can be done at home to give young children the opportunity to develop their fine motor skills. Children are attracted towards different objects, such as playing with vegetables, soap, and engaging with adults in their activities. Sometimes, being unaware of an object's real function, they get into trouble—for instance, they may jump on newspapers or, imitating their mothers, empty out huge quantities of soap powder. Such activities disrupt adult routines; however, this is how children naturally show their curiosity and explore.

Physical and motor development follows the principles of development. Development follows a directional pattern—large muscles develop before the smaller ones, and so children learn how to perform gross motor skills before they learn to perform fine motor skills. Muscles located at the core of the body become stronger and develop sooner than those in the feet and hands. This principle is called proximodistal development. Also, development is from the top down, from the head to the toes; this is called cephalocaudal development. Therefore, young children are able to throw a ball before they learn to kick it.

While physical and motor development occurs in an orderly manner, it is also important to realise that the rate at which these milestones are reached can vary. Some children learn to cycle before their same-age peers, while others may take a bit longer.

Parents should realise this variation is normal, and not worry or pressure their children to perform certain motor tasks. However, unless there is some disability, nearly all children exhibit these motor skills at a fairly consistent rate. In the event of a lot of delay, it is advisable to visit a doctor to rule out any form of disability.

Refining Motor Skills

By the age of **two and three**, young children stop 'toddling' (the hallmark of new walkers) and develop a smoother gait; they also develop the ability to run, jump and hop. Children should be given the opportunity to participate in throwing and catching games with larger balls. Riding toys, which give them a chance to push themselves around with their feet while sitting, will promote motor skills.

Children of **three and four** will try to climb stairs by bringing both feet together on each step before proceeding on to the next, while a watchful adult stands close by. The ability to climb down comes later; initially, infants tend to turn around and climb down the stairs backwards. By the age of three, children hold railings or the wall to climb down.

Three to four-year-olds can jump and hop higher as their leg muscles grow stronger. Many can even hop on one foot for short periods of time. Also, at this age children develop better upper body mobility, which results in an ability to catch and throw with speed and accuracy. They can also hit a stationary ball with a bat. As whole body coordination improves, children enjoy cycling. In large families, children play with older cousins and cycles are often given away to younger children in the family.

By the ages of **four and five,** children can climb up and down stairs alone, their running continues to smooth out and increase in speed, they can skip, and have more control and speed when riding their cycles. Children aged **five to six** continue to refine the earlier skills and run and cycle faster, and begin mastering new forms of physical play, such as the jungle gym, see-saw, slide, and swings. Many children of this age enjoy playing organised sports, such as cricket or swimming, and participate in physical extracurricular activities such as karate or dance. Communities should recognise the importance of outdoor play for young children, and develop safe play areas in every neighbourhood. Once children get into the habit of going out to play every evening, they make up their own games, which allows them to practice their large muscles activities.

Opportunities for Fine Motor Skills

Gross motor skills require less precision and accuracy. In fine motor skills, however, children engage in smaller, more precise movements, using the hands and fingers. By the ages of **two to three**, children can build towers out of blocks, mould clay into rough shapes, and scribble with a crayon or a pen. They can also insert objects into matching spaces, such as placing round pegs into round holes. Two to three-year-olds often begin showing a preference for using one hand more than the other, which is the beginning of becoming either left or right-handed. It is important to let them use the hand they prefer. Opportunities to handle material by either tearing it into small pieces, folding, or colouring can keep them busy for hours. Using old newspapers and material around the house enables children to be creative. Sand play is very important for children to imbibe sensory stimulation, and engage in fine motor tasks.

Children at the ages of **three to four** use zippers and gain independence in dressing and undressing themselves. At this age, children can also begin using scissors to cut paper, but should be given blunt scissors for safety reasons. Three to four-year-olds start drawing with crayons, and can make twisting motions with their hands, useful for opening door knobs or twisting the lids off containers. During the ages of **four to five**, children continue to refine their fine motor skills and build upon earlier skills. For instance, they can now button and unbutton their clothes by themselves.

There is a marked improvement in perceptual motor skills as children engage in visual representations. Their artistic skills improve, and they can draw simple stick figures and copy shapes such as circles, squares and large letters. Drawing more complex shapes, however, may take longer. As by this age most children will be attending preschool, they will get a lot of opportunity to use these fine skills. At home, too, parents should keep colouring and pasting material to engage children and enhance their skills.

Figure 4.3: Building confidence

Source: Rajkumari Amrit Kaur Child Study Centre collection

COGNITIVE AND LANGUAGE DEVELOPMENT

Understanding Children's Thinking

Early childhood is also a time of amazing development in children's thinking. Changes take place as memory, reasoning, problem-solving, and thinking continue to evolve. Cognition in childhood can be understood through Piaget's descriptions of the basic stages that children go through as they mentally mature. He believed that children are like 'little scientists', actively trying to explore the physical social world through their experiments. We often notice children moving around, touching and examining anything that looks new to them. Through such activity, they are building information that will enable them to know their surroundings.

Children do not simply wait to be told passively. A key concept in Piaget's theory is the notion of mental frames known as schemas, which help people organise and interpret information. As the child interacts, new information is added to or completely changes previously existing schemas. For example, a young girl may have a schema about a type of bird, such as a sparrow, as something that flies and has wings. When she first encounters a crow, she might initially believe that they are all birds. Soon, she learns to see the difference, either through adult intervention or her own skill, which is when she learns about several types of birds.

Stages in Cognition

Between birth and two years, an infant's knowledge of the world is limited to her/his sensory perceptions and motor activities. The gathering of information through sensory experiences during infancy is known as the sensorimotor stage.

As children grow, their increased mobility gives them some autonomy in exploring. They now enter the **preoperational stage,** which builds upon and adds to earlier sensory learning. Children also begin to develop the ability to use language.

During this stage (two to six years), a child does not yet understand reasoning, cannot mentally deal with information, and is unable to consider the views of other people.

According to Piaget, through the advantages provided by language, young children in the preoperational stage make big strides in knowing their physical world. They build and use the knowledge gained from their senses during the sensorimotor stage to start thinking more symbolically about things that may not be open to their immediate experience. This is evident as children turn a block into a train or a walking stick into a horse. Imitative behaviour reflects symbolic thinking, and facilitates language development and make-believe play. However, the preoperational child lacks abstract thinking skills and their reasoning skills are not fully developed either, and so to learn, they still rely largely on concrete evidence. One of the most important achievements of the preoperational stage is symbolic thinking, which then facilitates language development.

Vygotsky's Perspective on Advances in Children's Thinking

The Russian psychologist Vygotsky studied children's cognitive skills around the same time as Piaget. In his writings, he emphasised that children gain immensely from being part of a socio-cultural context, with the presence of a more experienced other. Vygotsky introduced the notions of guided mediation and the zone of proximal development. He focused attention on the fact that children not only learn through exploring and imitation, but also seek intervention. As the child explores, the adults—often referred to as 'more experienced others'—provide labels, and suggest some meanings that support children's journey of getting to know the world around them. This supportive role is what Vygotsky termed 'guided mediation'.

With regard to the Zone of Proximal development, Vygotsky pointed out that children are able to do certain things independently at each age, and that there are certain aspects that they can achieve with a little support. For example, a child trying to stand is given a walker by adults, and this support allows the child, through assisted attempts, to enhance her/his skill. Another example is of children learning words reading a book with an adult and thereby learning many new words; this experience of reading provides a zone of proximal development. The adult can be any experienced person, including siblings or, as children grow, older friends. Together, Vygotsky's socio-cultural perspective and Piaget's perspective of the individual child as a young explorer help us to build a more holistic understanding of how children learn.

Box 4.3 The Relevance of Vygotsky's Concepts for Early Childhood Learning

The Zone of Proximal Development (ZPD) is the best-known Vygotskian concept. To successfully apply it in a classroom, it is important to know not only where a child is functioning now and where s/he will be tomorrow, but also how best to assist that child in mastering more advanced skills and concepts. This is where scaffolding comes in. Although not used by Vygotsky himself, the concept of scaffolding helps us understand how aiming instruction within a child's ZPD can promote the child's learning and development.

The ZPD describes the area between a child's level of independent performance (what s/he can do alone) and her/his level of assisted performance (what s/he can do with support).

Skills and understandings contained within a child's ZPD are the ones that have not yet emerged, but could emerge if the child engaged in interactions with knowledgeable others (peers and adults), or in other supportive contexts (such as make-believe play for preschool children). According to Vygotsky, the most effective instruction is the kind that is aimed not at the child's level of independent performance, but within the ZPD. This instruction does more than increase a child's repertoire of skills and understandings; it actually produces gains in child development.

To aim instruction at the child's ZPD, the teacher needs to know the child's developmental level at present, as well as the skills and concepts that will develop next. To know these, the teacher needs to understand the developmental trajectories for these skills and concepts. Successful instruction within the child's ZPD also involves making sure that the child will eventually be able to function independently at the same high level at which s/he was previously able to function with adult assistance. Once this is accomplished, the teacher can start aiming instruction at the new ZPD.

Even when children have developed new skills and competencies sufficient to perform a task with adult assistance, it may not mean that they will be ready to perform the task independently the next day. For most children, the transition from assisted to independent learning is a gradual process, involving moving from a great deal of assistance to slowly taking over until eventually, no assistance is needed. To facilitate this transition, a teacher needs to scaffold student learning by first designing and then following a plan for providing and withdrawing appropriate amounts of assistance at appropriate times.

Source: http://www.toolsofthemind.org/philosophy/scaffolding

Observing Children

Young children below the age of six are usually in the midst of others, either in homes or in institutional settings like early childhood centres. Children are largely seen playing, by engaging with objects or through more structured activities. Children play with each other, converse and respond to questions. They may ask questions as they encounter different situations. Babies and small children are usually with adults, who directly and indirectly guide, watch over their behaviour, and help them. Besides physical protection, adults structure the daily rhythms for children in a manner that allows children's development to progress in accordance with their needs.

Box 4.4 Children's Minds and Thinking Processes

Children need time to work out their observations, and what they think the world is all about. 'Why do cats walk on fours?' 'Why do we not live on trees like the birds?' Needless to say, these innocent queries need immediate resolution from the child's point-of-view, but often leave adults wondering at the child's depth and width of inexhaustible curiosity. Children's questions are windows to their minds and permit us to develop an understanding of how they think and feel. We need to ensure that our children receive the appropriate guidance to acquire new competencies, opportunities, as well as time to just be: to learn, to know and grow. As important as it is to expose children in a guided manner to skill-building, it is also important to let children be. Child-rearing is a balance between watchful mediation and watchful freedom.

Factors Influencing Children's Communication

The emergence of language in children during early childhood is fascinating. From cooing and babbling as babies to a few words in infancy, children start speaking in full sentences in a very short period during early childhood. Researchers have found that language development begins before a child is even born, as a foetus also responds to sounds and is able to identify the speech and sound patterns of the mother's voice. The story of Abhimanyu in the Mahabharat learning certain facts in his mother's womb is one that all Indians are familiar with. By the age of 10 months, children begin to recognise the speech sounds of their native language. By the time a child reaches the age of three, s/he will have a vocabulary of approximately 3,000 words.

Several different **theories** explain how and why language development occurs. B. F. **Skinner** suggests that imitation and reinforcement facilitates the emergence of language, while the nativist theory of **Noam Chomsky,** in contrast to the behaviourist approach of Skinner, suggests that language is inherent in human beings, and that children are born with a language acquisition device that allows them to produce language once they have learned the necessary vocabulary.

Parents and other family members facilitate language development through different ways as they interact and play with children. Talking, guiding, asking questions, and providing information are some of the different features of adult-child interaction. Such adult-child engagement also creates a language environment.

Most cultures have certain ways to socialise children, which involve the creation of a language environment. Adults often use a style of speech with infants known as *motherese* or baby talk, which is really infant-directed speech. Baby talk may be higher-pitched intonation, shortened sentences, or a vocabulary that is child-specific. There is greater use of shortened sentences and exaggerated vocalisations or expressions. Infant-directed speech often also conveys affection, and is noted to be more effective in getting an infant's attention as well as aiding in language development. Researchers believe that the use of motherese helps babies learn words faster and easier. As children grow, parents naturally adapt their speaking patterns to suit their child's growing linguistic skills.

Stages of Language Development

By the time children reach the age of two, the **prelinguistic stage**, the initial stage of language development, has provided them with ways to communicate. Crying, cooing, and babbling help to create nurturing relationships with mutual levels of language exchange. The second stage of communication, known as the **holophrase stage** of language development, is when children use single words. Around 10–13 months, children begin to produce sounds that are close to words (often understood only by their parents). Infants begin to comprehend language about twice as fast as they are able to produce it. Around 18 months, the child enters the third stage—often called telegraphic speech—when children begin to use two-word sentences, akin to the old telegrams. These sentences usually consist of just nouns and verbs, such as 'Where daddy?' and 'Puppy big!'

When they enter early childhood, or the preschool years, there is a quick leap in communication, and children enter the **multi-word sentences stage.** They begin to speak in short, multi-word sentences with a basic grammatical structure. For example, a child might say, 'Papa is nice' or 'Want more fruit'. As children age, they continue to learn new words everyday. By the time they enter school around the age of five, children typically have a vocabulary of 10,000 words or more.

Box 4.5 Major Features of Communication

Let us summarise some of the basic steps that lead to children's proficiency in language and communication.

Between birth and six months

- Child communicates and bonds by crying, cooing and then babbling. The first sounds may be ah, oh, and a few more, intentionally produced through control of the speech muscles
- Watches others when talked to
- May laugh out loud, either along with another person, or as a reaction to stimulation
- Child is comforted by sounds in different pitches and tones, and responds to a voice by becoming quiet, listening, turning the head, opening eyes, or waking to the sound of a familiar voice in a quiet room
- By three months, can distinguish between the voices of his mother and other females
- Makes sounds in a bid for attention—sticks out tongue, coos, babbles, or gurgles, in addition to crying
- By four months, babies react to the rhythm of the speech of caregivers
- Makes three or more sounds in one breath, such as *bababa* or *dabaka*
- Says at least two different sounds, like *da* and *ba*. The babbling sound may have their own order, such as *baba* first, followed by *dada*, or the reverse. The essential feature is the production of sounds using the repetitive movements of the lips, also called labial sounds
- Responds to own name by looking, listening, smiling and quietening down, vocalises for attention
- Can locate the source of a bell rung out of sight
- Laughs, gurgles and coos with familiar people, especially in play
- Turns to look for new and unfamiliar sounds

Between six and 12 months

- Repeats sounds
- Listens carefully to different sounds
- May respond by nodding
- Uses two or more words with parents
- Uses Mama or Dada as names for caregivers
- Uses babbling combination of sounds from the language environment
- Waves bye-bye or folds hands to greet
- Enjoys interactive games, such as peek-a-boo
- Looks towards objects when called by name, showing the skill to recognise objects/pictures. May point to objects
- Responds to simple instructions, such as give me your hand, where is your nose?
- May have a receptive vocabulary of about 100 words

It is important that children be talked to and family members expand their conversations with them. Children growing up in joint or extended families have the company of several adults and young children, who become their readymade teachers. It is also important for parents to tell stories and read books, which will help to expand the child's vocabulary. Reading to the child every night will not only influence the child's language development, but will also help in socio-emotional development. A quiet time with parents, where children have the space to share their thoughts, is good for emotional development.

Social and Emotional Development in Young Children

Emotional expression is about comprehending feelings and behavioural reactions. Being in a social environment amidst care and experiencing need-fulfilment from an early age fosters emotional understanding. Children grow up happier and develop high emotional skills if there is active interaction with parents and other family members. The child imbibes feelings of being loved, and feels safe to express her/his feelings.

One of the tasks in early childhood is for children to understand their own feelings, learn to regulate them, and realise that others, too, have feelings and needs. We often note that children pick up objects and put them in their mouths. If an adult feels an object is harmful, the child is told 'no'. This can upset the child, who might want to persist. Or if a child snatches a toy away from another child, s/he will be rebuked; both children may be upset, one at being denied ownership and the other at being disciplined. Early childhood experiences, coupled with appropriate interventions, teach children to share, care, take turns, and respect other people's choices. Such learning is part of children's socio-emotional development.

A child's ability to express emotions appropriately, interpret other people's emotions correctly, and understand the triggers and outcomes of certain emotions is described as 'emotional intelligence'. Several factors—fewer children in families, fewer adults in social proximity—have led to the absence of natural forms of sharing or cooperating for mutual harmony. Thus, interpersonal conflicts need to be resolved with care to help children acquire the optimal levels of emotional intelligence. Managing and regulating emotions also relates to the ability to cope with their own or other people's emotions in a way that creates positive social connections. During early childhood, with interventions, most children show great improvements in interpersonal developmental skills. Advances in emotional intelligence help in team-building and learning interdependence, lifelong goals that can help people maintain emotional health and prosocial, cooperative behaviours.

Socio-emotional development in early childhood can also be explained by Erikson's theory of psychosocial development. In early childhood—the Piagetian preoperational stage of cognitive development—children are high on exploring and experimenting, which may lead to crossing the boundaries of social conduct. In the Eriksonian stages, young children go through an 'initiative versus guilt' stage of psychosocial development. During this period (ages three to six), with the correct intervention, young children develop a healthy eagerness to tackle new tasks. With encouragement and guidance, they can join in activities with peers, and try things without the help of adults.

However, with too many instructions or rigid rules, they may develop inhibitions and a strict sense of self-control and guilt related to their actions, and approach the world timidly and fearfully. Children do not have the skills to understand what they cannot do. Coping with limitations is important; it is equally important to see that they do not develop a sense of failure. Children also need to learn the value of persistence as a way to overcome limitations.

Bronfenbrenner's **ecological systems theory** deals with processes of socialisation in early childhood. It explains how the interaction between children's genetic and biologically influenced personality traits interact with their environment to affect how they grow and develop. An encouraging and nurturing environment will set the stage for optimal maturation. In addition, how a child acts or reacts to the environment will affect how others treat her/him in return. For example, an easy-going child may be treated more positively by caregivers than a child who is difficult to soothe; also, children often do not understand the frustrations of parents after a bad day at work, and may become irritable for want of attention.

In Bronfenbrenner's theory, there are three levels of influences—micro, meso and macro—corresponding to the immediate environment, indirect influence of adult orientations, and invisible forces of socio-cultural history. In early childhood, the micro-level of a child's environment consists of parents, siblings, grandparents, and other extended family members. Children growing up with caregivers who show warmth, compassion and understanding display empathy and pro-social behaviour. On the other hand, children growing up with caregivers who tend to be angry, punitive and cold tend to have trouble in emotional responses, and struggle to develop empathy and prosocial behaviour.

At the meso-level, the culture of the local community will also have an effect on children's emotional development. The meso-level includes the characteristics of a child's neighbourhood, school and community; if children grow up feeling unsafe, or are focused primarily on meeting basic survival needs, the fear of violence or sense of insecurity will influence their emotional reactions and beliefs. But a child living in a safe, supportive community will have a more positive view of and emotional response to that environment. In terms of a macro-level influence, the child's traditions, and the culture and ethos of the country affect her/his emotional development.

DEVELOPING EMOTIONS

All children come with their own temperaments; however, the harmony between a child and caregiver is very unique. This bond is known as attachment. Many theorists have argued that right from birth, children need to develop trust, which is born out of consistency and continuity of interactions. The give and take between babies and caregivers needs to be both regular and in response to the child's need.

Box 4.6 Some Facts About Children

The first five years is when basic skills are being acquired, tested and encouraged. Along with the natural unfolding of growth are small gestures that ensure emotional strength and security—for instance, a child needs to be fed on a routine and sometimes on demand. Schedules for young children are important, as children feel an affinity for rhythms and repetition. Such gestures create positive bonds, and provide a sense of trust in the social environment. Rhythms provide children with continuity and consistency, so they can make their own connections. There is something magical when a child with limited vocabulary looks at a painting of a woman and says 'mama', displaying a basic ability to make connections, or when a toddler goes to the kitchen and asks for 'milk' or goes near the computer and says 'gana', indicating a growing sensibility for recall of past experience.

Children display sensitivity to their experiences, discipline, and family and concerned adults from a very early age. A discerning adult can make inferences about young children's passionate desire for immediate attention; a 2-year-old might accidentally break a flower vase and exclaim, 'Oh no'! Or a child might jump up and down the stairs, repeating, 'You will fall, you will fall'. Such expressions create visions of children in playful activity being coaxed to be slow. Children feel secure within such watchful freedom, and gain confidence and initiative.

The First Two Years

During infancy, babies experience the world through touch, sounds, the rhythms they experience, and kinesthetic movements. This harmony and rhythm helps them to feel secure and emotionally at peace. The first social action is the social smile, before which babies communicate through crying and cooing. Through gazing, s/he connects with primary caregivers, and soon learns to catch their attention by crying when in distress. Soon, babies make gurgling and happy cooing sounds. With consistent exposure, babies laugh and respond to caregivers. Slowly, by five months or so, the baby seeks attention, starts to show an interest in other babies, and can imitate sounds and different inflections. S/he cries when separated from the caregiver.

In the latter part of the first year, s/he intentionally makes sounds, attracts attention and plays interactive games. They will search for absent objects and people. By 10 months, s/he can respond to a goodbye kiss, and indicate the need to be picked up, even showing anger if they are not picked up. By 15 months, they can imitate actions around the house. By the age of two, babies begin to recognise themselves and become assertive, and this when the stubborn phase begins. Children cannot delay gratification and want immediate returns, which lead to frustration and aggression. Children also do not know the ownership of objects; tasks of emotion regulation are to be learnt to respect the rights of others, the importance of taking turns, and understanding limitations. Appropriate interventions broaden the child's emotional repertoire.

During early childhood, children typically start to develop self-conscious emotions as they begin evaluating themselves, instead of purely reacting to caregivers' and other adults' evaluations. For example, the child will feel pride when praised by parents in front of other relative, and will feel shame or guilt when faced with disapproval. As children become increasingly self-aware, more effective at communicating, and better at understanding the thoughts and feelings of others, their social skills increase. Children at this stage become skilled at modifying and expressing their emotions to fit different social situations. For example, Rohan may feel angry at school, but will stop himself from throwing the same tantrum that he would at home. Changing or controlling one's emotions in social situations is an important skill, which allows children to fit into groups and start to create interpersonal relationships.

Another emotional capacity, **empathy**, develops during early childhood, and is also an important component of positive social behaviour. Empathy is the ability to see from another person's perspective in order to understand what they are feeling. Children start understanding cues—facial expressions, spoken thoughts, or behaviours such as laughing or crying—that suggest what another person is feeling. Young children might also be able to predict someone's emotional response from the context of the event, such as anticipating that someone who is hurt will be in pain and feel sad.

Any child's emotional development is influenced by both internal and external factors. The innate or genetic component of an individual's personality refers to the internal temperament, which can affect how children respond to the world emotionally. Temperaments are developed largely in response to healthy physiological functions, and responsive care practices, such as not remaining wet for long, being fed adequately, and affectionate playful interactions can help.

Children with easygoing temperaments can regulate their own emotions as well as respond to other people's emotions more positively. Sometimes, children may be irritable and slow to warm up, which is when they find it difficult to regulate their own emotions and tend to react to other people's strong emotions by becoming distressed themselves. The nature of role models and the interactive dynamics of the environment strongly influence how children react to the world emotionally.

In early childhood, it is important to teach children to cope with emotions and appropriately express and deal with anger, aggression. or even fear. Emotional regulation is a valuable skill, and caregivers need to be alert to 'teachable moments' to show children how to deal with intense emotions and difficult situations with calm and resolve. Children are continuously observing adult behaviour, and parents and caregivers have a social responsibility to transfer approaches to problem-solving and conflict resolution. Frustration, anger or aggression in response to situations (or to children themselves) on the part of caregivers may contribute to negative behaviours.

Frustration and assertion of one's needs often leads to aggression, and is usually observed during the early preschool years, especially around age four. Children below four will often just snatch, hit, kick, or shout for a desired object or action, as they have no other skill at this point. This is known as 'Instrumental Aggression'. When aggression is more acute and takes the form of intentional injury to peers, it is known as 'Hostile Aggression'. This is further divided into Overt Aggression, threats of, or actual physical injury, and 'Relational Aggression', which is when children exclude someone in peer relationships, or spread rumours.

Through open talks on the incorrectness of violence, which can lead to a public scarring of image, and with appropriate direction and guidance, preschoolers soon learn ways to regulate themselves and attempt to get along with others. A balance of scolding and explanations helps children to grow out of using instrumental aggression to get what they want. A certain amount of hostile aggression may increase between the ages of four and seven. This may be gendered, with boys being overtly aggressive, while girls may use relational aggression to harm someone else.

Through being in social groups, children learn effective ways to deal with interpersonal conflicts. Play and participation in team events teach children that each person needs to have their own turn. Such situations benefit children's social growth and interpersonal relations. However, some children need to be helped as they may continue to use physical and verbal aggression, which may get them into trouble, both at school and home. It is important for caregivers to convey that there are peaceful ways to resolve differences. Violence and aggression defy basic social rules, and are unacceptable. As adults, care needs to be taken to avoid any demonstration of physical or verbal aggression, with no name-calling, shouting, or use of physical punishment in response to negative behaviours. Children should be restricted from watching violent media content on television, or playing video games for long hours.

Fear is a strong emotion that many children experience intensely during early childhood, as they are still unaware of the consequences of new and unknown encounters. Unable to differentiate between reality and make-believe, young children with active imaginations often fear lightening, thunderstorms, 'boddha baba', or other scary dangers their minds create, or are sometimes used by the family as disciplining tools. Many children also have nightmares during early childhood.

Parents often respond to a child's expressed fear with an extra hug; this does not ignore or dismiss the fear their children are experiencing. Their proximity and action offers extra emotional support. For example, caregivers can put a night light in the child's room to help lessen shadows, and not insist on ways to discipline them. Nightmares or storms can be moments for caregivers to offer support and physical comfort, such as hugs. Sometimes, if a child's fear becomes very intense, persists for a long time, does not respond to a caregiver's attempts to reduce it, and significantly interferes with daily activities, professional treatment may be needed.

The responses of caregivers to the trials and triumphs of childhood often help children to internalise the attributes, abilities, attitudes, and values that they believe define them. Developing a **self-concept** is another important event that takes place during early childhood. By the age of three, children have developed their **Categorical Self**, which is a concrete way of viewing themselves through labels, such as 'I am a girl and my name is Lata'. Three to 5-year-olds are not yet aware that a person can have many characteristics. For example, it is difficult for them to know that they can be good and bad, depending on their actions.

Slowly, children store pieces of information in their long-term memory, developing, a continuity of experiences, This is when children gain a sense of the **Remembered Self**. This self incorporates memories by way of listening to a recounting of good and bad actions, and this information about personal events contributes to building a sense of the self. Adult narratives about children make them feel special, and they develop positive self-worth by listening to such descriptions of their acts or pranks, which momentarily turn them into heroes.

The **Inner Self** comprises private thoughts, feelings and desires that a child develops. This inner self may be in harmony with external expectations, when we see a happy, interactive child. At times, children may have conflicts and disharmony, which the child might display through restless behaviour or other forms of discontent.

Along with the child internalising a view of her/himself, many external factors influence how children view themselves. Positive feedback about children's abilities by adult caregivers, along with guidance in moments of error enable a realistic **self-esteem**. However, if parents, peers or teachers react only with negative or punitive comments, ignoring children's attempts to succeed, they do not gain in confidence, Regular ignoring or downplay of children's achievements will lead to poor self-image and a lower self-esteem. Each child is unique, and they respond to different environments in different ways.

Even in their developmental trajectories, some young children are not as vulnerable as others. At times, children are naturally emotionally 'resilient', and are able to cope with negative or harmful experiences and go on with life without any damage to their self-worth or emotional development. As parents and caregivers of young children, it is helpful to remain alert to differences in temperament, and be encouraging and warm towards children who are not naturally resilient.

GENDER IDENTITY IN EARLY CHILDHOOD

In certain cultures, gender identity begins with what babies wear or the toys they are given. Such gendering is adult initiated. In India, ceremonies and celebrations might vary with gender; for instance, there might be more pomp and show and special functions for boys. The kind of objects that children are given promotes growth and progress. Certain theories have interpreted the construction of gender identity, which cuts across the dimensions of physical, cognitive, social, and emotional development. Kohlberg describes how young children learn to understand their gender, and what gender means in their everyday life.

In the early preschool years (ages three to four), **gender labelling** begins with the consciousness of being a boy or a girl, which usually relates to what you wear, how your hair is tied, and to an extent, what you play with. However, there might be a faint belief that gender is not permanent, and can change. Preschool children may have trouble understanding that males and females have different body shapes, and yet might have similar characteristics. For example, seeing female teachers all around might lead children to disagree that 'men can be teachers too'.

As young children mature, their understanding of **gender identity** stabilises, and they learn to deal with individual preferences. Children soon learn that gender is stable and constant; however, they might still believe that changing one's physical appearance or activities can change them into the other sex. For example, Meher might believe that if her mother drives a truck or cuts her long hair short, she will become a boy.

Box 4.7 Anecdotal Narratives of Gender and Childhood

Five-year-old Chamki was watching her uncle shave. The shaving brush and the lather of the shaving cream fascinated her, especially when it vanished with the application of the razor. She imitated the action, lathering her face with the brush. Her older cousins and siblings started teasing her, telling her that she would soon have a beard. Chamki spent some anxious days watching her chin for emerging hair, till her Mother assuaged her fears by explaining the functions of the body and the inability of small external acts to result in gender change.

In a small project aimed at understanding children's gender identity, a summer camp leader decided to play a game of *Ladka Ladki Adal Badal* (Boy Girl Changeover) in New Delhi. The children were told that two days later, they had to make a gender switch in dress codes—boys had to come dressed in girls' clothing, and vice versa. The woman instructor, too, would come dressed in male clothes. There was stunned silence, especially among the boys. Parents were distressed, too, as some of the boys, particularly the 6-year-olds, wanted to stay away from the camp. Some parents were dismissive of such a venture.

On the designated day, all eight girls came dressed as boys, while of the six boys, two were absent, three decided not to participate, and the only boy who dared wear female clothing did so in the changing room, but did not emerge outside. He only presented himself to the camp instructor, and changed back into his clothes. Many of the societal beliefs associated with male and female roles were contained in this performance, including the dominance of male superiority. Another interpretation is that girls are more adventurous and willing to experiment, while boys are satisfied with sustaining their position and status.

Source: Asha Singh.

By the early school years (ages six to seven), children begin to understand the fact of gender consistency. Other theories also help in understanding the development of gender identity by examining young children's play and social interactions. By the age of five, children tend to play with 'gender-specific' toys. Young boys often play together in larger groups, while young girls tend to play more in pairs and smaller groups. During this age, children reflect the images of stereotypical gender-related activities and behaviours. Early beliefs about the possibility of transition in gender roles may aid in inculcating gender equality or equity as children grow. Families, schools and media play a very important role in forming beliefs about gender roles.

LEARNING AND PLAY

Play is the work of children in the early years. Play activities are a natural and essential part of childhood. Research shows strong links between creative play and language, physical, cognitive, and social development, and its positive effects on early childhood learning. As they grow into their early childhood years, young children increasingly engage in play activities that expand their knowledge of the world, and develop their motor, physical, emotional, and cognitive skills. Playing with other children provides many opportunities for learning crucial social skills like sharing, taking turns, problem-solving, and conversing with others. Through play, children explore their environment, and this contributes to their understanding of the expanding world. Children are naturally curious and far more capable than adults at learning important concepts through exploring and playing.

Box 4.8 Guiding, not Microscopic Scrutiny: Role of Parents

Children's play is their learning institute. It is through play and games that children learn to take turns, share, ask questions explore, experiment, and invent. While at play, adults ensure supervision to avoid physical injury. It is equally essential to become involved in what children are thinking, saying, watching, and the meanings of some of the things they are creating. In urban metropolises, television has a powerful social impact. Are children watching content relevant to them? Co-viewing serves to involve parents, and through active engagement, regulate, respond, and guide or diffuse unresolved understandings. Crucial for parents is to be interested, but not interfere in their children's well-being, by maintaining a watchful distance and through engaged proximity.

- Understand that children are active meaning-makers
- Must nourish overall growth and development
- Value children's play, and the functions of playfulness in interactions
- Use art as a medium of teaching and learning
- Draw on learning through stories
- Inculcate an appreciation of differences
- Generate dignity and respect for work
- Understand the errors that children make
- Use local crafts, art and performance to infuse cultural pride
- Practice awareness of and respect for the diversity of Indian people, and those around the world

Source: Asha Singh.

Vygotsky believed that children developed social competence through play, which helped them to re-play the cultural norms, expectations, and values of a society. Through play, they discover the workings of the world, and negotiate their way through their surroundings. Play teaches children about themselves, others, rules and consequences, and how things go together or come apart (Klein et al. 2004). Play is how children learn to socialise, to think, to solve problems, to mature, and most importantly, to have fun. Play connects children with their imagination, their environment, their parents and family, and with the world. Parental involvement in a child's world of play is extremely beneficial for both the child and the parent. Parent-child play establishes and strengthens bonds that opens doors for the sharing of values, increases communication, allows for teachable moments, and resolves differences, as well as family-related concerns and issues.

Children often do not need commercially bought toys; they play enthusiastically with any material they can find. However, it is important to remember that play that encourages active engagement is far more favourable for childhood than material that supports passive entertainment. Sometimes, play materials are not needed at all; preschoolers develop creativity by engaging in **pretend play**, creating imaginary friends or exploring alternative worlds. Through this, they learn what people are like, what they do, and how they think. Similar to pretend play is **fantasy play**, where children try new roles and situations, experiment with languages and emotions, and learn to think and create beyond their world. They assume adult roles and learn to think in abstract ways, thereby stretching their imagination.

Another kind of play observed during early childhood is **social play,** whereby, through interacting with other children in play settings, children learn social rules such as give and take, and cooperation, and are able to share toys and ideas. In **motor or physical play,** children run, jump, and play games such as hide and seek, which offers them a chance to exercise and develop muscle strength. Children also learn to accept winning or losing. Another type is **constructive play,** where children create things, which allows them to explore objects and discover patterns to find what works and what does not. Children gain pride when they accomplish a task during constructive play.

Parten also discussed categories of play. Two categories that fall under early childhood are **Associative and Cooperative play**. In Associative play, children around three to four years become more interested in other children, and start to socialise with them. Associative play helps the preschooler learn the dos and don'ts of interaction, teaches sharing, and encourages language development, problem-solving skills and cooperation. In associative play, groups of children have similar goals. They do not set rules, although they all want to play with similar toys and may even trade toys with each other. There is more formal organisation in **Cooperative play,** which begins in the late preschool period. The play is organised by group goals. When children move from a self-centred world to an understanding of the importance of social contracts and rules, they begin to play organised games with rules.

Play assists children's development in many ways, and the undisputed role of play in enhancing skills and abilities is well-recognised. Play influences development in an integrated manner, and gives children the opportunity to practice fine motor skills like gripping a pencil or cutting with scissors, as well as gross motor skills like walking, jumping and running. Play in group settings also encourages children to cooperate with each other through negotiation and problem-solving, allowing them to develop self-confidence while forming important relationships with their peers.

Children gain knowledge through their play. They learn to think, remember, and solve problems. Make-believe play can stimulate several types of learning; children strengthen their language skills by modelling other children and adults. Playing 'house' helps children to create stories, which in turn helps them to learn about the different roles of family members. An understanding of size, shape and texture is also learned through play. Play allows children to be creative, while developing their own imaginations. It helps a child to master skills that will develop self-confidence, and the ability to recover quickly from setbacks. For example, a child may feel pride in stacking blocks, and disappointment when the last block makes the stack fall.

Figure 4.4: Learning in a classroom

Source: Rajkumari Amrit Kaur Child Study Centre collection

Play allows children to express their views, experiences, and, at times, frustrations. Children practice decision-making skills, move at their own pace, and discover their own interests during play. Children's readiness to learn and their cognitive development are enhanced when they are allowed to practice their skills without fear of failure. Children develop a sense of self, learn to interact with other children, and learn how to make friends. Children take up adult roles in their games, and play out quite detailed observations of adults in action. Social play is crucial for children to learn how to interact with others as they grow up.

INTERCONNECTION BETWEEN AREAS OF DEVELOPMENT

All areas of development—physical, motor, cognitive, language, social, and emotional—are interconnected, rather than being separate, isolated skills. The interconnection between cognitive skills and emotional development is particularly important. As children's abstract thinking and language skills increase, they become better able to label and discuss their emotions with others. For example, they can let adults know that they are scared to go to the bathroom alone in the dark, instead of crying when asked to go by themselves.

Language also allows children to regulate their feelings better, soothe themselves in response to negative feelings, and exert control over emotional situations. They also start developing the ability to understand other people's viewpoints, and begin to change or cease behaviours that might hurt someone else's feelings. Again, as with other emotions, the development of empathy depends on cognitive and language development. Children who cannot engage in abstract thinking or take someone else's perspective are typically unlikely to respond with empathy.

SUMMARY

- As discussed in this chapter, children continue to grow and change in amazing ways as they move from infancy into early childhood. During the preoperational years (between the ages of two and six), young children make several gains in their physical development, and grow taller as their bodies take on adult proportions. They gain the ability to run and climb stairs independently, as well as cut with scissors and grip a writing tool. Cognitively, young children learn how to think symbolically, which leads to make-believe play, and their language explodes and matures. Emotionally, children learn to express their own feelings and feel reflective empathy. Socially, they begin to cultivate relationships with peers, and deepen family ties. Morally, they begin to understand 'right' from 'wrong', and to understand that they have the choice about which way to go. Sexually, young children continue to form their gender identity, and begin to understand what it means to be male or female.
- At this point, it is important to remember that children develop at their own paces. Development occurs over a wide range of ages, and even if a child seems a little behind the norm (the average ages at which specific developmental tasks tend to occur), it is not something to worry about as individual variations are also normal. However, parents must discuss any noted delays in their children's development with pediatricians, even if certain delays turn out to be normal. For example, girls tend to develop slightly faster than boys, and in some families, some children start walking earlier than others. Concerned parents should consult a doctor, as s/he can determine whether additional assessment and/or treatment are necessary.

KEY TERMS

Early childhood – Period between birth to six years

Early childhood development – Development during the early years, significant for the rapid changes that occur during these years

Early childhood care and education – Term coined to stress the need to convey the importance of creating responsive environments for children

Early communication – Initial ways that children use to convey their needs and responses

Responsive environment – Understanding of caregivers while watching young children closely and responding to their needs

Zone of proximal development – Events and actions that provide challenge and support building on the immediate competencies of children

Play as learning – Importance of the role of play in initiating self-directed learning.

EXERCISES

1. What are the appropriate theories to explain early childhood development?
2. What is the significance of ECCE? Why is there a worldwide movement to promote awareness of early childhood care and education?
3. Describe the views of some Indian thinkers on early childhood.
4. Observe one boy and one girl aged two. Note in about 15 minutes:
   The ways in which they move.
   How many things they pick up.
   How they talk, and with whom.
   Take a diary record of the 15 minutes. Analyse observations with what you read.
5. Watch children in a Nursery school. Identify how the materials and classroom activities promote developmental processes. Write a record and discuss in class.
6. What are the stages of language development in infancy? How do babies develop early communication?
7. Discuss the cognitive skills of preschool children.
8. In a nursery school, ask children to draw and ask them questions about what they draw. Note the narrative. What do you understand about children's thinking? Does it reflect their reality, fantasy, or does it relates with cartoons?
9. Identify two mothers who have babies under two. Ask them how they come to understand the needs of their babies. Ask them specifically about the cues babies use to attract their attention. Analyse the two descriptions, and show how it helps you to understand about the communication skills of babies.
10. Watch a 6–9-month-old baby for 15 minutes each over two days, and record her/his vocalisations. Match it with the verbal sounds listed in the box item.
11. Watch a few 3-year-old children and collect 8–10 sample sentences they use, noting who they are speaking with. Analyse their sentences for the average number of words. Discuss the content of their speech in relation to the context. Comment on the nature of the child's responses to the two different ways of storytelling.
12. Read a story to children, choosing an appropriate book for 4-year-old children. Note the children's reactions to the book. Ask the child to recall the story. Show some pictures to assist recall. Note the differences in spontaneous and assisted recall.
13. What is the role of play in early learning?

REFERENCES

Aggarwal, J. C., *Early Childhood Care and Education: Principles and Practices*, New Delhi: Shipra, 2007.

Arni, K. and G. Wolf, *Child Art with Everyday Materials*, TARA Publishing, 1999.

Doherty, J. and M. Hughes, *Child Development: Theory and Practice*, Canada: Pearson, 2013.

Heckman, J., 'The Economics of investing in children', Policy Briefing No. 1, Dublin: UCD Geary Institute, 2006.

Heckman, J. J. and D. V. Masterov, 'Invest in Kids', Working Paper 5, Working Group Committee for Economic Development, 2004 available at http://jenni.uchicago.edu/Invest/FILES/dugger_2004-12-02_dvm.pdf (accessed 24 November 2014).

Klein, T. P. D. Wirth and K. Linas, 'Play: Children's Context for Development', *Young Children*, 58 (3), 2004, Washington National Association for the Education of the Young Child.

McCain, M. and F. Mustard, *Reversing the real brain drain. The early years study*, Final Report, Toronto: Ontario's Children's Secretariat, 1999. Available at http://www.founders.net/ey/home.nsf (accessed 21 February 2010).

Mohanty, J. and B. Mohanty, *Early Childhood Care and Education*, New Delhi: Deep and Deep Publication, 1996.

Morrison, G. S., *Fundamentals of early childhood education*, Virginia: Merrill/Prentice-Hall, 2003.

National Council for Educational Research and Training (NCERT), Position Paper On ECCE National Focus Group 3.6, 2006.

Parten, M., 'Social participation among preschool children', *Journal of Abnormal and Social Psychology*, 28 (3), 1932, pp. 136–47.

Schweinhart, L. J., H. V. Barnes, and D. P. Weikar, 'Significant benefits: The HighScope Perry Preschool study through age 27', Monographs of the HighScope Educational Research Foundation, 10. Ypsilanti: HighScope Press, 1993.

Schweinhart, L. J., J. Montie, Z. Xiang, W. S. Barnett, C. R. Belfield, and M. Nores, 'Lifetime effects: The HighScope Perry Preschool study through age 40', Monographs of the HighScope Educational Research Foundation, 14, Ypsilanti, MI: HighScope Press, 2005.

5

Development in Middle Childhood

HIGHLIGHTS

- Discusses the growth and development of more complex attributes in all domains during the ages of 6–11.
- Theoretical perspectives on middle childhood are described with reference to achieving developmental tasks.
- Provides a domain-wise study of development in middle childhood.
- Discusses the widening social network of the school-age child, behaviour-related difficulties, learning disabilities, and school performance.

THE GROWING YEARS

As children grow, they gain in physical competence, which leads to an independence in mobility that produces a pronounced change in their sociality and width of experience. During this stage, they begin to take small steps towards creating social groups, without their parents or family. This chapter will capture the growing child's position in the enlarging physical and social spaces.

Centuries ago, the notion of childhood was very different from the way we understand it today. Our understanding of childhood has been evolving in more ways than one. From early pictorial references and descriptions in Euro-American literature, it seems that childhood as a distinct developmental phase was given little recognition. Even where childhood was considered special, it was mostly thought to be till the age of seven. In the study of the developing child, 'middle childhood' or 'elementary school years'—or simply, 'school years'—is recognised as a stage with unique needs and developmental achievements.

Middle childhood lasts a good six years in a child's life, the most often quoted range being 6–11 years. Some texts quote the school-age period as falling between 6–12 years, or even 7–11 years. Although a child may enter formal school at the age of five, these age divisions for middle childhood are done on the basis of 'developmental changes' in a child, in different domains such as the physical, cognitive, or even language. These divisions do not signify that all children enter formal school at the ages of six or seven, as the age for entry to school depends on the national policy. In India, children enter formal school around the age of six. Middle childhood or school age is thus, for the purpose of the developmental study of the child, the period that follows preschool years and precedes adolescence. This stage falls in between two stages of rapid growth and change, and serves to consolidate acquired skills and abilities as well as nurture the inculcation of complex skills in all domains.

Middle childhood brings about unique changes and developmental gains. We could use the notion of physical mobility, which allows for social independence. This is the time when the 'little personality' is thought to emerge, giving children a sense of their unique self. That is, the child's personality may for the first time reflect what s/he would be like as an adult.

In most parts of the world, it is during this period that children begin to engage in a socially organised world. With the start of formal schooling and initiation into basic survival processes for children in disadvantaged settings, middle childhood essentially engages a child's self-help and social skills. Gradual and steady physical growth and qualitative leaps in thinking and cognitive processes shape the child's interactions with the world. Family, community and peers help in fine-tuning interactions and deriving an understanding of the world and its dynamic processes. During these years, children develop a moral stance, learn to use their creative skills, and experience the transformative power of language. This is also the time when a child may encounter specific difficulties in schoolwork, or even in social interactions. Adults around the child act as resources to assist her/him in overcoming challenges in learning and day-to-day living.

We will now take a look at domain-wise development in children during the elementary school years.

PHYSICAL-MOTOR DEVELOPMENT IN MIDDLE CHILDHOOD

By the time children are four or five, they have acquired basic mobility skills—they can walk, run, jump, and climb. As they grow, they attempt to create complexities in locomotor skills, such as try and hop on one foot, walk on a line, or try climbing fast. During this period, children build control, regulation, precision, speed, and balance. Children try to do complicated physical tasks, considering them challenges to be mastered. In these years, children use skills to regulate both strength and speed.

Physical development in middle childhood is most often described as 'slow and steady'. Apart from changes in height, weight and body composition, children learn to practice many new motor skills. Sport activities take on a prominent role in the child's life. Where organised sports are missing, children learn to devise games and sports with local materials or engage in other indigenous games, depending on the socio-geographic setting. An absence of resources often leads to creative thinking. Gender, social setting, resource availability, and individual differences in growth, development and learning are vital factors in children's physical motor outcomes.

Pattern in Growth

As you will have learnt in the earlier chapters, physical motor development is guided by the cephalocaudal (head to toe) and proximodistal (centre to extremities) trends or principles. An infant has a large head, and in proportion to the rest of the body, the head seems to be quite big! However, as the child advances in age, the rest of the body becomes more pronounced and the proportions change. During middle childhood, a child adds 2–2.5 inches per year in height. This means that in the entire period of 6–12 years, a child may become taller by 12–15 inches—or more, or less, depending on individual pace or growth rate. Weight will also see an increase by 2–3 kilograms per year, or 12–18 kilograms in the entire middle childhood.

Diet plays an important role in children's physical development. Food-related beliefs, cooking and eating practices, and activity levels of the child will affect the course of weight gain and distribution of body weight. Individual differences in children's physical growth are also genetically guided, along with influences from the environment. For example, a child with good cumulative nutrition will more likely reach her/his genetic potential for height.

In the first half of middle childhood, girls and boys show comparable physical growth rates, after which girls surpass boys in physical development. At the start of middle childhood, children may be at 65–70 per cent of their eventual adult height. And at the end of middle childhood, they may have achieved 85–90 per cent of their adult height. They may also achieve their adult foot size. So much for slow and steady growth! Compared to adolescence and its changes in physical development—brought about by puberty and sexual maturity, which leads to a marked transformation in physical appearance—growth in middle childhood appears to be actually quite slow and steady.

Appearance and Other Bodily Changes

What really contributes to changing body proportions is the growth of a child's legs. During middle childhood, both boys and girls are long-legged. Boys at this age sometimes put up a resistance to wearing shorts, as they begin to be conscious of their bare legs and arms. This trend continues till early adolescence, when children may sometimes be referred to as 'all arms and legs'! Increase in strength and stamina in middle childhood improves body posture, and movements become more precise. The child's face also elongates as a permanent set of teeth are accommodated in the lower jaw. By the end of middle childhood, a child will have all permanent teeth, except perhaps for the second and third molars. Girls are ahead of boys in teething.

In keeping with the cephalocaudal trend in development, head growth slows down during middle childhood. The first 12 years of life constitute the critical or the sensitive period for brain development. By the end of middle childhood, brain growth and development is technically complete. Lateralisation or hemispheric specialisation has also taken place. That is, left brain and right brain functions are quite distinctly established. Children's bones are more pliable than those of adults, and ossification is an ongoing process during middle childhood. Children are especially prone to injury due to high activity levels and soft pliable bones. Middle childhood tends to be most accident-prone, given the advent of play groups and the slowly reducing presence of adult caregivers.

Box 5.1 Culture of Childhood: Play, Adventure and Games

Play in school-age years is usually outdoor and social, with other children. Every culture and social setting has their own games, such as hopscotch or *Stapoo*, Catch-catch or *pakdan-pakdai*, *oonch neech*, corners, elastic, L-o-n-d-o-n LONDON, and many others. Each game sets rules, challenges and simple competence in being attentive, responsive, and executing one's role. In India, games like Chain, Khokho and marbles are very popular, and teach children strategy through planning and quick decision-making.

All cultures have local games that children learn on their own. These games naturally foster all-round development, as natural peer groups are created in neighbourhoods and schools. During the middle school years, children develop a strategy of winning and losing. Cognitive planning and strategising is made possible through physical skills, mobility and precision. Play is an important source for promoting development.

Another aspect introduced in children's play is the making of teams and competition. Social interaction is on the rise, and so the size of the group also expands. Games are governed by setting challenges and common goals, which the teams have to achieve. Sometimes the group identifies one person to carry the game; for instance, in catch a child, the rest of the group runs, and the game moves if the child who is 'caught' carries the game forward by catching another child. Children devise ways to identify the 'den' or 'it', and use vocabulary specific to the game. Such systems or culture of childhood is learnt by successive generations of children in the play field. Childhood games and play is learnt by immersion in outdoor settings and as members of a neighbourhood, and the rules of games require no formal teaching.

At times, children are excluded for several reasons and find themselves at a disadvantage. The reasons for exclusion could be ability, personality or unfamiliarity, and the exclusion can be short-lived or long-term. At times, some sensitive intervention by adults helps children transform this exclusion into inclusion, which is necessary as the culture of childhood is a small aspect of 'society'. Children learn social skills, emotional control and regulation, besides nurturing their physical growth and exercising their physical skills.

In this play, children often get hurt by falling, or while meeting challenges such as scaling a wall or climbing a tree. They may be learning to ride a bicycle and may not balance well. Children in groups may explore together and go beyond the immediate boundaries of their play areas. We often read in newspapers that a child fell into an open drain or did not estimate the extent of play space, leading to hurt and injury. It is important that play spaces for children be safe.

Growth and Gender Variations

There are differences in the physical development of boys and girls during middle childhood. Boys gain more muscle tissue and girls have more fatty tissue in their bodies. Although muscle size and strength increases in both boys and girls, boys have more strength at the onset of adolescence. The heart grows slowly in this period, and blood pressure stabilises. A child's body image is of significance during middle childhood, as children may be influenced by current trends in socially approved body types. This will have a direct bearing in adolescence.

However, even during middle childhood many children battle with health as well as body image issues, such as obesity or being excessively thin, both of which are examples of malnutrition. Material and environmental deprivation in many parts of the world may lead to other physical development issues, such as stunting. It is important to recognise emotional, social and selfhood correlates along with nutritional deprivation to understand health and disease in a holistic manner.

Figure 5.1a: Physical development in 7–8-year-olds

Source: St Mary's collection

Physiological Functions and Physical Skills

Children's digestion improves during middle childhood as the gastrointestinal system matures. Their stomach capacity also increases. The respiratory system sees changes, as their breathing becomes steadier. Lung capacity increases and the respiratory rate slows down. By the end of middle childhood, children will have attained 20/20 vision, and an adult-like auditory acuity.

Figure 5.1b: Physical development, 10–11 years

Source: St Mary's collection

Middle childhood sees leaps in children's motor skills. There is enhanced strength, precision, flexibility, speed, as well as stamina, and they participate in a greater number of sports and other physical activities of interest to them. An increased impulsivity and low reaction time helps them to improve their performance in outdoor sports. The gross motor skills they master are running, jumping, catching, throwing, balancing, and controlled foot movements. Improved visual-motor coordination aids children's gross motor movements.

Fine motor skills are used in craft activities, board games, playing musical instruments, or pursuits such as painting or needlework. Improved hand-eye coordination is the key to good fine motor performance. Children may also express likes and dislikes vis-à-vis particular activities, which is a part of their exploration of the world. Children begin to show a preference for not only certain kind of activities, but also skill at tasks and how they perform them. By this time, it is clear if the child is left-handed or right-handed. The clarity for handedness is well-established by the time the child is seven. Even though the child shows greater precision and range of movements, at times there is physical clumsiness. This may be due to the changing and awkward body proportions, social shyness, or even boredom.

Towards the end of middle childhood, a child is pre-pubescent, that is, ready for pubertal changes or sexual maturity. There is a great deal of individual variation in these physical changes. Some children may already have experienced the appearance of certain primary and secondary sexual characteristics. For example, girls may start menstruating at the age of nine or 10. This is also the time when many schools feel the need to begin sex education lectures for their students. You will read more about this in Chapter 6.

COGNITIVE DEVELOPMENT DURING MIDDLE CHILDHOOD

Much of the discourse on cognitive development is dominated by Piaget's cognitive developmental perspective and Vygotsky's socio-cultural theory. Both theories have implications for school education and teaching-learning practices. The previous chapter discussed Piaget's preoperational period, which describes cognition in the preschool age. You would also have studied how, at each stage in the discontinuous theory of cognition given by Piaget, there are qualitative changes in the nature of cognition. That is, the preoperational period is very different from the sensorimotor and concrete operational periods, which describe cognition in infancy and middle childhood, respectively. The preoperational period is dominated by a lot of imaginary references; a child in the concrete operational period, however, is dominated more by facts and logic. Let us take a look at cognition in the school years, as described by Piaget's concrete operational stage.

Figure 5.2a: Stage of learning and consolidation of skills: Society organises institutions for skill building

Source: Children in their classroom, Ganeshpuri (Site).

Figure 5.2b: Learning together independently and building relationships

Source: Dimple Rangila

The years between five and seven show a definite transformation in a child's thoughts. From being arbitrary and imaginative in their reasoning and thinking, children become more consistent and logical in their arguments. At this stage, children begin to think logically about the real world or concrete events. They begin to understand the operations and rules underlying physical state transformations, as well as relationships. They also understand ideas of age, time, numbers, distance, speed, supernatural phenomena, and human and animal mortality more concretely. They may start applying the concepts of science to everyday life, and developing their own theories about cultural and social phenomena. According to Piaget, the prime ability that a concrete operational child acquires is decentration, that is, the ability to shift focus from one aspect of a situation (centration) to many other aspects. The ability to decentre allows the child to evaluate situations, objects, people, and phenomena using more than one parameter. Their understanding of a phenomenon or process is therefore no longer limited. They have realised that there can be multiple possibilities and directions, including multiple viewpoints and perspectives, in everyday life situations.

During middle childhood, children are able to move beyond their perception-bound cognitive evaluation of things, events or phenomena. They use their knowledge of rules, their learning from past experiences, as well as cultural information to arrive at conclusions and take decisions. In other words, they stretch their mental operations in order to act on the given information or a cognitive problem from multiple vantage points. The concrete operations stage brings with it the important ability of 'conservation'.

Piaget's concept of conservation can be interpreted as the understanding that the core properties of a substance, person, event, or phenomenon may remain the same even when outward appearance changes. One of the most difficult aspects of sustaining the idea that nothing has changed in quantity despite a change in appearance relates to the conservation of volume. For example, when water is poured from a tall narrow glass to a flat-bottomed bowl, it seems as if the water has increased in quantity. However, nothing has been added or subtracted, and so the volume of water is unchanged. The water looks vertically greater in quantity or volume in the first instance, and horizontally more spread out in the other. A child who can confidently say, 'Nothing has been added or taken away, and so it is the same amount', understands this concept of the conservation of volume.

Conservation of other dimensions, such as mass, number, length, and weight, is also mastered during concrete operations. One of the criticisms levelled at Piaget's cognitive developmental perspective is that it underestimates the abilities of children at each stage; children do respond when questioned with an approach that is more child-like. For example, in the preoperational period, children's thinking is considered to be egoistic, and emerging from their limited world of experience. However, if questioned in a child-like manner, it may be possible for children to be able to conserve. Generally, the ability to conserve follows a developmental sequence, with the ability to conserve number and length preceding the ability to conserve mass and volume. Sometimes, younger children can be seen to carry out conservation, but their concepts of age, size, number, space, mass, volume, speed, time, and so on may be fuzzy. For example, an almost 3-year-old child remarked, 'If only I would eat more, I would become two years taller!' A school-age child would laugh at such a response, as s/he has comprehended the basic ideas of time and size.

Box 5.2 Conservation Exercises

Try the following activities with two children, one preschool-age child and one school-going child. Organise some basic materials like three tall narrow glasses, a flat-bottomed bowl, three pencils of equal length, 20 stickers or paper cutouts in shapes such as stars or circles, some clay or dough, water, and a duster to clean up after the exercise.

Conservation of number:

Take the 20 stickers or paper cutouts. Arrange 10 of these in a close scatter, that is, do not spread them out too much, they should be bunched close to each other. Arrange the other 10 in a loose scatter, that is, they should be spread out over a greater area. Ask the child which pile has a greater number of stickers. If the child says there are equal numbers of stickers in both piles, it reflects her/his ability for conservation of number.

Conservation of length:

Take the three pencils and place them next to each other so that their tips and ends are in the same horizontal plane. Get the child to agree that the pencils are of equal length. Now place the pencils in such a manner that the second pencil is positioned slightly ahead of the first, and the third one is positioned slightly farther than the second pencil. They should all be placed horizontally in front of the child. Now ask the child which of the pencils is the longest. If the child says that all three pencils are of equal length (either from memory or after placing the pencils next to each other to match their length), the child shows an ability for conservation of length.

Conservation of mass:

Take the dough or clay and divide it into equal portions. Show it to the children and ensure

Box 5.2 contd.

Box 5.2 contd.

that they agree there is an equal amount of dough in each division. Make a round ball of dough of the first portion, and flatten out the other portion like a pancake or *chapati*. Now ask the child which portion has greater mass or amount of dough. If the child says there is an equal quantity of dough in the round ball and the *chapati*, this reflects her/his ability to conserve mass.

Conservation of volume:

Pour out equal amounts of water in two of the tall narrow glasses. Ask the child if the water is equal in quantity. After the child has agreed that there is an equal amount of water in both glasses, pour water out from the first glass into the third empty tall narrow glass, and pour the water from the second tall narrow glass into the flat-bottomed bowl. Now ask the child which of the containers has a greater quantity of water. Conservation ability will be reflected if the child says there is an equal quantity of water in both.

Cognitive Gains

Piaget has introduced the concept of decalage. Decalage means that there may be similar changes occurring in cognitive development at different ages. He talks of two kinds of decalage—vertical and horizontal. Vertical decalage is traced from one stage to the next in the continuity the child shows in learning and mastering a concept. For example, the child may have an idea of the location of home and school, distance between the two, and the route needed to be taken to reach school from home. At the preschool age, this could be fuzzy and filled with imagined details. In middle childhood, the child can draw a cognitive map of the same. Horizontal decalage traces developmental sequences in the child's learning of a specific concept in the given stage. For example, the child learns the conservation of mass first and the concept of weight later.

An important ability underlying conservation (apart from decentration) is 'reversibility'. In the definition of conservation, we included not only substances, but also people, objects and events. Reversibility allows the child to think back in the sequence of events, or retrace a process from its beginnings. It also allows the child to see the basic unchanging identity of a person. For instance, if the child's teacher dresses up like an old man for a drama act, reversibility allows the child to understand that this person dressed as an old man is still the teacher, and has not actually become an old man.

We are familiar with children being called stubborn. In early years, there is no concept of time or logic with which to see consequences. Sometimes, when children are playing, they do not want to be interrupted and it is difficult to convey reasons to finish the ongoing game. They continue their actions as they are unable to comprehend perspectives other than their own. This habit may also surface when children need to share something they like. As they grow, children adapt, and they learn to be more considerate and social, both with reason and sometimes even with rule. Earlier, it may not have been easy to tell children that eating too many chocolates is bad, or that they cannot just eat sweets for a meal. Soon, they will be able to understand that their concept can lead to consequences. The child will show an ability to take the perspective of another person.

However, the loss of egocentrism and gain in perspective-taking ability may be limited. Children may still be rigid and stick to a particular hypothesis or perspective. Often, children will change facts to fit their beliefs or hypotheses. As they hypothesise, evaluate and accommodate facts, and experiment in their everyday worlds, children begin to form theories of the world. In doing so, they develop and use the important ability to reason inductively.

Inductive reasoning is the ability to apply reason or logic from a specific experience to construct a general principle. Inductive reasoning is achieved before deductive reasoning. Ability to reason by looking at facts appears during adolescence. Deductive reasoning is reasoning from the general to the specific, that is, applying a general principle to a selected situation. I felt bad when I was scolded and so will others if they are scolded, therefore scolding is a bad practice—this is an example of inductive reasoning. It is wrong policy to be harsh on children while disciplining, so I too do not deserve punishment—this is an example of deductive reasoning.

Children in middle childhood make many cognitive gains as they expand their social world and set of experiences. Apart from the concepts of number, size, volume, mass, and length, children also make gains in the understanding of space, time, distance, and speed. Recent research on autobiographical narratives suggests that children begin forming a sense of an autobiographical self (or a self with a life story) only after the age of two. Their concepts of time and timeline are vague, and only in the middle childhood years do they begin to arrange events along a timeline. They may not have a clear sense of history, and the past and the future, both recent and distant, may be clubbed. Futuristic thinking is better defined in formal operations or in adolescence.

New Cognitive Concepts

Time, distance and speed may still be confused during school years. However, the ability to cognise space improves. Children often take pride in arranging their personal space. They draw cognitive maps or visual representations of their cognition of real space, for example home, locality, school, daily route to a place, marketplace, and so on. They also like to solve mazes or draw imaginary places in their cognitive maps. They start noticing and using landmarks. They also show the first signs of independence in going to places like the market, friend's home, or the bus stop.

Apart from arranging objects in physical space, children also begin to arrange and categorise objects according to dimensions. Seriation is the ability to arrange objects according to size, in ascending or descending order. As children begin to understand the concept of ascending or descending size, they may make 'ordered pairs' of one big and one small of the objects being arranged, before they are finally able to arrange the objects in ascending or descending fashion.

Categorising objects based on their properties is a more complex ability of concrete operations. Piaget called this hierarchical classification. Children learn to classify according to colour, size, shape, and number, in terms of the more basic dimensions. This ability assists in the child's solving of complex jigsaw puzzles at more advanced levels of cognition. Another ability that evolves during concrete operations is that of class inclusion, which is really an ability to see more than one attribute, or multiple factors, to make categories often said to be 'a category within a category'; for instance, blue tables and red tables are all still within the category of tables. So a classic 'class inclusion' question would be: Are there more tables, or are there more red tables? Such a poser may potentially cause the child confusion, and at the same time be a misleading question.

Testing this skill of class formation is one of the controversial investigations of Piaget's cognitive developmental perspective. Class inclusion refers to the understanding that there are sets and subsets of objects in this universe, and that an object may be categorised under a 'class' of objects. Piaget famously asked children questions about class inclusion using flowers, which were heavily criticised for being misleading. For example, we show a child a bunch of red flowers and a bigger bunch of white flowers and ask, 'Are there more flowers or are there more red flowers?' Children may invariably be led to answer that there are more flowers. The child who says that both red flowers and white flowers belong to the larger class of flowers, implying that the question is incorrect, is said to have an understanding of class inclusion.

Researchers often see that children seldom question adults, but tend to view the adult proposition as true. Such examples in theory formation are placed to help you understand that no one theory becomes the only way to understand behaviour. Children often surprise you with their responses and their ability to inquire, reflecting the leaps in their thinking and skills in meaning-making.

SCHOOL PERFORMANCE AND LABELLING

School years are also a time for academic performance. In the past, children have often had to sit through IQ (Intelligence Quotient) tests in order for school authorities to determine how best to teach them. IQ tests were first conducted in the early 1900s to screen out children with intellectual disabilities, and design remedial coaching for them. Although the original motive for IQ testing was a noble one, things took an ugly turn when IQ testing led to the labelling of children as 'low' or 'normal' in intellectual functioning.

Labelling children can not only impact their performance or abilities, but more importantly can hamper their sense of well-being or self-esteem. Labelling also changes the expectations of people around the child (parents, educators, peers), and children psychologically tend to pick up cues and act or perform to fit their label. 'Intelligence' and IQ have also been at the centre of the debate on heredity and environment as influences on development. Focusing on intelligence and IQ does not tell us much about 'how' children learn, even as these tell us much about 'what' children learn or 'how much' they know. More than the products of learning, we need to focus on the process of learning. Intelligence testing is still quite common during school years. It can be significant as a way of screening children with learning disabilities and other special needs, and designing an inclusive school curriculum. Assistance in improving learning and academic performance can boost a child's self-esteem and confidence. IQ is also a fluid concept and shows variation over time, and according to circumstance. It may therefore not be a very reliable long-term indicator of a person's abilities or success.

Testing and Cultural Issues

The WISC-R—the revised Wechsler's Intelligence Scale for Children—and the Bhatia Battery of Performance Tests for Children are two commonly used intelligence tests in school years. Most intelligence tests have specific components or scales—the verbal scale and the performance scale. The full-scale IQ is calculated using the verbal and performance scale scores. The Bhatia Battery has only performance items. Sometimes, language or medium of instruction may make a test difficult to use in a particular culture. For example, a test using English may be incomprehensible to a rural Indian child.

Even if the test is translated and standardised, there may be certain concepts that are true to a particular culture only. Such concepts, even when translated, will have little relevance for other cultures or places. One of the questions in the WISC asks, 'How many cents are there in a dollar?' Few schoolchildren in India may have a theoretical knowledge of how many cents make a dollar, as it is not part of practical everyday exchange. Also, a question like, 'Do you like to eat cereal in the morning?' may draw a blank response, as people eat different kinds of breakfasts in different cultures. In a nutshell, there are few tests that are objective and culture-free!

Many Intelligences and Creativity

Instead of using a composite indicator like IQ, it is often more rewarding to look at the construct of intelligence in terms of its various manifestations. Different theorists have pointed out that there are multiple dimensions to intelligence. Gardner's theory of Multiple Intelligences sees intelligence as multiple abilities, and not just scholastic performance. The multiple intelligences are musical-rhythmic, visual-spatial, verbal-linguistic, logical-mathematical, bodily-kinesthetic, interpersonal, intrapersonal, naturalistic, and existential. It is during the middle school years that children's varied potential is displayed in classroom transactions and other contexts.

An ability closely associated with the study of intelligence is that of creativity. Creativity literally means original thinking. It essentially requires the skill of divergent thinking, that is, looking for alternative, multiple and novel ways to approach a task or solve a problem. Like intelligence, creativity has also been the subject of the heredity-environment debate. Creative thinkers are not necessarily born; the mind can be taught or trained to think creatively. In other words, creativity can be cultivated in the classroom! Along with emphasis on assisted learning or remedial teaching for children with intellectual and learning disabilities, it is also vital to focus on promoting learning that is suited to the potential of children who may be intellectually gifted or more advanced than others. Enrichment of the learning programme to suit their individual needs is important.

Learning disabilities are commonly noticed in schoolgoing children. These are specific difficulties in reading, writing, or mathematics. Children with learning disabilities may show hyperactivity, attention deficits, motor control problems, and perceptual limitations. Experiencing learning disability can impede a child's sense of self-worth.

LANGUAGE DEVELOPMENT IN MIDDLE CHILDHOOD

Cognitive and linguistic advancement show simultaneous leaps in middle childhood.

Did language come first, or did thought emerge first in the history of human beings? What do you think early man did to survive? Did he think out difficult situations or use the capacity for communication and speech to survive on a daily basis? And if he thought, what is the way in which thoughts occurred—as visual schemes or a silent inner speech? It is difficult to establish very clearly what came first in the language and thought debate. Taking a cue from this debate, one can say that it is difficult to ascertain whether language promotes cognitive gains, or whether cognitive gains result in the advancement of linguistic skills.

During middle childhood, vocabulary size expands considerably. There is increased use of conjunctions, more complex sentences, and greater flow in making connections between thought. By the age of 11 or 12, children can write essays and poetry on different topics. Children who learn grammar in formal educational programmes will show good skills in everyday construal, as will children who experience storytelling, poetry and rich conversations in their everyday lives. Language learning is culturally guided and socially reinforced (as discussed in Chapter 1). During middle childhood, children enjoy word play, rhyming, writing stories, composing poems and songs, and even inventing special languages. They like learning and using synonyms, antonyms, metaphors, and idioms. Class inclusion skills help children to understand and use language better. Decentration helps them to communicate effectively, as children who can decentre can take on other people's perspectives. They can therefore participate in purposeful debates, arguments and persuasive talk. The ability to recapitulate the details of an event or a story improves considerably during middle childhood.

A special aspect of language during middle childhood is the use of humour. Children begin to appreciate subtle forms of humour. They enjoy slapstick and understand culture-specific jokes. In their middle childhood years, children can have a huge repertoire of jokes, which they enjoy telling in public. They may be interested in school-related jokes, jokes about adults, jokes about other children and their weaknesses, common childhood fears, and so on. Humour and its use can get them to become popular. Some childhood humour can sound unkind or socially inappropriate, resulting in rejection from peers, behavioural difficulties like bullying, or social isolation.

MORAL DEVELOPMENT

During middle childhood, children follow rules keenly because someone in authority tells them to do so. This is identified as heteronomous morality or moral realism, as given by Piaget. In this stage, children become aware of rules, often taking them a bit too seriously—as seen in children's games, and the fights over breaking a rule. They see rules as unchanging, even sacred, developed by an unseen authority or all-powerful adults. Adherence to rules is essential under all circumstances. At this stage, children believe in imminent justice, that is, wrongdoing is invariably punished. They may make moral judgements using the consequences of the actor as a benchmark, and not the intentions of the person.

During the closing years of middle childhood, children make a shift from heteronomous to autonomous morality. This means that there is an understanding that rules in social situations are made by people, and not just by powerful authority figures. This shift also fosters a responsibility in creating rules. Heteronomous morality is when a child takes a moral decision because of the rules set by others, or follows a rule because of a fear of others. Autonomous morality is the moral judgement of the child based on ideas s/he believes in, or has internalised as the correct reaction. They start viewing rules as human constructions, subject to flaws and change. People are entitled to their viewpoints and ways of doing things, as long as it does not harm humanity. The motive or intention becomes more important than the consequence in making moral decisions. They are confused by the need for fairness on the one hand, and the inequalities of the world on the other. They may rely on some form of religious explanation, and not on abstract reasoning or extreme objectivity in their moral valuations.

Lawrence Kohlberg worked extensively on the development of moral reasoning, describing morality as a three-part internalisation. Beginning from a very rudimentary personalised experience of what is right, individuals develop an understanding of behaviours and phenomena that are good for humanity. Kohlberg describes the changes that take shape as children grow and adjust to expanding social networks.

In preschool years, led by egocentric thought and an absence of the ability to think of others, children almost behave as if might is right. As they grow, they learn to share and realise that objects that are not yours cannot be snatched. Respect for ownership and the rights of others are learnt by middle childhood, when children operate at the conventional level of moral reasoning (level 2 in Kohlberg's theory). They now function on the principles of 'right' and 'good'. They are concerned with being fair and gaining the approval of others. Societal conventions and social order are of paramount importance in making moral choices, and evaluating the conduct of self and others.

However, children at this stage may use more rigid standards of moral evaluation for others than they do for themselves. Parental disciplining, teacher expectations, culture, and experiences within the social and personal contexts influence children's moral decisions. Sometimes, children seem to have theoretical knowledge of morality—for instance, in the understanding of the moral of a story—but may have difficulty in applying moral knowledge to their real-life situations. All children have early experiences with what adults call lying, cheating and stealing. These behaviours, if consistently present or observed in an individual, are often referred to as conduct disorders. But for most children, such behaviour may be accidental, playful, or even triggered by their imagination and fantasy. For example, a child may see the answer for a test question from another child's answer book without realising that this is cheating, or is against the rules. Or a child may pick up an object that belongs to another child simply because it is attractive, not knowing that this amounts to stealing.

Most childhood lies could be the outcome of rich imagination, curiosity, and the rapidly developing mind. Sometimes it is seen that children who appear to consistently lie or steal have emotional issues with parents; for example, fear of rejection. It is the responsibility of parents and educators to discuss right and wrong, as well as moral rules with children. It is important to help children understand the need for such rules, how they may have originated, and to evaluate the validity of these rules in the day-to-day context. The child should be encouraged to see the role and perspective of the individual in relation to culture, in upholding moral standards. Reasoning and explanations are the preferred disciplinary strategies in this context, as too much punishment may adversely affect moral behaviour in children. It is important that parents and teachers keep communication channels open.

If school-age children are asked to share or distribute a resource, they might use different forms of reasoning to make decisions. For example, there are five toffees and seven children! In developing ideas of fairness, children show a special form of reasoning called distributive justice. In middle childhood, younger children focus on an equal distribution of goods for all, irrespective of special circumstances. Older children, however, take more complex distributive justice decisions, and may consider other factors, such as individual contribution within the group, purpose, responsibility, roles, age, disability or limitations, and so on.

In their school years, children also display a lot of altruistic or prosocial behaviour. They like to cooperate in group activities, can empathise with other children and with adults, and have the capacity to sacrifice small pleasures for the self. Prosocial behaviour and the development of empathy are facilitated by perspective-taking exercises and role play-based activities.

Social and Emotional Development

Middle childhood is when children spend more time with friends than with family. It may be the first time that children form true friendships. Also, as the child's social network expands, adults other than parents and teachers become important in the child's life. As the child comes into contact with more people, situations of conflict may also increase. It is important that adults around the child encourage independent actions and responsibility. Over-protection may lead to low self-confidence in the child. However, withdrawal of parental support, especially during failures, could be detrimental. Extreme criticism can also distance children from their parents. Parents need to continuously negotiate the boundaries between being a parent and being a friend.

School children take great pride in doing things on their own. Everyday tasks interest children, especially the everyday activities that adults participate in, for example cooking, shopping, cleaning, and so on. This is also when the child takes pride in and cherishes a personal physical space, be it a separate room, or a play or study area. Towards the end of middle childhood, children may also start running errands outside the home, such as going to the market, taking care of pets, or keeping younger siblings occupied. They may organise events with peers, such as a fair, charity event, picnics, and camps. Along with their interest in routine adult activities, they handle and learn about important concepts like money, first aid, and culturally sensitive practices.

Another dimension binding them to peers is style of dressing. In middle childhood, children across socio-economic strata may like to conform to the fashion trends followed by their group of friends. Some may even be the trendsetters! Children and families everywhere are inclined towards aesthetics, although a lack of resources may not enable them to keep their homes as aesthetically as they would like to. School-age children like beautiful possessions and nice toys. When we talk of poverty and plan programmes for children in poverty settings, we must not forget that along with mid-day-meals, free school uniforms and stationery, they must also have access to technology, high quality play or learning material, and enriching and comfortable environments at home and at school.

Figure 5.3: Socialisation into cultural values

Source: Dimple Rangila

School-age children learn about core familial and societal values, and become aware of human rights and civic responsibilities. They may start using their knowledge of rights, responsibility and values in a practical context. If children are made to understand the reasons behind, justifications for, and origins of such notions, they will negotiate the practical context better, and also start thinking for themselves. Once they learn that there can be different perspectives on an issue, they learn the art of debating, an important ability in cognising complexity.

All children have ideas about themselves. For example, they know 'who they are', 'where they live', 'who their parents are', 'what their parents' professions are', 'their own likes and dislikes', and so on. In other words, children have a self-concept—an understanding of selfhood. This self-concept may assume an evaluative dimension, that is, 'I am good', 'I am naughty', 'I am clumsy', and so on. This is children's way of evaluating the self, referred to as self-esteem.

Self-esteem will influence how children function in their environment and the quality of relationships that they form. Children develop concepts about themselves in social interactions with parents, or among peer groups. Children with high self-esteem generally reflect confidence, a positive outlook, initiative, interest in activities, and have good relationships with peers and adults. Children with low self-esteem may have difficulties with friends, and may show low initiative and interest in day-to-day tasks. They may also be withdrawn, expect failure, and reflect self-doubt. Children's everyday experiences and how they are received and/or appreciated by significant others go a long way in the development of their self-esteem.

ROLE OF FAMILY

The family is the first context of socialisation for the child, and continues to hold importance throughout life. In the middle childhood years, family may begin to take a backseat as peer influence starts to develop. When children experience warmth, encouragement and appreciation within the family, their basic emotional needs for security and love are met. This builds their sense of trust; however, family relations need not dominate to an extent that prevents them from looking for bonds outside. On the other hand, attachment relationships outside the family have to be balanced within the parameters of individual needs. Friendships and relationships outside can be nurturing, yet not always geared to individual affective needs. Hence, dependence on any one context may not be nurturing for the child, and children need to be aware of primary ties. Family provides the child with the strength to go into the world and carve out a personal niche. It also provides the essential guidance and counselling that a child may need from time to time.

As the child experiments with freedom and independence, sensitive parenting guides her/him in understanding boundaries and regulating behaviour. Children may cherish secrets, and may not want to reveal the content of their conversations and interactions with friends. During middle childhood, children's relationships are further defined with parents of the same and opposite sex. While mothers are seen as constant close companions, fathers may be sought out for a specific range of activities.

Parental depression, stress, family living arrangements in single-parent families, and other difficulties such as illness or disability will affect children's familial experiences in different ways. Death of a parent and parental separation can be traumatic for a child. School-age children will be able to cope with the stress as they have a better social understanding of situations and a repertoire of competencies to manage everyday affairs. If financial constraints are fewer or facilities greater, children will do reasonably well. They may, however, experience anger, fear of rejection and moodiness. If their coping mechanisms are not very strong, they may experience falling grades and difficulties in interpersonal interaction.

Figure 5.4: Family activities give emotional strength

Source: Galli Galli Sim Sim, Season 1.

Remarriage of a parent and living in 'step-families' with step-siblings can be stressful for children. They may experience turbulent emotions that they find difficult to deal with. Step-family experiences may also be gendered. Sons and daughters may adapt differently to the presence of a stepmother or a stepfather. The quality of the interpersonal relationships shared by the parents will also influence the adaptive behaviour of the child.

Parental Preoccupations and Varying Family Configurations

Absence of a parent due to work, lack of involvement, and ambivalence in intra-family interactions present a challenging context for the child. Maternal employment often leads to the child taking on more responsibility for activities relating to the self, school and home. The child may also experience inconsistence in parental disciplining and expectations.

Parental satisfaction with their own work will also affect their childcare approach. It may be unfair to compare the academic performance of children of working mothers with those of mothers not employed outside the home, using IQ as an indicator. Research has shown that IQ may be a poor yardstick for assessing intelligence, as it also varies over time and with situations. Research shows no significant differences in the academic performance of children of working mothers, vis-à-vis those with mothers not employed outside the home. In poverty settings, children may often be homeless, and with or without families. Street children are the most disadvantaged in terms of material resources and nurturing adults. Research on resilience has shown that the presence of a single mentor or nurturing adult goes a long way in securing positive developmental outcomes.

During middle childhood, it is critical to ensure an environment for the street child that is not abusive or exploitative. At this age, children may be more vulnerable, as they come into contact with people from a wide range of settings, including people who indulge in deviant behaviour, and with law enforcement agencies. The daily stress of not having a permanent home, a nomadic life, insufficient food, lack of access to education and healthcare, and abusive interactions has a deleterious impact on the child. Very often, street children have to work, usually in situations identified by law as hazardous. Child labour is, of course, not limited to street children.

Box 5.3 Sibling Relations

Piya and Venky were two siblings. Vivacious and outgoing Piya was four years younger than 11-year-old Venky, who was a quiet and serious child. They studied in the same school. Usually, the two were at loggerheads at home, vying for parental attention. However, at school Venky would be busy sorting out some last-minute discussions with teachers, and would often be late catching the school bus home. It was Piya who would ensure that the bus driver waited for her errant older brother. Siblings do stand up for each other in situations that herald inconvenience.

Source: Asha Singh {conversations with children in theatre workshops}.

Sibling Relations

Another critical component of family life is sibling interaction. Relationships with siblings may assume new dimensions in middle childhood as children's peer networks expand. Increased responsibility may also spill over to sibling care. While some children enjoy caring for younger siblings, others may detest it, as they have their own goals and interests. Poor sibling relationships at this age could predispose children to difficulties in interpersonal relations outside the family. Younger siblings are more likely to imitate older ones.

Box 5.4 Developing Friendships

Vignette 1

One day, Raghav came home from school and announced that he wanted to spend the night at his schoolmate's home. His mother said that Raghav's friend should bring a letter inviting him over. Later, she asked Raghav if he could brush his teeth, get ready in the morning, and take care of his clothes. Raghav was only a little over five. He had been studying in kindergarten for two years. The first pajama party took place successfully, and the two boys have remained friends ever since. In fact, there are reports that some lifelong friendships have begun during middle childhood.

Vignette 2

Disha joined school a little late, in Class I. During lunch, everybody sat down to eat, and Disha opened her lunch box. Her mother had given her sandwiches, with ketchup packed in a small glass bottle. Priya was fascinated by the bottle, and pulled it from Disha to inspect it. Unfortunately, it fell from her hand. At this point the teacher entered the room and assumed that Priya was bullying Disha. However, Disha explained that Priya had wanted to see the bottle, and that it fell while she was handing it over. The teacher did not scold or punish Priya. Priya looked at Disha and thanked her. Disha remembers this incident, as it marked the beginning of their friendship. Friendships become possible because children now begin to understand perspectives, and move away from being egocentric.

Source: Asha Singh.

Gender is another factor defining sibling interactions. Same-sex siblings are more likely to share interests. Two sisters may argue a lot; two brothers may indulge more in rough and tumble play and physical fights. The most harmonious relationship is supposed to be between different-sex siblings, as they may have completely different goals and interests. However, they may still be competing for parental affection and attention. Sibling rivalry tends to be an important developmental experience. Disability in one sibling may evoke varied reactions in the other. While some siblings may be very supportive, others may be prone to rejection. The age of the siblings, gender and parental resourcefulness will also define sibling relationships.

The importance of the peer group in the life of a child cannot be overemphasised. To the school-age child, peers may be somewhat more important than the family. The influence of the peer group assumes primary importance in middle childhood. At this age, the peer group may be loosely formed, with few formal rules. Towards the end of middle childhood, the peer group may be more structured, cohesive, and sometimes exclusive. Since children enjoy leadership roles and group activity during school years, the peer group provides ample opportunity for both. There are few gender differences in peer group formation during middle childhood. Both competition and cooperation are acted out with peers. Membership of a peer group marks the child's partial autonomy, and provides the base for emotional self-regulation. Peers are powerful socialising agents, and transmit attitudes and values and provide models for behaviour.

Conformity and compliance may be big issues in middle childhood, as parents and peers appear to pull in different directions. The pressure to conform to peer group values might be so strong that children may indulge in risky behaviour. Productive peer group values may lead to high achievement motivation. Conformity may be required more strongly with regard to physical appearance and social attitude. Early or late attainment of physical maturity can affect peer group acceptance and rejection. Although children who mature early may gain popularity among peers, they can sometimes face rejection and ridicule for appearing different. Depending on the situation and group values, late maturing children may also face rejection.

Figure 5.5: Making life-long relationships

Source: Chembakolli.com (22 January 2015)

The first 'true friendships' are formed during middle childhood. These are long-term and intimate; at this age, children have 'best friends'. Friendships are reciprocal and more mutually satisfying. Same-sex friends are common. Children without friends may feel lonely and depressed. Childhood depression is more observable at this age. Reduced self-confidence, feelings of rejection and withdrawal on the one hand, and aggression, hostility and deviant behaviour could result from a lack of friends.

Play during middle childhood is more of a rough and tumble variety. There are also cooperative group games, organised sports, and formal indoor and board games. Make-believe elements in play may be fewer. Competition and cooperation enter the world of play. Children also gain popularity and rejection through play activities. Another form of 'play' or recreation is the child's interest in 'hobbies' or pursuits like craft creations, painting, sketching, sculpture, sewing, doll-making, toy-making, learning a dance form, music, gathering collectibles, and so on. These pursuits are mostly undertaken alone by the child, that is, as an individual activity. The child may take great pride in sharing these skills with others, and showcasing these at events. Reading is another pleasure of childhood, which, if encouraged, becomes a life-long source of joy. Children at this age also enjoy conversations with other children and adults. They may like to 'just talk', in order to have a good time. Online social networking is another way of social expression. Most social networking sites have age limits specified. Parents also have access to mechanisms to monitor their child's online activities.

Box 5.5 Popular Childhood Activities: Team Games

A popular sport among Indian children, KhoKho is a basic game of strategy to catch an opponent, and can be played with any number of people.First, you need to divide all players into two equal teams. The team that chooses to be the 'catcher' should crouch in a line with enough space between each person for players of the other team to run between. One person from this team is the catcher, who can only run around the line of people and try to catch three people from the other team. Once anyone is caught, one more person joins in.

The catcher starts the game by running around the line three times. The person chasing can only go around the line, but people from the other team can pass through the spaces between those crouching in the line. The catcher, when tired, can swap with another person in their team by coming up behind them, tapping them on the shoulder, and saying 'kho'.

The entry of another member may lead the runners in the other team to be caught by surprise, which is a strategy for gaining victory. When all three have been caught, another three from their team should take their places. When everyone in the team has been caught, the two teams exchange roles.

Second only to family, school is the other vital, naturalistic and socio-cultural context for development. As we have seen, middle childhood is also known as the elementary school years. At this age, children spend a good part of the day at school. An enriching classroom environment, sensitive teaching approaches, opportunities for self-expression, and good friendships make the child's schooling experience very positive. On the other hand, ill-equipped classrooms, low teacher motivation, bullying, low encouragement for initiative and expression, and insensitive disciplining can make schooling a negative experience.

Difficulties with particular academic subjects can also mar the child's positive schooling experience. If a child has a learning disability, remedial assistance can be helpful. Good school practices will have a learning disabilities screening programme in place. Early identification facilitates early intervention. Effective schools also have a philosophy that is sensitive to children's learning and developmental needs, and emphasises parental partnership in children's education.

EMOTIONAL DEVELOPMENT IN MIDDLE CHILDHOOD

Children are emotionally impressionable during middle childhood. Their expanding social networks require them to negotiate a range of emotions, both in themselves and of others. Not only does children's emotional expression improve, but their capacity to comprehend emotions also enhances. They may also learn to differentiate between fleeting feelings and deeper emotions. With experience, children learn to watch their moods and practice emotional self-regulation. Moodiness may remain a characteristic emotional state well into adolescence.

Most irrational fears in children will have subsided by middle childhood. They are, however, still fearful about selected personal and social issues, for example fear of failure or rejection, parents' health, accidents, death, and so on. Sometimes children may experience intense or extreme fears known as phobias, for instance, an extreme fear of heights, or of darkness, crowds, or animals. Fear of school can be a tricky one to deal with for parents. Childhood fears are often expressed in terms of physiological symptoms, such as nausea, stomachache, a dip in body temperature, diarrhoea, and so on. When the fearful stimulus is removed, the symptoms go away. Children, however, may need to face the fear gradually and overcome their negative feelings.

Aggression can be a definite emotional difficulty in childhood years. Often accompanied by hyperactivity, aggressive behaviour may be the first form of antisocial behaviour that a child either experiences or acts out. Aggressive behaviour may be the fallout of certain co-occurring conditions, such as falling grades, low self-esteem, parental discord, depressive home environment, and so on. Aggression can be both physical and verbal, and could be intended to hurt others. This is known as hostile aggression.

Aggression could also be goal-directed, or directed at removing frustrating obstacles from the environment. Such aggression is known as instrumental aggression. Boys may be seen as more aggressive than girls. Bullying involves physical and verbal aggression. Research shows that children who indulge in bullying may have self-esteem issues. A disturbed home environment or having been bullied in another context can also lead to bullying behaviour in a child. Aggression can also be modelled from television programmes.

According to Freud, middle childhood is a stage of latency. During latency, the child's development follows a hidden pattern. Sexual impulses and sensory urges are curbed as the child indulges in day-to-day activities. According to Erikson, middle childhood is a stage of Industry vs. Inferiority, wherein the child is engaged in play, work and society. Feelings of competence and worthiness encourage productivity in the child, while experiences of failure lead to low self-worth and inferiority.

SUMMARY

- After reading this chapter, you will have learnt what is developmentally significant in the elementary school years. Middle childhood is a period of unique achievements for a child. The child becomes increasingly autonomous, participating in varied ways in family and community life. Utilising physical capabilities to the fullest (through games and organised sport) and a concrete grasp over the reality of the world (through experimentation and learning of facts) are the hallmarks of this age. Middle childhood is in some ways recognised to set the base for the child's future personality as an adult, as the ways and modes of learning and functioning acquired in middle childhood stay with the child for a long time to come. Also, this is when formal learning, whether through school or apprenticeship to a trade, becomes a vital part of the child's life. The child learns the importance of 'work', and finds expression through various forms of play and recreation.
- During this period, the child is well-initiated into the rituals of school and learning. This age period is also sometimes referred to as the elementary school years. While exercising and mastering their physical-motor skills, children can often encounter small accidents. The safety of children in middle childhood years needs to be ensured in the day-to-day context. While there is a lot of latent physical growth, their bodies need adequate and optimal nutrition. Children of this age enjoy dabbling in facts and learning new concepts, and enhancing their knowledge of things. They enjoy working on group projects and organising social and recreational activities with friends.
- As their social network expands, they may sometimes experience difficulties like bullying, quarrels, feelings of rejection, inadequacy, and so on. They may even develop positive attributes, like an enhanced sense of self, faith in their competencies, and skills in socialising. Much will depend on guided social experiences, in which parents and teachers have an important role to play. During middle childhood, school and curriculum-related learning difficulties also need to be looked into by sensitising curricula and using inclusive and special teaching methods. Middle childhood, well-lived, with enriching social and learning opportunities, sets the child on the journey towards adolescence on a positive note.

KEY TERMS

Middle childhood / elementary school years / school years – The period between the ages of 6–12, following preschool years and preceding adolescence

Concrete operations – A stage of cognitive development given by Piaget, which describes cognitive changes during middle childhood

Conservation – According to Piaget, the cognitive ability of the child to understand that the properties of a substance will remain the same even when the outward appearance changes

Seriation – According to Piaget, the cognitive ability of the child to arrange objects in order of a chosen dimension, like length or size

Horizontal decalage – A concept given by Piaget, which explains that a particular ability acquired by the child is not immediately applied to all situations and problems; the child will apply learning gradually, with experience and experimentation

Vertical decalage – A concept given by Piaget that explains that a child may use a cognitive ability or function across various stages of development.

EXERCISES

1. Define middle childhood. What are some of the major developmental goals of the childhood years?
2. How do children go to school? At what age do children start going to school? In different parts of the country, are there different ways in which children go to school? Think about these issues and plan and prepare a project titled 'Going to School'.
3. Approach a child in the age range of 6–12 years. Over an informal conversation or a game talk about the child's daily routine and experiences at school and home.
   Do children have friends?
   What games do they play?
   Are the games individual or team?
   Balanced diet
4. Approach a child between the ages of 9–12. Talk with one boy and one girl about the physical changes they have noticed in themselves in recent months. You could discuss topics like becoming taller, body weight, strength, the budding of breasts in girls, and breaking of voices in boys. You could also explore satisfaction with body image, or their performance in special skills such as sports, dance or gymnastics.
5. Explore patterns of play and nature of interaction in two groups one each of boys and girls. Note
   The types of games
   Number of children
   Duration of play
   Number of interruptions and reasons
   Nature of conversations
6. Can children carry out conservation tasks at a preschool age? Compare the nature of their conservation abilities with those of an elementary school child.
7. Enlist the cognitive characteristics of middle childhood years. How does culture play a role in the developmental of cognitive concepts in schoolgoing children?
8. Approach a child of 10–12 years. Ask the child to share some jokes with you. Ask questions, like where was the joke learnt, does the child enjoy jokes on self, are jokes important, and so on. Ask the child to help you invent a new joke!

9. Describe the roles played by school, family and peers in middle childhood. What are some of the ways in which the child affiliates with parents, siblings, teachers, and peers? Use examples from your observations, as well as your personal experience.
10. Write notes on the following:
    a. Learning disabilities in schoolgoing children
    b. Language during the elementary school years
    c. Intelligence and IQ assessments of schoolgoing children
    d. Behavioural difficulties
    e. Friendships in middle childhood
11. Describe physical-motor development in the middle childhood years. What are some of the issues children may face in relation to early and late maturation?

REFERENCES

Berk, L. E., *Development through the life-span*, Boston: Allyn & Bacon, 2010.

Kohlberg, L., 'Stage and sequence', in *Handbook of Socialization Theory and Research*, New York: McGraw Hill, 1969.

Papalia, D. E., S. W. Olds and W. Duskin Feldman, *Human Development*, 9e, McGraw Hill, 2004.

Rice, F. Philip, *Human Development*, New York: Prentice Hall, 2000.

Santrock, J. W., *Life-Span Development*, 13e, McGraw Hill, 2010.

6

Development in Adolescence

HIGHLIGHTS

- Describes the universal aspects of growth and developmental changes during teenage years.
- Focus on the specific social contexts of India.
- Focus on the transitions and changing role of larger societal factors on growing individuals, and how they transact and deal with emerging demands.
- The role of family, peers, and other social factors are discussed.
- Describes the physical, social and emotional changes experienced by individuals from the onset of puberty.
- Contemporary definitions and tasks of adolescence are described.
- Developmental issues and concerns of adolescence are discussed with special reference to India.

WHAT IS ADOLESCENCE? A HISTORICAL PERSPECTIVE

Historically, like the contemporary understanding of childhood, adolescence is also a notion of modern life influenced by industrial growth and consequent urbanisation, as well as a reconfiguration of family dynamics. The first use of the term was in the fifteenth century, and stems from the Latin *adolescere*, to grow into maturity. Each society, primitive or modern, has systems to help individuals make the transition from childhood into adulthood. In the pre-industrial era, families were occupied together in occupations, in their personal spaces. All generations contributed according to their competence, and learnt tasks of living and livelihood as they grew. With the invention of machines, new social structures emerged, and social roles were redefined. The influences of laws on child labour and education led to the emergence of new social tasks, specifically for children above the age of 11. G. Stanley Hall is credited with the discovery of this stage of life, especially as a point of rapid growth and change. Hall is often called the 'father of adolescence', and had a large repertoire of empirical work focusing on issues of teenage years. He also shaped themes in the study of adolescence. In post-industrial societies, adolescence is a phase of life that spans a few years. In many other cultures, the significance of adolescence lies primarily in capturing the transition from childhood to adulthood.

Hall did not view this period very positively. According to him, individuals went through mood disruptions, conflict with parents, and risky behaviour. Adolescence was dramatised as a stormy and stressful period in developmental literature. Individuals face trials of identity and social adjustment in their move from being children to adult members of a community. While the way adolescence unfolds in different societies varies, the universal feature lies in the transition from being a child to learning to become a self-reliant member of the cultural group. All cultures recognise this transition as being an important phenomenon. Anthropological studies on childhood have identified rites of passage, which are marked by certain celebrations or ritual events to facilitate this transition.

The vocabulary in different cultures is also indicative of how society views the different phases of life. Most cultures have terms for things, events and phenomena. Brown et al. (2002) noted an absence of any word denoting the stage of adolescence till recent times in East Asian countries. Societies that are mainly agrarian initiate children from young ages into adult responsibilities. Within Indian culture, too, early initiation into adult roles can be observed in certain traditional communities, like the weavers in Benaras. In many social groups, it is not uncommon to see children attend school and return to help in the family trade, such as toy-making, selling vegetables, or assisting a washerman and delivering ironed clothes to local residents. *Kishore-avastha* relates to the stage of youth in the lifecycle, and initiates individuals from the primary learning-dominant stage of *bal-avastha* to building an understanding of social roles and responsibilities.

In cultures where the transfer of skills begins early, the storm and stress that Hall talked about is negligible, and the transition to socially responsible adult is quite smooth. In post-industrial societies, the segregation of age groups leads to a lowered exposure to adult icons and roles. An absence of role models during adolescent years often results in an inability to resolve conflicts. The role of peers and mixed consequences in shaping the young personality is discussed in a later section.

SOCIAL EXPECTATIONS DURING ADOLESCENCE

Adolescence is an age of qualitative transition in many areas of development. It is a time for self-discovery. As an adolescent undergoes tremendous physical and physiological changes, corresponding changes take place in social expressions. The quest for understanding the self and one's place in the world is important during adolescence. Sexual maturation and its implications—in terms of the desire for intimacy—is not always in consonance with societal norms, and can lead the adolescent to experiment with roles and relationships.

Adolescence is also a special time for planning the future and developing the necessary skills for a chosen field of specialisation. Advancing cognition and language assist the adolescent in knowledge construction, and an application of what is learnt in practical contexts. Research in recent years has contested the traditional view of adolescence, which begins at around the age of 12 and ends at 18 years. Many of the tasks of adolescence, such as finding intimacy and living independently, are continued well into young adulthood. It therefore remains debatable whether adolescence should be expanded as a period in terms of age range.

Gender-related experiences of adolescence make for important research themes, from a developmental and cultural perspective. It is understandable that boys and girls may have different interests, as a result of gender-role socialisation in childhood years. Such differences are more pronounced during adolescence—a time characterised by sex-role experimentation and gender-specific expectations on the part of the family, which set culturally defined norms for boys and girls. For example, in the Indian setting, it may still be the prevalent belief that by the end of adolescence, parents should get girls married, or not allow them to pursue academics beyond a certain age, or even live independently from their families for work or education. Boys are largely faced with the pressure of preparing to be breadwinners, obtaining a conventional degree, and a decent job. There may be little acceptance for maverick individuals who go against the trend, or attempt to chart a unique course of life for oneself.

Box 6.1 Coming of Age: Lifecycle Changes

Events to mark the transition from childhood to adolescence are present in most cultures, as part of religious tradition or community rituals. Often, this is referred to as *coming of age*, with the event being termed *rite of passage*. The community recognises and facilitates individual evolution as the change opens many new freedoms and brings in new responsibilities. Growing is a process, and at this juncture individuals find themselves leaving the dependency of childhood and strict adherence to family codes, and moving towards areas of independence and self-direction. Young people find new responsibilities, new roles, and new things to do to mark the entry into adolescence.

Box 6.1 contd.

Box 6.1 contd.

Often, during this period, children go through initiation ceremonies. In India, certain groups across regions, especially Hindus, perform the *Upanaya*. Different rituals in the presence of the larger family and community help children to find their niche in the adult world. Ceremonies require families to identify a Guru, who serves as a role model. Seeking blessings from the mother and other elders functions to create direct bonds of affection.

Ceremonies for girls are more specifically connected to attaining menarche. At this point, celebrations mark the transition from girl child to girlhood, and further, to becoming a woman. The girl receives blessings in cash and kind, as do boys. Such rituals vary between communities. Tribal groups, such as the *Ghotuls* among the Muria tribe in central India, have different ways which appear more liberal, such as permitting the mixing of the young to explore their need for intimacy. Such social arrangements facilitate social roles, assisting individuals in their adjustment and movement towards independent adulthood.

The Muria is a sub-caste of the Gonds, and their customs seem almost too forward and permissive. The Murias live in north Bastar in central India. The Ghotul consists of many huts, where boys assemble after sunset. Unmarried men and women (mostly men) invite each other for the evening with drum beats. The tribe sanctions Ghotul interactions and permits the free exploring of sexual relations. The anthropologist Verrier Elwin writes that there are two kinds of Ghotuls, one where the young develop permanent relations that end in marriage, and the other where the young people continue to explore attachments.

The idea of the Ghotul is linked to a legend about a boy, Lingo Pen, who used to play the drums. As Founder of the Muria tribe, he taught drumming to the boys. It is said that Lingo Pen is a phallic deity. Amongst the Murias, a good drummer is regarded as a good lover. A Muria proverb says: 'One who can beat a drum knows how to beat a girl in love'. In mythological accounts of the Murias, Lingo Pen is all-powerful. No witch or ghost can invade the Ghotul because of his invisible presence. Since Lingo is also the God of love, sin has no place within the boundaries of the Ghotul. Such a custom recognises adolescent sexuality and fosters community togetherness allowing the youth to mingle.

Source: Adapted from Gupta 2002.

BRAIN DEVELOPMENT AND ADOLESCENT BEHAVIOUR

Neuroscience research is providing new information and a fresh thrust to the understanding of early childhood development. Similarly, there is new research regarding brain development influencing behaviour and the growth spurt during teenage years. It was earlier believed that the brain stops developing at puberty; however, it has been found that the brain continues to develop well into the 20s (Dobbs 2011).

Interestingly, in legal language, the adage 'womb to the tomb' refers to the human lifecycle, implying a concept of stage-related competencies. In fact, modern science states that the brain begins to develop in the womb, which is why you hear pregnant mothers report different responses of the foetus to different stimuli. First, the brain stem begins to function, providing instructions for basic actions such as breathing, blood pressure, or regulating body temperature. After birth, the mid-brain grows rapidly, regulating eating, sleeping, and comfort in being dry. Responsive care-giving in the first few months facilitate brain growth, and there is massive development in the early years. Nurturing, talking and playing with babies assist all-round development, laying strong foundations for later growth and progress.

By the age of three, children have developed almost 90 per cent of their brain size, and over the next six to seven years, there is slow and steady growth of brain functions. After that, there is growth in the limbic system in the lower part of the brain, as well as in the front brain, known as the cortex. These two areas stoke the emotional features and the thinking or reasoning skills, respectively. The cortex is that part of the brain that signals what is correct and what is wrong; however, it is not fully developed till the mid-20s.

The activation of the limbic system stimulates our emotions, attachments and sexuality. The fast pace of brain growth creates an emotional rush, leading to friends and relationships being sought with little regulation from reasoning skills. This can be noticed in the way teenagers seek the company of peers, identify with role models, and often get into conflict with parents. The developing brain also processes the functions of the cortex, the frontal lobe responsible for concrete and abstract thought, discovery, chance, and the search for novelty. Often, the teen brain is characterised as a 'work in progress'. The executive functions of the pre-frontal cortex are in the process of developing, while the sub-cortical parts of the limbic system are highly active. This area controls the joy of rewards, deriving pleasure, and seeking risk and adventure. Teenagers with a highly activated limbic system and slowly maturing pre-frontal cortex are more oriented towards emotional behaviour, which outweigh reasoning skills.

Adolescence becomes a prime time for experimenting, taking chances, and perhaps indulging in risky behaviour. The promise of the potential rewards of trying new skills and the admiration of peers often override the fear of consequences. Youngsters get high on new and exciting things, and sensation-seeking. In recent years, 'risk taking' has been classed as adaptive behaviour, which allows adolescents to move from the safety of the home to the complicated world outside.

Box 6.2 The Developing Brain

In a famous quote, Mark Twain writes: 'At 14, I thought my father is quite ignorant while at 21, I realized that the old man had learnt a lot.' Modern brain research can be contained and understood through this quotation. At 14, youngsters are full of zest and impulsiveness, and are ready to try new actions, explore, invent, and experiment. With maturing brains, thinking matures too, and individuals are able to dwell on the consequences and perhaps see reason in the statements made by adults.

There is some concern related to social pressure, such as the inability to deal with stress in the absence of an ability to comprehend the range of consequences. Most youth, in the course of socialisation, are able to cope with social-cultural demands, while in some cases youth is the stage where mental disorders might begin. As mentioned earlier, adolescents are not always capable of understanding the dangers of 'dare' and adventure. Parents need to use caution in dealing with their children, both in terms of their freedom to make choices, as well as providing appropriate counsel within the boundaries of competencies and social position.

PHYSICAL AND PHYSIOLOGICAL CHANGES

One of the ways to estimate the age range of adolescence is to mark the beginning of pubertal or sexual changes, and continue till physical growth comes to a halt and sexual maturation is complete. Physical development shows great individual variation at this stage. The importance of socio-cultural and economic influences on physical development, such as type of food, opportunities for physical activity, and gender-related differences in expectations of and opportunities for physical expression, cannot be overemphasised. Physical maturation is a process that begins with conception. As brain development advances, the brain sends the body messages to increase hormone production. The hypothalamus causes the pituitary gland to increase the production of growth hormone. The pituitary also causes the release of other growth-related and sex-related hormones by the thyroid, adrenals, testes, and ovaries. The changes produced by these hormones start becoming visible towards the end of middle childhood.

The timing of puberty has seen changes over the past few decades. Changes in diet, lifestyle and environment have been responsible for the early achievement of sexual maturity, and advanced physical maturation during childhood. Girls now achieve puberty sometime towards the end of middle childhood. Early achievement of physical maturity over generations—due to changes in diet and food habits—impacts health status and genetics, leading to a lowering of the age of menarche, and is known as secular trends.

In a recent book in which he describes adolescent psychology around the world, Arnett (2012) explores the age of puberty and questions the notion of adolescence. In many countries, societies recognise adolescence with the onset of puberty, or with changes in the physical characteristics of children. Cross-culturally, there are variations in the age of attaining puberty. While most countries can identify the age of menarche, there is little data available on spermarche, which is the onset of male puberty. Arnett provides details of the experiences of adolescents in friendships, family relationships, education, love, sexuality, age of marriage, employment, media, and politics.

Adolescence is a time of growth spurt. The first such growth spurt occurs during infancy. In adolescence, the rapid changes in the physical and sexual aspects of development characterise growth spurt. There are individual differences in the achievement and nature of this growth spurt. Girls show a growth spurt early, compared to boys. The hands and feet of adolescents may appear larger than the rest of their bodies. Girls will have achieved their adult height by the end of adolescence, but boys may continue to gain height in their early 20s as well. Compared to girls, boys have larger muscles, heart, lungs, and general body frame. By the age of 14, boys may surpass girls in height and weight. Both boys and girls experience a redistribution of body muscle and fat. In girls, the existing fat is redistributed to the thighs, hips, buttocks, and breasts. Boys lose fat and add more muscle.

Sweat glands become fully functional, and body odours are more pronounced. Boys may sweat more than girls. Skin changes are common in adolescence. Girls' skin is softer and smoother than that of boys. Oil-bearing glands become more active in adolescence, often causing acne in both boys and girls. Among girls, an aggravation of acne is often a result of stress, hormones, drugs, the weather, and emotions. Self-treatment often worsens the condition

Puberty

Puberty is the term defining the process of physical change as a child's body matures, leading to the growth of the reproductive system. This growth spurt facilitates the maturing of the body into an adult body, capable of sexual reproduction and fertilisation. The initiation is through signals from the brain to the ovaries in females, and to the testes in males. The gonads, that is, the reproductive organs, produce hormones that stimulate the body to transform. The first signs are the accelerated growth in height and weight, and this physical growth is complete by the end of puberty.

On an average, pubertal age for girls is 10–11 years, and is complete by 15–17 years. Many African countries report puberty as early as nine years. Boys begin puberty around 11–12 years, and complete it by ages 16–17. The first sign of male puberty is ejaculation from the penis. From the nineteenth to the twenty-first century, there has been a drop in the age of puberty, from 15 years to 10–11 years among girls, and from 16 years to 11–12 years among boys. There are several reasons—besides improved nutritional status—that lead to rapid physical growth and fat deposits. Modern foods are processed and contain artificial preservatives, referred to as 'endocrine distractors'. Early puberty is known as precocious puberty, while delayed puberty occurs when the pubertal changes begin late.

Accompanying morphologic changes make the body look different, and during puberty, these bring about secondary sex characteristics, such as the development of breasts, fat deposits and pubic hair in girls, while in boys the penis increases in size, there is a growth of facial and pubic hair, and a change in the voice. There are visible differences in male and female reproductive growth.

Sex Differences in Reproductive Growth

Two significant differences in male-female puberty are the age of onset and the sex steroids that initiate sexual development. Among females, the chief steroid is oestrogen, and among males, it is testosterone. The interplay of hormones is different in boys and girls. Hormonal changes in girls are more complex, and the process is faster and starts earlier. Boys begin later, and at a slower pace. Pre-pubertal boys are almost 2 cms shorter than girls; however, by the end of puberty, boys are 13 cms taller than girls. Most of the male gain in height can be attributed to a later and slower progression in reproductive growth.

Primary and Secondary Sex Characteristics

Puberty begins when the pituitary gland in the brain increases the secretion of the follicle stimulating hormone (FSH). In girls, the FSH stimulates the ovaries to start producing oestrogen, and in boys, it causes the creation of sperms. The FSH stimulates the primary sex characteristics to develop—these are the anatomical parts involved in sexual reproduction, and constitute the reproductive system as a complex organism.

For boys, the changes are gradual and do not occur as a single event.

- Beginning of puberty: about 9 to 9.5–14 years
- First pubertal change: enlargement of the testicles
- Penis enlargement: starts approximately one year after the testicles begin enlarging
- Appearance of pubic hair: 13.5 years old
- Hair under the arms and on the face, voice change, and acne: 15 years old
- Nocturnal emissions (or 'wet dreams'): 14 years old

Girls also experience pubertal change as a sequence of events; however, it is well-known that sexual maturity in girls begins before boys. While differing individually, the events still follow universal trends.

For **most girls,** pubertal growth tends to be somewhat as follows.

- Beginning of puberty: 8–13 years
- First pubertal change: breast development
- Pubic hair development: shortly after breast development
- Hair under the arms: 12 years old
- Menstrual periods: 10–16.5 years old

Sexual maturation during adolescence is reflected in the appearance of secondary sexual characteristics. These are the appearance-related features of sexual maturity. Facial hair and cracking of the voice in boys, and budding breasts and pubic hair in girls are examples of secondary sexual characteristics. Primary sexual characteristics include the development of body parts and organs involved in human reproduction. In boys, androgen stimulates voice changes, the appearance of body and facial hair, skeletal growth, chest enlargement, and the narrowing of hips. In girls, progesterone and oestrogen stimulate the widening of hips, fat redistribution, growth of the uterus and vagina, and skeletal maturation. Both sexes possess oestrogen and androgen.

Secondary sex characteristics follow puberty, but are not involved in reproduction. These changes also follow a sequence.

- The enlargement of the scrotum and testes is the first pubertal change in boys. The penis does not enlarge as yet. The testes and scrotum continue to enlarge, which is when the penis gets longer. The penis continues to grow in both size and length.
- In girls, puberty changes begin with the development of breast buds, in which the breast and nipple grow in size. The areola (dark area of skin around the nipple) increases in size at this time. The breasts continue to enlarge and the nipples and areolas elevate again, forming another projection on the breasts. In the adult, only the nipple remains erect.
- For both girls and boys, pubic hair develops in similar ways. To begin with, the hair is soft and long and only on a small area around the genitals. This hair slowly becomes darker and coarse, spreading over the genital area. Soon, pubic hair looks like adult hair. Sometimes, pubic hairs are found on the thighs and the stomach.

Variations in the Experience of Menarche

Menstruation can be a difficult experience. Much will depend on cultural attitudes, the age of onset, and support from the mother or a family member. Very early onset of menstruation can be confusing and problematic. Menstruation is also known to be more painful in the first five years after onset. Very painful menstruation is known as dysmenorrhea. In the early years, it may not be very regular. Irregular or delayed menstruation is called amenorrhea. Pre-menstrual syndrome (PMS) is the name given to a collection of physical and emotional symptoms that occur prior to menstruation, and may continue through the menstrual period. An adolescent girl will benefit from awareness and knowledge of the menstrual process. Talking to a family member, counsellor, or sensitive peer provides essential social support.

Traditionally, in India, menstruation is seen as a time of 'pollution'. Menstruating girls are therefore often not allowed to take part in certain activities, like preparing food, touching plants, visiting a place of worship, and so on. While cultural beliefs and traditional practices deserve respect and acknowledgement, it is important to change such practices if they are seen to inhibit the freedom of women or disrespect their personhood.

In recent times, many countries have been reporting a lowering of the age of menarche among girls. In some parts of the world, improved nutrition is reportedly lowering the age at which children enter puberty.

Early and Late Maturing

While there are individual differences in the attainment and experience of puberty, adolescents may face specific situations by virtue of early or late maturing. Generally, early maturing boys will display greater confidence in social situations, and be able to develop better skills. They may also take on leadership roles. Early maturing adolescent boys may become involved in heterosexual relationships sooner. They may even be more popular and skilled at sports and athletic skills. Late maturing boys, though, are less likely to be treated their age, and may be at a disadvantage in social situations as well as in activities like sports. They may feel inadequate and rejected, and suffer from low self-esteem. Some late maturing boys could resort to aggression to make up for their comparably immature stature.

On the other hand, early maturing girls may become the object of teasing and ridicule. They may be dissatisfied with their physique, particularly their weight. They may feel awkward and be compelled to hang out with older girls. They may also involve themselves in sexual experimentation before they are ready, and have a lot of restrictions imposed on them by their parents. Late maturing girls could become very negative about their appearance. They may need a lot of emotional support to maintain positive self-esteem. The expectations and values of peers will also impact their sense of self. Whether early maturity is a greater advantage for boys remains a question that needs continuous cultural evaluation.

Mood Swings

Mood swings are often believed to be caused by hormones. However, this may hold true only in early adolescence; later, environmental factors also influence changes in mood. Mood swings are common features of personality and social interactions during adolescent years. Sometimes, adolescents may seem to be on an emotional rollercoaster, and act on impulse in even crucial matters. Self-consciousness, confusion about the future, junk food, and conflicts with peers and parents might lead to bad moods. Although mood swings are a typical adolescent expression, prolonged low, sad, or aggressive moods may be a sign of depression or neurotic disorder.

Gender-related differences in moods are also evident, with girls exhibiting more low or sad moods than boys. Adolescents may also experience physiological symptoms such as headaches, bodyaches, lethargy, and nausea, which they might be unable to explain, but occur with changes in moods. If depressive feelings continue over a period of time or are severe in nature, a sense of hopelessness and suicidal tendencies may set in. It is important that parents and teachers inform themselves adequately in order to manage adolescent mood swings, and seek professional assistance if needed.

ADOLESCENT SEXUALITY

In most cultures, adolescence is a time of sexual experimentation and interest in one's sexuality. The nature of interest and experimentation may vary, depending on the cultural sanctions and beliefs prevalent about adolescent sexuality. While some adolescents may indulge in intercourse, others may indulge in physical, but not sexual, intimacy. Masturbation is another sexual activity that adolescents indulge in. Adolescents must have access to information on safe sexual behaviour, sexually transmitted diseases, and the hazards of very early pregnancy. Sexual orientation, societal response to homosexuality, and the legal status of homosexual relationships are other concerns that must be discussed in an educative and sensitive manner. It is important to help them know the difference between voluntary sexual behaviour and sexual abuse. They must know their rights, and be equipped to determine the boundaries of physical intimacy.

Adolescents often suffer from eating disorders. Obesity has a damaging influence on not only physical health, but also self-esteem. Obesity puts stress on the kidneys, lungs, heart, skeleton, and joints. The adolescent may also experience social rejection. Weight loss must be under supervision or guidance. Sometimes, adolescents are just not satisfied with their physical appearance, and depend too much on perceived standards of 'beauty'. Some adolescents suffer from anorexia nervosa, a condition characterised by an obsession with food, a distorted body image, self-starvation, and low self-esteem. Parental demands related to food and nourishment often clash with societal standards of beauty and body image. This puts the adolescent under pressure—they have to appease parents, as well as meet the standards of body image set by peers and the media. Often, such pressure interferes with the adolescent's search for identity.

Another eating disorder, characterised by gorging followed by compulsive purging, is called Bulimia. The food binge in bulimia can be huge, and focused mostly on sweet, high calorie foods. Persons suffering from bulimia often force themselves to exercise excessively, or depend too much on laxatives. Depression may further complicate the condition. Psychotherapy and promoting an appreciation of a realistic body image may contribute to reducing the intensity and occurrence of the condition.

BRAIN DEVELOPMENT DURING ADOLESCENCE

The brain experiences a final growth spurt and changes during adolescence. The brain and sensory systems reach their adult size (even though the brain reaches 95 per cent of its adult volume by the age of five). The brain is an evolving organ, and continues to develop substantially in adolescence and even into young adulthood. Changes during this period enhance its functioning by eliminating unnecessary brain cells and connections, which may reduce the ability to react to new functions. The formation of myelin sheaths around the nerve fibres is completed, allowing messages to travel faster in the brain. Functions of the right and left brain are localised, and the connection between the two hemispheres strengthened. These changes provide new thinking abilities, as suggested by many theorists; there may be greater memory and problem-solving abilities among adolescents.

However, the brain does not recover from shock and disharmony easily during this period. If certain experiences have not occurred before adolescence, the skills associated with them may be more difficult to acquire. For example, learning a new language—even though most secondary language instruction happens during adolescence, our brains are actually more receptive to learning this material earlier in life. Sometimes, children take time to adjust to family problems if they happen during adolescence.

Box 6.3 Dealing with Stress

A leading male journalist and a successful female management consultant were married for 15 years, and had two boys aged 12 and six. They decided to separate. The boys were shattered, as they admired both parents and were equally attached to both. Both boys were also doing well in their studies. After the family broke up, they were uprooted in more ways than one. The younger boy bounced back sooner, while the older boy took longer, and was unable to get over it completely. He developed certain socially awkward traits, which prevented the development of long-lasting friendships. He immersed himself in writing, and created a niche for himself by becoming an investigative journalist.

At times, it is difficult to cope with new situations after a certain period. Social adjustments or learning new coping skills require critical timing.

Source: Asha Singh.

Teenage years bring in many changes. With the difference in physical appearance, social reactions, and thus people's expectations, also change. Faced with more challenges, adolescents are charged with new thinking skills. There is an enhanced ability to think abstractly, and eventually plan for and set long-term goals. Progress may vary for individual children, and each may have a different view of the world. In general, the following abilities may be universal during adolescent years.

- develops the ability to think abstractly
- is concerned with philosophy, politics, and social issues
- thinks long-term
- sets goals
- compares one's self to one's peers

An adolescent may seek independence and control, and these strides in autonomy may cause trouble within families. Issues and concerns within the family and social dynamics may cause the individual to

- want independence from parents
- accept peer influence; acceptance also becomes very important
- hold male-female relationships as important
- may be in love
- has long-term commitment in a relationship

COGNITIVE DEVELOPMENT DURING ADOLESCENCE

Adolescents show a marked transition in their cognitive stance vis-à-vis the world, compared to children in elementary school years. The most distinctive change is that adolescents master the ability for abstract thinking. They begin to comprehend the intangible elements of everyday and natural phenomena at the start of adolescence. This ability advances, and they handle more complex abstract relations later in adolescence. According to Piaget, adolescence is the stage of Formal Operations in cognition. In this stage, the adolescent's thinking becomes more sophisticated, and the capacity for higher-order reasoning develops. The adolescent finds it easy to mentally manipulate ideas without dependence on concrete evidence.

Formal operations involve thinking creatively, carrying out mathematical manipulations, using abstract reasoning, and imagining the outcomes of particular actions. While school-age children accept the first hypothesis given to them, adolescents have the capacity to form and evaluate multiple hypotheses related to a problem. Adolescents can deliberate over global issues, hypothetical situations, and futuristic scenarios that they have not directly experienced. They understand that the world has multiple realities. They are often moved by injustice and wrongdoing, and may participate in activities to demonstrate their feelings and bring about a change in the status quo.

Adolescents use what Piaget has termed hypothetico-deductive reasoning, via which they deduce all possible scenarios of a problem or situation, and then decide upon the best course of action or solution. They demonstrate considerable flexibility in thought. Piaget's famous pendulum problem highlights adolescents' hypothetico-deductive reasoning. This task involved a length of string and a set of weights. Participants had to decide what determines the speed of the pendulum's swing. They were required to experiment with varying lengths of the string in combination with different weights, and the release height and strength of the push. Pendulum speed is measured by counting the number of swings per minute. Adolescents were systematic in their evaluations of the pendulum task, manipulating one variable at a time. Younger children were more random in their approach.

Adolescents also demonstrate propositional logic, or the ability to evaluate the truth of a logical relationship. They can compare analogies and logical statements, like 'p is equal to q, q is equal to s, therefore p is equal to s', and see the relationships between the elements of a logical statement without taking it at face value. Adolescents have their own theories of the world and its processes. They value their opinions, and may expect others to do so as well. The ability to communicate their ideas effectively and generate a healthy affirmation or even opposition is an important part of their cognitive appraisals. They also use a lot of futuristic thinking with regard to their personal, professional, or vocational goals. They may also be worried about the future of the world, and how it will impact their lives. Culture, socialisation, areas of work interest, and training are significant influences on the expression of formal operational thought.

Adolescents can be very inventive in their thinking. Piaget used the 'Third Eye problem' with adolescents and younger children. They were asked: If they were given a third eye, where would they place it? Younger children mostly said they would do so on their foreheads, whereas adolescents answered more inventively, saying they would like to place it on their hands, or on the back of the head, and so on. During this period, young minds are most keen to explore the many facets of ideas. Adolescents are capable of looking at many perspectives and taking decisions. However, cognitive advancements are also guided by social development and social behaviour patterns.

Formal operations among adolescents are also governed by an enhanced sense of self-consciousness, which often leads to adolescent egocentrism. While adolescents show concern about social issues, they may do so in relation to an enduring sense of self. David Elkind describes how adolescents are possessed of a sense of 'personal fable' (or invincibility or uniqueness) and feel surrounded by an 'imaginary audience' (the feeling that everyone is watching them and thinking about them). Adolescents are often preoccupied with the self, and feel others are evaluating them. They may believe in a personal fable—that they were born for some higher purpose—and may look for perfection in their world.

During these growing years, adolescents strongly believe that they are always under scrutiny. To some extent, this self-consciousness is prompted by bodily changes and an awkwardness that transforms into egocentric attention. We often note the significant time that young people spend on their looks, presentation, and self-appraisal. At times, the amount of time young people spend inspecting their physical appearances appears illogical.

Social behaviour patterns are a close outcome of cognitive growth. The growth spurt leads to many interrelated representations in the presentation of behaviour. There is a universal quality to an enhanced perception of the self. Theoretical speculation also recognises the attention paid to the dominance of the self. Box 6.4 explains self-indulgent behaviour.

Box 6.4 The Imaginary Audience

The emergence of the social self seems to be marked by a period of heightened self-consciousness, during which adolescents are thought to become increasingly conscious of their appearance. The change in body structure initiates a self-consciousness that makes teenagers believe that all eyes are watching them. It is an 'as-if' situation, compelled by the bodily changes that make an individual adolescent think that the visible transformations attract others' gazes. This development has been described in terms of phases of egocentrism during childhood and adolescence, and is based on Piaget's stages of cognitive growth (Inhelder and Piaget 1958). It is proposed that after children develop internal representations of objects and referential thinking during early childhood, they reach the stage of the 'emergence of concrete operations'. Between the ages of 7 and 11, children's abilities to deal with classes and hierarchies are restricted to concrete, physical entities, and do not extend to abstract thought. Children of this age group therefore manifest an inability to distinguish between a mental construction and perceptual phenomena. By age 11, the emergence of 'formal operational thought' enables children to differentiate between the perception of an object and their own mental construction of it, allowing them to objectify their own thoughts and reason about them. Piaget proposed that this new form of thinking allows early adolescents to conceptualise other people's thoughts and take their perspectives (ibid.).

The development of adolescent egocentrism is therefore thought to be a dialectic process: it is the ability to represent other people's thoughts as distinct from their own. The skill to recognise the thoughts of others is also the developing ability to move away from egocentrism, as an understanding of 'other perspectives' allows individuals to decentre. However, learning about the thoughts of others initiates a new form of egocentrism, leading teenagers to often think that 'all attention is on them'. In other words, as soon as they are able to understand that other people have distinct thoughts and perspectives, they become preoccupied with the notion that other people's thoughts are focused on their own behaviour or appearance (Elkind 1967). Elkind's original theoretical model of

Box 6.4 contd.

Box 6.4 contd.

adolescent egocentrism delineates two ideation patterns thought to arise as a consequence, and to characterise common adolescent social behaviours: the 'imaginary audience' and the 'personal fable'. The 'imaginary audience' refers to adolescents' belief that they are the object of other people's scrutiny. According to Elkind, this belief results in increased self-consciousness, a tendency to anticipate the reactions of other people in relation to the self, and a feeling of being the focus of attention, regardless of whether a real audience exists or not. The 'personal fable', a related construct, denotes adolescents' convictions of their own personal uniqueness, giving rise to the sense of being 'special' (ibid.).

Cognition and Cultural Behaviour

Cognitive behaviour is often attributed to academic performance, and other performances related to literacy skills. Cognition has many facets, depending on social situations and individual orientations. A well-known and often cited example is that of Steve Jobs, the founder of Apple Computers, who was a school dropout and yet rose to become a powerful world figure through his own search and explorations. The universalisation of education has created conformity and uniformity in assessing cognitive competence. Youngsters' skills can be seen in how well someone repairs a household gadget, or develops relations good for mutual teamwork. Business acumen and skill in the arts may use skills of literacy, as well as other aspects of higher thinking, such as investigating, making connections, judgement of strategies, abstract thought, ability for foresight, planning, and attention to detail. An assessment of language, body signals, making associative connections, and deriving inferences provide insight into social relations, or while venturing into new tasks. The Bollywood film *Bunty Aur Babli* is a good example of youth exploration, and an investigation into the world of the unknown through experimentation, conviction, and the ability to dare and decide.

SOCIAL DEVELOPMENT DURING ADOLESCENCE

The onset of adolescence also marks a change in patterns of social behaviour. They begin to increasingly enjoy the company of friends and want to spend less time with family. The opinion of friends is important, and their responses are affected by the presence of friends. There is also a tendency to take more risks in the company of friends. Recent researches indicate that adolescents indulge in more risky behaviour in the company of friends, rather than with adults, such as skipping a traffic light and driving fast; in the absence of their friends, though, the behaviour of adolescents is all that different from that of adults (Gardner and Steinberg 2005).

Box 6.5 Case Profile. Dare me and I will: Arjun, Class VII

Arjun was part of a theatre workshop at school. One of the exercises required students to share their 'Unforgettable Moments' in small groups of five to seven. In each group, members would select one incident to share with the larger group of 35–45 in the classroom. The number was contingent on the attendance for the day. All the children were between the ages of 12–13, at the brink of their growth spurt. Many incidents related to injury and accidents, as a result of venturing into new tasks or trying tricks were narrated. Arjun's story was a little different, as it entailed jumping from the second floor to show his commitment to a friend. Arjun reported getting slightly hurt, but had no bones broken. He was very categorical that it was important for him to demonstrate physical prowess, as he was not active in sports. Some female classmates teased him, and dared him to show physical competence. Arjun said unhesitatingly that he would attempt it again, and no amount of explaining the dangerous consequence of such acts could deter him.

Source: Asha Singh (conversation in a theatre workshop).

The search for self dominates adolescents' social experience. As we have seen earlier, adolescents continuously evaluate their self in relation to others. This is especially true of collectivist societies. Although the self is defined by many things, including a sense of achievement, vocation, physical and personality attributes, etc., affiliation to relationships remains a core standard for understanding selfhood. As in other domains—such as cognition and language—adolescents experiment with social relationships, too. According to Erikson, they are in search of an identity. In Erikson's Psychosocial Theory, adolescents are in a stage of identity vs. identity diffusion. Through experiences, formal learning and self-examination, they arrive at a sense of identity, or, unable to do so, develop a confused or diffused identity. According to James Marcia, adolescents go through this identity moratorium, or search for an identity. They may even experience identity foreclosure if parents, adults, or others decide the adolescents' future course of life, and literally hand down an identity to them, not allowing the search for identity.

Language Development in Adolescence

Language during adolescence is an interplay of cognitive competence and a changed social structure, which confines homogenous age groups within an institutionalised setting for a long time. As youngsters stay with children of a similar age for a prolonged period of time, their language takes on a special character. We have established that adolescence is a product of modern industrial society, and a society that has universalised education. Employment or vocation for large numbers of children is delayed or even denied, as gaining qualifications serves as a prerequisite to seeking jobs. Adolescents are adept at communication and in the use of language. In fact, in keeping with the dominance of exploring and inventing, there is a predominance of innovative communicative styles.

Language during adolescence is grammatically sound, with a certain level of proficiency that is quite well-established. Language provides pathways to explore the social and physical world. It is also through language that teenagers reflect their identity in specific styles. Distinct in this age group is the use of language for group identity, for expressive behaviour, and for experimentation in communication. Teenagers recognise that there is an established form of communication that links to socially desirable forms.

As school is the dominant social landscape, a certain vocabulary is necessary for classroom discourse and verbal exchanges with adults. We all know that 'there is a particular form of address and language' that is socially permissible, and this is well understood among the young across cultures. Another form of communication expresses the intensity of peer togetherness, through the use of local, created and coded words among peer groups. There is an increase in the use of slang, and where the official language differs from the local language, there is a mix of several languages, such as Bangla in Hindi, or Hindi or Gujarati in English. An element of social identity pervades the way social groups use language during adolescent years.

Box 6.6 Young People's Conversations: The Language of Social Bondedness

Anuja: Let's go to Knags. I am famished.
Priti: No way! Can't even drag.
Anuja: *Chal*, we'll take a rick. Hot samy will do me good.
Priti: Got to Xerox DC notes.
Anuja: Ok, I will exit while you be in study mode.

This conversation was reported just after a lecture between two fresh college entrants. It would be difficult for a non-Delhi resident to make sense of the conversation; 'Knags' is an abbreviation for Kamla Nagar, the local marketplace (and residential area) close to Delhi University, 'samy' is short for samosa, DC stands for Development Communication, and 'rick' is rickshaw. The language is laced with slang and metaphoric use of words and phrases—famished instead of hungry, 'can't drag' instead of tired. 'Exit' and 'study mode' give the dialogue a contemporary spin.

Besides having the cognitive ability to conceptualise and adapt, young people are also conveying intimacy and need for affection. The coded language alludes to a small coterie, and provides a sense of group membership.

Source: Students File Work as part of practical assignments.

The creation of this language does not create boundaries; rather, it functions to express group intensity as well as organise groups for action and management, both emotionally and socially. Through the use of abbreviations, the group creates an emotional bond, while they quickly generate social action. Another example is the use of cell phones—to send messages, to gather students for assembly, or to convey the presence of a teacher. Such actions protect group identity in relation to the maintenance of social order.

Adolescents are abstract thinkers, and this is reflected in their written expression as well. They are able to write on an issue from multiple perspectives. Much adolescent writing is heartfelt, and may have a personal orientation. Their writings may also bring to the fore issues of concern to humanity in general. Adolescents may rapidly advance their vocabulary and linguistic expression, and become adept at deciphering social meanings at various levels. They understand understated and subtle expressions, and attain a good grasp over humour, satire and metaphors. The use of slang and cuss words may at times seem fashionable. Speech difficulties, like stuttering or lack of fluency, may lead to difficulties with peer groups, as well as issues with self-esteem.

MORAL DEVELOPMENT IN ADOLESCENCE

According to Piaget, adolescents are in a stage of autonomous morality. Their moral decisions are guided by values that have been internalised. They may not act out of a fear of authority, but are self-directed in their moral actions. They see rules as flexible, which can be changed for the benefit of others or oneself. Intentionality of action may be the major criterion in their moral judgement. According to Kohlberg, conventional moral reasoning dominates the thinking of most adolescents. They may feel the need to conform to stereotypes, and win the approval of society at large.

The next level of post-conventional moral reasoning may see adolescents going beyond social norms and conventions, often questioning societal values and their relevance. Human rights and one's own conscience may take precedence over other matters in moral decisions. Culture, education, societal pressures, peer group influence, familial expectations, and individual experiences shape moral understanding at all ages.

FAMILY RELATIONSHIPS: CHANGING CONTOURS

Family is seen as the most significant unit for the socialisation of children and adolescents. Typically, adolescents growing up in extended family units may be part of a hierarchically organised web of relations, with a natural exposure to vertical roles and responsibilities. Exposure to many adults provide a range of role models, which in turn provide young, growing individuals the opportunity to derive their own prescriptions for identity, or for future roles. In nuclear set-ups with double-income parents, children may not get enough time and exposure to intimate relations. Maternal employment influences family life, especially for girl children, by modelling spaces in the economic sphere.

Adolescents experience a continued sense of love for and affiliation to their parents, even though they may at times find it difficult to clearly understand or express their emotions. The rapid changes they experience may lead to conflict when their needs, desires and expectations do not match those of their parents. Girls and boys may handle such differences in separate ways, with girls focusing more on emotional issues and boys on material and objective issues. Some adolescents may experience extreme feelings of negativity around their parents. Parental friendliness can often help them to handle complex feelings. It is essential that parents be good communicators, express optimal interest in adolescents' activities, value their child's freedom, set good examples, and be firm yet reasonable in disciplining.

Sibling relationships could be a mixed bag of experiences. Some amount of conflict is inevitable; during adolescence, the need for personal space, privacy, and hanging out with one's own friends may take precedence over shared activities with siblings. Positive sibling relationships can be very rewarding. Much about sibling relationships will depend on birth order, sex of siblings, disability in a sibling, differing levels of achievement among siblings, and parental response to conflict between them.

Adolescents may experience complications in the living arrangements and emotional life of a family if they are in single-parent households, or have seen parents go through a divorce. It may be difficult for them to come to terms with such a situation, and they may also feel pressured if asked to shoulder too much household responsibility. In such situations, adolescents often experience feelings of alienation or aggression. Sometimes, propelled by circumstances and egged on by peers, they may take the path to truancy or drug addiction, and may even come in conflict with the law.

Authors researching adolescence across nations report variations in family configurations. The family is changing in form, with more divorces, single-parent homes, remarried families, or multi-residence families (Brown et al. 2002). Smaller families and families located in geographically distant spaces reduce the chances of family guidance, as the exposure to multiple adults is drastically low. When youngsters leave deprived home situations, they live in unfamiliar settings, and are deprived of the emotional support and physical facilities natural to family life.

PEER RELATIONSHIPS DURING ADOLESCENCE

'Peer pressure' is a value-loaded term, and indicates societal ambivalence towards the functions that same-age mates could serve for the growth and development of individual personalities. Peers do offer companionship and emotional relief; however, they also promote consumerism, negative attitudes towards school and life, compromising situations like drugs, sexual license, violence, and other delinquent acts (Brown et al. 2002). Sometimes, societies restrict peer interactions outside the kin group, especially for girls (Booth 2007), and schooling takes place in gender-segregated schools. Romantic relations are also closely monitored. Such gendered social positioning of peers is common in India, along with a prevalence of arranged marriages.

In several contexts, where the focus is on the development of the self and independence from an early age, there is a primacy of peers. As often reported in parts of Europe and the United States, peers provide a substitute for parental roles, and play a substantive part in adolescent development.

Just as in middle childhood, adolescents also tend to spend more time with peers than with family. At times, adolescents can be so influenced by peers that they will not express their individual choices and opinions. As their sense of self and identity become more definite, they may find it easier to express their individuality. Being connected to peers is important for most adolescents. They also tend to hang out in groups and indulge in fun activities like playing music, dancing, visiting cafeterias, outdoor games, partying, and so on. The availability of resources will make a difference to the activity they select. They might even like planning their future vocation with friends.

Social networking is very important for adolescents today. While social networking has its benefits—providing a platform for individual expression, sharing feelings, ideas and activities—it could also lead to depression, generalised anxiety, and social isolation in extreme cases. Participation in such platforms can lead the individual astray from real-life goals. On the other hand, social networking can encourage extremely shy people to express themselves. Ensuring a balance between real-life interactions and online social networking will bring about harmony in an adolescent's life.

Often, adolescents like to follow their biorhythms and may like to sleep a lot or even while away time relaxing, and doing nothing. This could be a normal part of growing up, if not overdone. Peers could also include a lover, or potential life partner. Adolescents may indulge in close relationships with sexual overtones. Knowing their boundaries and keeping future goals in mind are essential in order to keep safe in such relationships. Adolescents may be attracted to like-minded people, with whom they can share pleasurable activities and even a sense of identity. They will look for compatibility and loyalty in long-term friendships. Across cultures, there is an increased leaning towards friends during teenage years in urban societies.

Emotional Development During Adolescence

During adolescence, emotions can be intense. They can centre on the self and relationships, as well as on personal and professional achievements. There are gender differences in emotional expressions, with girls focusing more on relationships and boys on objective achievements. Adolescents may have more memorable emotional experiences with friends, than with family. Romantic love may be a salient emotion, and bouts of anger and frustration when things go wrong are also common. Often, anger is directed more towards parents and family.

Adolescents may suffer from disturbed emotions, which can sometimes lead to depression and anxiety disorders. They may need counselling and psychological—sometimes even psychiatric—help to deal with their condition. Extreme feelings of isolation or depression could lead to suicidal tendencies. This may also happen if the adolescent suffers from extremely low self-esteem, and feelings of failure in personal or vocational domains. It is important to talk about such feelings and sensitise them on how to pick up cues on the onset of depression and suicidal feelings, and deal with these in an appropriate manner. A critical attitude on the part of parents and little affection from family can lead to depressive feelings, as does repeated failure. Extreme withdrawal from reality can take the form of schizophrenia, which is usually due to extreme physical or psychological stress. Such onset is sudden, rather than gradual. It is characterised by disordered thinking, difficulty in forming meaningful relationships, and obsessive-compulsive and hostile behaviour.

ADOLESCENCE IN INDIA

While many adolescents in India—as well as Indian adolescents in other countries—value the Indian cultural heritage and hold tradition close to their hearts, they are almost equally influenced by global trends and changes. Gender, urban-rural contexts, and social class are pervasive variables in adolescents' lives, although there are numerous instances of adolescents defying such socially constructed barriers. For example, most adolescents use technology extensively, follow fashion trends, and show a keen sense of independence in choosing a future.

Nevertheless, there are ample stories of oppression and closure of opportunities for self-discovery and growth. Girls all over India are married during adolescence, often before they attain the legal age of maturity, and coerced into motherhood. The girls usually have little opportunity to acquire skills for financial self-reliance, and little or no say in reproductive choices. Boys often bear the brunt of unrealistic social expectations; there is evidence of boys being forced to be responsible for the major practical concerns of family life, such as carrying on the family trade, marrying according to parents' wishes, and caring for ageing relatives. With little concern for their emotional well-being and individual needs, they are forced to conform to stereotype of male 'strength'.

Early entry into employment may leave adolescents with little time for higher education or refined skills. In affluent settings, adolescents may be faced with more opportunities than they can handle. They may be spoilt for choice, and might not learn to develop a work ethic or socially adaptive behaviour. The question remains: Are more adolescents in India experiencing identity foreclosure, or do they have an adequate platform from which to search for an identity? Resource availability, parental attitudes, perceived societal expectations, and individual motivation influence adolescents' search for identity. Urban Indian parents are increasingly becoming well-informed about the emotional and psychological needs of adolescents. Newspapers, magazines, films, and TV shows take up myriad themes linked to adolescents' lives. Openness to consult psychologists, therapists, psychiatrists, and other mental health professionals has also increased.

Schooling and Adolescents

In India, there is a difference in the socio-cultural profile of children who attend public/private schools, and those who enrol in state-run schools. State-run schools are non-fee paying and attract the lower-income groups, while fee-paying schools are chosen by groups with resources, which include educated families. Schools can cater to children of the same sex, or be co-educational. The gender groupings impact adolescents while forming relationships, as well as in understanding what it means to be a girl or a boy. Children experience a growth spurt during middle school and well into the secondary school stages. Pubertal changes might be experienced differently in same-sex and co-educational schools.

There are anecdotal accounts of school friends who eventually married and had families. However, other pressures prevail in the contemporary world—boys and girls have to choose streams that will directly impact the careers they choose as adults. The boys find themselves stressed out by the competition and expectations, as they continue to be cast as the 'breadwinners'. A large number of girls are now performing well and choosing non-stereotypical options, despite the societal restraints on their performance.

Globalisation and Adolescents

Children are growing up in a social world where knowledge of and exposure to other cultures is only a click away. Adolescents live in world with multicultural forces. The varied lifestyles and different values in dress and cuisine are often a part of the daily experiences of certain sections of society. In situations of exclusion—geographical location, economic deprivation, or being part of marginalised groups—exposure may come from films, posters, and intra-country regional experiences. Globalisation has created a shrinking universe, where the world is as familiar as one's family. Regional foods such as *dosa*, *idli*, *dhokla*, *sarson ka saag*, etc., are common across the country, while international food chains are making their presence felt in large metros and small towns.

Culturally varied ideas, goods and people are present everywhere. Growing children are exposed to cultures and ways of life different from their own local customs, which might lead to cultural conflicts. There might be norms for dressing in families, and growing children defy those prescribed rules to conform to social trends and peer culture. In India, religious values may require specific hairstyles, restrict the cutting of hair, require the head to be covered, or a turban worn. Adolescents are familiar with such practices in the Indian socio-cultural environment, and often display both conformity and assertion of individual identity in their choices. Valentine's Day, Rose Day, Friendship Day, etc., are hugely popular among senior school children. Equally, the exhilaration over local festivities has not decreased; rather, most local festivals and celebrations have seen a massive rise in the extent of revelry and merriment.

A confusion in cultural identity may be a reality. Adolescence is a period of choices, and identifying a suitable path through decisions. This path needs to be informed and guided by adequate counsel, or sometimes by restricting new choices.

The State and Adolescence

The Government of India has several programmes for the protection, education and skill development of adolescents. Through programmes such as the Adolescence Education Programme (AEP), the Adolescent Girls' Scheme under ICDS (Integrated Child Development Services), and National Nutrition Mission's Nutrition Programme for Adolescent Girls, the State reaches out to rural and urban adolescents living in disadvantage and distress. There are also numerous services in both the government and the voluntary sector that provide rehabilitation, vocational guidance and educational inputs for adolescents.

Education for girls is being encouraged in various states through schemes that provide incentives, for instance, bicycles to facilitate travel or the *kishori yojana*, which gives cash benefits to girls after they finish secondary-level education. The latter uses the cultural symbols of marriage as an incentive to increase female education.

SUMMARY

- This chapter described the universal aspects of growth and development during teenage years, with special reference to the specific Indian social contexts. It focused on the changing roles of larger societal factors on the growing child—family, peers, etc.—and the physical, social and emotional changes experienced from the onset of puberty. Social expectations during adolescence, and the different ritual and ceremonies associated with this 'coming of age' was also discussed, as were the sex and gender differences in reproductive growth during adolescence. Adolescent sexuality, brain development during these years, as well as cognitive growth and cultural behaviour have been described in detail. Particular attention has been paid to language development among adolescents, and the changing role of the family during these years.

KEY TERMS

Adolescence – The period between 12–18 years

Identity – A person's perception and expression of her/his individuality and affiliation with others

Identity foreclosure – According to James Marcia, when a person ceases the search for identity or does not even begin such a search because s/he has accepted roles specified by parents or significant others

Identity moratorium – According to James Marcia, a stage of crisis where adolescents actively explore alternatives in an effort to form an identity

Identity diffusion – According to James Marcia, this is when adolescents with an undefined sense of identity show no effort to explore identity

Personal fable – According to David Elkind, an adolescent's feeling that s/he is of noble descent, invulnerable, unique, and worthy of much more that s/he has

Imaginary audience – According to David Elkind, the feelings of the adolescent that s/he is the focus of everyone's attention

Puberty – The process of sexual maturity during adolescence

Pubescence – The state of being in or reaching puberty

Menarche – The onset of menstruation in girls

Spermarche – The beginning of the development of sperms in the testicles of boys during puberty

Formal operations – According to Piaget, the period describing cognitive development during adolescence.

EXERCISES

1. Describe the understanding of adolescence in different parts of the globe.
2. Talk to an adolescent you know about any physical appearance issues that s/he may have. You could focus on physique, height, weight, facial features, choice of clothes and accessories, as well as peer standards and parental expectations vis-à-vis physical appearance.
3. Ask a 13-year-old boy and girl to write their experiences of growing up, and the differences they note in their relationships with parents and friends.
4. Enumerate the features of reproductive growth and highlight male-female differences.
5. Talk to a 12–13-year-old and a 16–17-year-old about her/his eating pattern, activity level and general health. Find out their views about body image in relation to media images, and what they observe around themselves in real-life settings. Explore their perceptions of the relationship between body image and identity in adolescence.
6. Present any hypothetical situation describing a relationship conflict to an adolescent—a need for money, or making career choices, etc. Ask for her/his views on how to solve the matter.
7. Try and talk to the parents, too, to get an intergenerational perspective on conflict management.
8. Conduct a survey in your neighbourhood among boys and girls in Class X to understand the nature of their career options.

   Explore the preferred choices of parents for their children in Class X. What would they suggest for their children, and why? Note the gender differences. You will have to identify parents who have boys and girls completing Class X.
9. What are some of the protective mechanisms for adolescent issues and concerns?

10. Discuss specific features that foster cross-cultural variations during adolescence.
11. Collect pictures of young people engaged in different activities to create a frame for adolescence in different parts of the globe.

OBJECTIVE QUESTIONS

1. Fill in the blanks:
   a. Adolescent brain is in a stage of ____________.
   b. The comprehension of logic occurs in ____________ part of the brain.
   c. Menarche is the initiation into ____________ among ____________.
   d. Spermarche is when males mature to produce ____________.
   e. Adolescent language is replete with ____________ and ____________ words.

REFERENCES

Arnett, J. J. (ed.), *Adolescent Psychology Around the World*, New York: Psychology Press, 2012.

Booth, M., 'From the Horse's Rump to the Whorehouse Keyhole: ventriloquized memoirs as political voice in 1920's Egypt', *Maghrep Review*, 32 (2–3), 2007.

Brown, B. B., R. W. Larson and T. S. Saraswathi, *The World's Youth Adolescence in Eight Regions of the World*, New York: Cambridge University Press, 2002.

Dobbs, D., 'Teenage Brains', *National Geographic*, August 2011.

Elkind, D., 'Egocentrism in Adolescence', *Child Development*, 38 (4), 1967, pp. 1025–34.

Gardner, M. and L. Steinberg, 'Peer influence on risk taking, risk preference, and risky decision making in adolescence and adulthood: An experimental study', *Dev. Psychol.*, 41, 2005, pp. 625–35.

Gupta, R., 'Kingdom of the Unmarried', *The Tribune*, 2 March 2002.

Hall, G. S., *Adolescence: Its Psychology and Its Relations to Physiology, Anthropology, Sociology, Sex, Crime, Religion, and Education*, 2 vols, New York: Appleton, 1904.

Inhelder, B. and J. Piaget, *The growth of logical thinking from infancy to adolescence*, London: Routledge and Kegan Paul, 1958.

Mussen, Henry Paul, J. J. Conger, and J. Kagan, *Child Development and Personality*, New York: Harper & Row, 1974.

Papalia, D. E., S. W. Olds and W. Duskin Feldman, *Human Development*, 9e, McGraw Hill, 2004.

Rice, F. Philip, *Human Development*, New York: Prentice Hall, 2000.

Santrock, J. W., *Life-Span Development*, 13e, McGraw Hill, 2010.

7

Adulthood: Transitional Roles and Responsibilities

HIGHLIGHTS

- Discusses the physical, intellectual, social, and emotional facets of transition from adolescence into adulthood.
- Discuses the rites of passage that prepare an adult to move through various life events.
- Focuses on the journey of adulthood—career, intimacy, nurturance, retirement—and successes and failure.
- Parenthood, which gives adults the opportunity to confront new challenges, test themselves, and display diverse competencies.

TRANSITION FROM ADOLESCENCE TO ADULTHOOD

Adolescence and, more significantly, the transition from adolescence to adulthood, is often challenging as individuals gain independence, face new tasks, take decisions, and become responsible for others. Socialisation into adult roles is learnt by being in families, watching adult role models, and being part of responsive environments. Adulthood may be difficult if young people have had to cope with significant losses or stresses during their early life. Even with optimal support, the shift from adolescence to adulthood presents trials and tribulations, and so the absence of a secure sense of belonging and encouragement can often lead to ruptures in transition. Some young adults in this transitional phase often find it difficult to make choices, which become progressively tougher—for instance, choosing a vocation, finding a life partner, creating a family, and making childcare choices. Profound physiological and psychological changes sometimes unwittingly impinge upon the need for a developmental space in which to think and reflect, often leading to a weakened identity.

The process of becoming an adult begins in adolescence and continues till you reach adulthood, in your own eyes, in the eyes of your parents, the law, and the society. When you reach the age of majority, you acquire the legal responsibilities and privileges of adulthood. All known human societies have identifiable stages of life that define responsibilities and privileges within families, communities and societies. Maturing from one stage to the next is often distinguished by rituals called rites of passage (as discussed in previous chapters). Many cultures attempt to understand changes in the lifecycle. Some Indian thinkers have also presented descriptions of the possible influences and adjustments made by individuals in adult life.

Box 7.1 Stepping into Adulthood

Rahul, Amrita and Mitu were busy filling forms as the last date for scholarships was only a couple of days away. Rakhi was unsure of what she wanted to do. She went along with her friends and watched them identify universities, and frantically discuss their statements of purpose and course selections. She was also worried about the exams, which were only a couple of months away. It was the final year of college. Her friends had looked at all the possibilities

Box 7.1 contd.

Box 7.1 contd.

and explored their options through discussions with seniors and their families. Raghav wanted to be a journalist, but would be forced to join the family business. Rakhi thought she would decide after clearing her exams.

The young adults here represent different ways of arriving at decisions about future training and building capacity. The group with the forms has clearly decided on a future course of action and collected the necessary information. Raghav's decision is a foreclosure to his career by being compelled to join the family business. Rakhi is postponing decision-making and taking it as it comes.

In another social group is a tailor who was trained by his father. The young son, however, finds the job unexciting, and is working for a company that sells aluminium foil. As a child, his father's shop was an enthralling place, and having spent time there, he knows much about the basics of stitching garments. However, he believes that the ready-made industry is very invasive, and small tailoring units will no longer be lucrative. He has thus made an informed choice to not further his father's profession. His choice was self-directed and the family seemingly did not object.

Source: Asha Singh.

Emerging Adulthood

Society is always in a state of flux, that is, there are many social forces that make social change a natural process. In the past 40 years, there has been an increase in the years of schooling. Till the late 1970s, children finished school after Class XI, around the age of 16–17. Often, by the age of 21, many young adults would be employed, and ready to start a family. However, with the addition of one year, as well as an increase in the age of entry to schools, most children finish school only at 18. Compulsory schooling has brought in changes in the duration of life stages, and the concurrent ages at which individuals adopt the social roles and responsibilities of adulthood. Around the globe, there is now a shift in the emergence of adult roles. The teenager may not move directly into adulthood, as training and skill-building continues well into adult years (between 19–24).

Till the late 1970s, young people were joining the workforce by the age of 22, and making the difficult decisions of finding a life partner and setting up separate homes—or continuing to be part of the Indian joint family. However, with the increasing years of education and specialisation, there is now a delay in the age of marriage. Girls especially are delaying marriage as they want to complete their education and take up employment. It is only after getting a job that they look at settling down and setting up home.

Arnett (2000) claims that emerging adulthood is a stage in post-industrialised, developed countries. In Western societies, youngsters spend an increasing amount of time in carving skills to make a living. The notion of adolescence is closer to Erikson's idea of 'prolonged adolescence'. According to Erikson, during this phase, through free experimentation, individuals find a niche for themselves with a psychosocial moratoriu. Erikson appears to have distinguished a phase wherein individuals dealt with the search of adolescence while also taking on a few adult roles—jobs and household responsibilities.

The notion of 'emerging adulthood' is possibly universal in a globalised world. In India, too, many young people are living on their own in a spirit of search and experimentation. In fact, there has been a redefining of relationships, with live-in relations and same-sex couples. There are many dimensions to emerging adulthood, in terms of social, socio-sexual and socio-economic influences. There are five main features facing the emergence of adulthood:

Identity explorations
Age of instability
Self-focused in life
Feeling in between
Age of possibilities

FOUR STAGES OF THE TRADITIONAL HINDU LIFECYCLE

Vedic scriptures elucidate four significant stages in the Hindu lifecycle. As per the traditional Hindu approach, the stages relate to pre-industrial civilisation, and are based on the Hindu philosophical beliefs of duty and rebirth. Although these stages and rites are revered by many, contemporary Hindus are governed by new forces of social life. The understanding of the human lifecycle in the Hindu belief system relates to the social roles and responsibilities encountered by individuals as they progress in age. Each role also takes the form of a stage in life, and serves as a cultural script for social expectations from individuals. The cultural reference to stage is denoted by '*ashrama*', that is, social institution.

Brahmacharya: The Preparatory Stage

The first stage, Brahmacharya, begins around the age of 10, and lasts for about 10 years. Before that, it is believed the Hindu child is not fully formed. During this first stage, the primary expectations of the individual are to remain celibate and become educated, particularly in religious matters. In terms of socialisation, the individual is to be prepared with the skills and competence to become productive adults in society.

Grihastha Ashrama: The Stage of Production

The second stage, called Grihastha Ashrama, can be translated as the stage of the 'householder'. It corresponds to economic, biological and social production, and is marked by marriage, employment, and the imparting of skills to the young. During this stage, married Hindu men and women nurture their children, and ensure that they thrive.

Vanaprastha: The Service Stage

At this stage, individuals have fulfilled their roles and are expected to pass the baton on to their children, who have now grown up and are perhaps in the Grihastha Ashrama stage themselves. The mature adult now needs to watch and reflect. As prescribed in tradition, once the children have established themselves, Hindu parents enter the third stage of life, Vanaprastha, which literally translated would mean 'going to the forest'. Metaphorically, however, it implies the transfer of power to the next generation. In this stage, they focus more on religious beliefs and rituals, and begin to separate themselves from their families. They might gradually give away their material wealth and worldly possessions in preparation for the next stage.

Sannyasa: The Retirement Stage

Sannyasa, or the stage of detachment, is akin to the modern notion of retirement. It is the fourth and final stage of life. Some Hindus move away from their families and start living as religious *sadhus* (holy men) and *sadhvis* (holy women). Detachment from loved ones and dependence on the charity of others in the community are significant characteristics of this stage of life. Traditional Hindu beliefs describe a lifecycle in which individuals mature, marry, and raise their children. The cycle continues over generations. The philosophical grounding signifies a belief in rebirth and in living one's life well. A well-lived life with high morals and a deep sense of duty is what might provide liberation from worldly desires, known as '*moksha*'. The life-course approach that focuses on the growth and development of an individual from infancy to old age is useful not only in practices of sociality, but also in the investigation of the transition to adulthood.

Box 7.2 Family Narratives: Gita and her Home

Gita was married at the age of 18, when she had barely finished school. She agreed to marry Prashant, whose secure job in the Indian Railways and pleasant demeanour had impressed her parents. After their wedding, Gita came to live in her parents' home to complete her college education. She would meet her husband during vacations. The couple had their first child after she finished college. Gita continued to study, and had a second baby. She was helped in childcare by her mother. During holidays, she went with her children to her husband's home, where

Box 7.2 contd.

Box 7.2 contd.

the paternal grandparents spent a lot of time with them. The children were happy to listen to stories about their grandfather' experiences as the Head Administrator of a Central Jail. The retired life of the grandparents provided a slow pace to the family routine. The children enjoyed the elaborate celebration of festivals, and learnt many skills such as floor drawings, as well as the different songs associated with festivals. They returned to their home in a metropolitan city and adapted to their school routines. Meanwhile, with schoolgoing children and time at hand, Gita joined a school as a nursery teacher.

The children completed their college education and got married, and Gita became the Vice-Principal of the school. Her husband is soon to retire. Her daughter and son-in law both work, and Gita helps her daughter with her own child, who is looked after by a helper till Gita comes home from school. Gita often feels tired taking care of the baby, but soon recounts joyfully that her mother had no difficulty as, being a homemaker, she did not have the pressure of dual duties. They laugh at the changes.

Source: Asha Singh theatre workshop.

BECOMING AN ADULT

Departing from the customs and values of their own childhood, or the expectation of their families in the process of individuation, some young persons may face conflict by seemingly opposing psychological, social and practical needs. Some adolescents and young adults may rebel, often deviating dramatically from any expectations that they perceive others may have of them, or alternately, becoming anxious, depressed or quiescent. These processes can be stressful, not only for a young person, but also for her/his parents, whose own fears and insecurities may be activated during this transition. Parents may be plagued by questions such as: 'Am I preparing my child adequately to be successful?' Or adults may over-protect the child by prescribing solutions that do not take into account the child's temperament, interests or needs, but are led by parental anxiety or dreams for the children's future. The span of adulthood comprises distinguishing features; this span can also be understood as three phases, based on age and social expectations. These are approximations, and liable to vary with individuals.

Early Adulthood: 20–40 years
Middle Adulthood: 40–60 years
Late Adulthood: 60–80 years

Early Adulthood

Adulthood is a period of optimum mental functioning, when the individual's intellectual, emotional and social capabilities are at their peak to meet the demands of career, marriage and children. During the mid-30s, people develop a sense of changing trends, relevance of social norms, as well as an awareness of 'what is contemporary'. Individuals are largely flexible. Quite often, previous behaviour patterns or beliefs may be given up in favour of new ones. This change is necessitated by the forging of new roles and relationships, which address the need for intimacy and procreation. During this period, young adults are at the peak of their physical, sexual and perceptual functioning. Maximum muscle strength is reached between ages 25–30, while vision, hearing, reaction time, and coordination are at peak levels in the early to mid-20s. Although many physical capacities decline in the mid-30s, the changes are not noticeable until years later.

Middle Adulthood

We often notice that adults begin to wear glasses or start eating regulated diets as there is a growing awareness of the changes and decline in physiological functioning. Middle-aged adults are still in excellent health and are very active. The growing experience of challenge and competition in jobs and recreational skills can offset many age-related declines. Certain functions do begin to wane. These changes begin during middle adulthood. During this period, physical status begins to decline, visual acuity often decreases, and muscles become stiffer and weaker. Around 40, basal metabolic rate also slows, which creates an increased tendency to gain weight. The efficiency of oxygen consumption decreases, and it is harder for middle-aged adults to maintain physical endurance. Regular and sustained exercise builds reservoirs for building stamina.

Middle age is a period of adjustment between the potentialities of the past and the limitations of the future. The experience of limitations leads to anxiety and dissatisfaction, and understanding and accepting the fact that the body is slowing down is not easy. As individuals age, they refuse to accept that there will be decreased energy, and that the body requires more preparation to act or react, which leads to unnecessary physical challenges, and often to defiance. For example, a lady in her late 20s asked her 60+plus father to carry a walking stick and be careful on the slope as it was raining; however, the suggestion was refuted with an indignant 'I do not need a stick'.

Some adults go through emotional rebellion or mid-life crisis, which emerges from a feeling of urgency at the less time left to be lived. There are gender variations here, too; in women, this stems more from a physiological change. There are dramatic fluctuations in hormone production that lead to the onset of menopause between the ages of 40 and 50. Men remain fertile, but this gradually declines in middle age. Often, couples whose children have grown up or have left home experience the 'empty-nest syndrome', which makes them feel unwanted or not needed.

During the latter part of middle age, individuals become more aware of ill health, and thus may consciously or unconsciously alter the patterns of their lives. Individuals accept the limits of their accomplishments and derive satisfaction; however, if there is continued despair, they may become anxious over unachieved objectives. Social groups and interactions with adults of a similar age help to build a better understanding of the life skills needed during this stage of life.

Late Adulthood

Age is not that specific a marker, and as life chances and opportunities become more accessible, competencies become more stable. Late adulthood, which is classed as 60 years, begins to show pronounced signs of age-related changes. By the age of 70, the balance between lean and fat body mass (which has continued to reduce) may be 50–50. We all know that if older members of the family suffer a fall, recovery is difficult as there is a change in bone density. Bones become brittle due to a loss in calcium and are slower to heal; also, hardened ligaments make movements more stiff, leading to a slowing of pace. The brain also loses neurons, and in the 90s, the brain of a healthy adult has lost 5–10 per cent of its early adult weight. However, with good nutrition, regular exercise, and a positive attitude and well-being, a good proportion of adults are able to maintain physical vigour and an active lifestyle well into old age.

Box 7.3 Longer Healing to Get Well

In families, the care of grandparents is often a source of concern and worry. We always tell our elders to be careful, and even have handles put in around the house and bathrooms to support movement and mobility. In the case of fall and injury, the body takes longer to recoup and recover, and return to balance. An older person's body does not bounce back as readily as a younger person's from exercise, illness, surgery, or situational stress. Recovery or recuperation time is usually longer for older adults. Prevention, planning and regular exercise are the keys to feeling better as you grow old.

Physiological deterioration impacts sensory and perceptual skills, muscular strength and memory, and there is a tendency towards diminishing sensory reactions, although mental skills may remain intact. These changes, which coincide with retirement from formal work and active employment, render the lives of the elderly more dependent on children or other younger people, causing both emotional and physical lifestyle modifications and adjustments.

DEVELOPMENTAL TASKS OF ADULTHOOD

Havighurst has worked intensively in the area of human development changes to comprehend the individual cycle and its co-relation with societal expectations. In the stage of adulthood, tasks arise from a combination of social expectations and personal values. These tasks emerge as part of the lifecycle, and are interdependent with society. Society provides the role models, and individuals often act in accordance with role expectations. The socialisation of individuals is a continuous process. Social norms are largely guiding principles, as individuals have their own choices and preferences for the paths they follow. To foster development, educators need to introduce students to these critical tasks at the right time. The tasks offer teachable moments, and as Havighurst said, 'When the body is ripe, and society requires, and the self is ready to achieve a certain task, the teachable moment has come' (1953: 5).

Some of the developmental tasks of young and middle adulthood are:

1. Selecting a mate
2. Starting a family
3. Rearing children
4. Managing a home
5. Getting started in an occupation
6. Taking on civic responsibilities
7. Finding a congenial social group
8. Accepting and adjusting to physiological changes, such as menopause
9. Reaching and maintaining satisfaction in one's occupation
10. Adjusting to possibly caring for aging parents
11. Helping teenage children become responsible adults
12. Achieving adult social and civic responsibility
13. Relating to one's spouse as a person
14. Developing leisure-time activities

PHYSICAL CHANGES DURING ADULTHOOD

A decrease in physical strength, endurance and flexibility is influenced by a complex set of biological, genetic and anatomical changes. Muscle strength and flexibility decrease with age; a major reason for the weakening of muscles is the loss of lean muscle mass, and its shrinkage due to a lack of physical activity.

Biological Ageing in Early Adulthood

Aging is a process that every human being goes through. It involves changes that help individuals to mature. Aging occurs biologically and is called senescence, that is, it is genetically inclined and contributes to a decline in the performance of different organs and systems in the human body. The aging process is asynchronous, in that all organs do not age at the same rate—some organ systems age faster than others. The range in individual differences can vary with factors like genetics, lifestyle, stress, and culture.

Aging can take place at the levels of DNA and body cells. Free radicals are one cause of cellular abnormalities. These are naturally occurring, highly reactive chemicals formed in the presence of oxygen. When oxygen molecules break down within the cell, the reaction takes away an electron and creates a free radical. It destroys nearby cellular material to replace that electron. Free radicals are related to 60 disorders of aging, such as heart disease, cancer, cataracts, arthritis. This damage builds up over time. Antioxidants, vitamin C, E, and beta carotene can limit this damage. Radiation and pollutants also trigger cellular breakdowns.

Ageing at the Levels of Organs and Tissue

Changes in organs and tissues, such as a loss in tissue elasticity, slowing of the endocrine system, and weakening of the immune system cause ageing. This slowing process is explained by the cross-linkage theory, which states that over time, protein fibres that make up the body's connective tissue begin to weaken bonds, or links, with one another. When these normally separate fibres cross-link, tissue becomes less elastic, leading to negative outcomes such as loss of flexibility, clouding the lens of the eye, clogged arteries, or damage to the kidneys.

The endocrine system gradually reduces and fails, which also contributes to aging. Menopause affects many body functions and the drop in growth hormones leads to a loss in muscle and bone mass. Intervention with regular exercise and diet regulation can work against ageing, and can slow some of these losses. Some other outcomes of ageing are additional fat, thinning of the skin, and a decline in cardiovascular function, which can also be controlled by diet and physical exercise.

Box 7.4 Rhythms and Activities for Well-being in Late Adulthood

It is important to ensure that as individuals grow older, there is access to regular medical check-ups and appropriate actions for health and well-being. Taking medication as ordered is very important when the person is diagnosed with high blood pressure, even if you 'feel fine'. Generally, high blood pressure affects the organs inside without giving any physical warning signs. This is the danger of not being treated or maintaining proper medical care, which could result in a stroke and/or a heart attack.

There is an increasing presence of older people in gyms and in regular walks. In many residential colonies, groups of the elderly engage together in the evenings. Besides physical exercises, they meet for Yoga or engage in Laughter Therapy.

At times, men and women have come together and begun education initiatives, teaching children from underprivileged families. This often provides homework help for children who do not have adequate support at home, due to reasons such as low parental literacy and poverty. The diverse social settings often lead to compelling situations, in which children need support from as many sources as possible. Social and volunteer groups organise cultural events and celebrate festivals, all of which are special events for children in deprived situations. Such different endeavours sustain will and enthusiasm by setting the rhythms for interacting with sections of society in useful and productive ways. Adult groups can contribute to the socialisation processes in these unique ways.

Hormonal losses also impact immune system function, leading to an increased susceptibility to infections, risks of cancer, and changes in blood vessels. There is also a decline in the efficiency of organs, which undergo changes and often have reduced levels of functioning. For example:

1. The heart becomes a less efficient pump and requires more oxygen to do the same work. The risk of blood pressure issues increases as a person reaches the 50s, as there is an increased thickness and hardening of the arteries, causing blood pressure to rise slightly and stay at a changed level.
2. Loss in the elastic flexibility of lungs do not allow them to expand as well, and thus less oxygen gets into them. Smoking harms the lungs and causes an earlier loss of elasticity, worsening this problem at a much earlier age in people who smoke, versus those who do not.
3. As one grows older, the functions of the kidney also reduce. Kidneys take longer to process body waste and get rid of waste products, especially with the effect of medication for different functions. Urinary incontinence, that is, the inability to hold urine, is not a normal change with ageing. Many other problems, such as enlarged prostate, weak muscles, limited fluid intake, or constipation may cause incontinence.

Body Image and Sexuality

Physical appearance is impacted by the many changes that occur in the body. Skin colour may change due to pigmentation, besides wrinkling of the skin, which is the most common and visible sign of age. Wrinkling is due to a normal loss in elastic tissue, excessive sun exposure, smoking, and possibly heredity. Small skin haemorrhages are noted, which may look like small red dots just about anywhere on your body.

The reproductive system may undergo changes with the onset of menopause; however, sexual activity is not impacted. Both men and women continue to derive pleasure from sexual intercourse and intimacy. Male penile erection may be delayed and orgasm is infrequent, as is sperm production. However, men have been able to fertilise the female egg till quite an advanced age. In women, there is hormonal loss, which affects vaginal lubrication and may impact orgasm. Oestrogen therapy can help reduce such reactions.

Loss of Bone Mass

It is common to see people developing a stoop as they grow older. This is due to changes in the spinal column and the compressing of bones. Thinning of the bones makes the vertebrae shrink, and this compression of the spinal column is responsible for many people getting shorter as they age, and for the stooping posture of many older people. The severe extreme of this change in bone is called osteoporosis. While it is mostly women who are affected, current research has shown that men, too, are being affected in growing numbers. The change in bone structure also slows the movements of the joints. Changes in the central nervous system also slow the reaction time to stimulus. With age comes an increase in the time lapse between the brain receiving a signal, and the person's response to it.

Coping with Sensory Changes and Positivity

The different sense organs may also have decreased levels of efficiency. One of the signs of ageing is wearing glasses. Losses in hearing or vision are most significant as they can affect a person in several ways, including limiting their mobility and communication, which in turn influences independence and interaction with others. Impact on perception and response to the environment will regulate the accomplishing of tasks and the way adults feel about themselves. It becomes very important to spend time with ageing family members experiencing such sensory loss.

Hearing gradually diminishes due to a decreased perception of high frequencies and pitch discrimination. These problems can often be resolved with a hearing aid. Although adding implements to assist hearing is a bother, the benefits outweigh any appearance-related dilemma. Nothing is better than the ability to continue to optimally communicate through adequate hearing. Several elderly also feel embarrassed to wear a hearing aid or walk with the aid of a stick. With more age-related changes, this might become a cause of accidents or falls. Changes in taste and smell can cause a loss of interest in food, and in turn lead to weight loss and malnutrition. Maintaining an adequate calorie intake and making proper food choices can prevent this from happening.

As the skin ages, it flattens due to a loss in subcutaneous fat, skin cells, sebaceous (oil) glands, sweat glands, melanocytes (pigment cells), and hair follicles. The skin loses some of its effectiveness as a protector against bacteria, as an insulator, as a thermal regulator, and as a sensory receptor. Since these losses cause wrinkling and loss of elasticity, freedom of movement and expression are inhibited. The slowing of circulation results in slower healing. The loss of colour is also seen, as the hair turns grey.

THEORETICAL PERSPECTIVES ON ADULTHOOD

Erik Erikson was the first psychologist to follow a life span perspective. Erikson described the stages of human development from childhood through adulthood, listing certain age-related functions. In the psychosocial theory of development, he suggested that each stage presents a dilemma, in which the person is challenged to develop skills to adapt to new situations and circumstances in life. By resolving each dilemma, the individual acquires the basic strength needed to meet the challenges of the next stage. Failure to resolve a dilemma suggests that the person might face some difficulties later in life.

Erikson defines dilemma from adolescence through early adulthood as 'identity versus role confusion'. Every individual is challenged to define who s/he is, and will be in the future. This dilemma is continuous and frequent, and thus becomes demanding, because many individuals face countless decisions at this time in their lives. Adolescents and young adults choose what work to do, how to be a man or a woman, and what to believe in. It enables an individual to make choices that serve their own needs, strengths and interests, and later, those of others.

The dilemma of early adulthood is 'intimacy versus isolation'. Intimacy is being able to merge your identity with someone else's without losing yourself in the process. True intimacy is based on the ability to trust a person enough to reveal your personal thoughts and feelings; to do so, it is necessary to have a clear sense of who you are. Intimate peer relationships replace parents as the primary supportive relationships. Erikson suggested that without an identity, formed in the previous stage, relationships would not be trustworthy. An individual would feel lonely if s/he could not connect with others. The basic strength that is acquired by resolving the dilemma of intimacy versus isolation is love, that is, an overall sense of caring and generosity toward others (Erikson and Erikson 1997).

Erikson proposed that women might develop identity and intimacy at the same time, because they might develop their identities through relationships with others. Thus, they might acquire the enduring strengths of fidelity and love simultaneously. This idea has been supported by feminist Carol Gilligan (1982), in her book *In a Different Voice*. Based on her studies of young women in the 1970s, Gilligan concluded that women determine who they are, how to be a woman, and what they believe in terms of relationships, whereas men usually cannot commit to others until they are sure of their own identities.

Carl Jung, the Swiss psychoanalyst, proposed four stages of development. His thoughts about development in adults were influenced by maturity, an acceptance of sexuality, and a growing consciousness. These attributes of youth and early adulthood between the ages of 20–40 foster a realisation that the carefree days of childhood are gone forever. People strive to gain independence, find a mate, and raise a family by the age of 40. Middle life (40–60) creates tension and anxiety with the dawning knowledge that you will not live forever. Clinging to youthful manners decreases the process of self-realisation. Tendencies towards introspection and inward thinking need to be explored, and people often turn to religion during this period. The inclusion of religious influences seems to be common across theoretical understandings, and carries on in years beyond 60; however, at this stage in the Jungian analysis, consciousness is reduced. There is more self-search and thinking.

Levinson's Life Structure Theory

Adult development has been studied in detail by Yale psychologist Levinson. He gathered empirical evidence through a series of intensive interviews with men (1,978) and women (1,987). Levinson proposed a theory of stages that adults go through as they develop, based on their rhythms and patterns of life at any particular time. The social and physical environments people live in shape individual lives. Family and work are primary factors, but religion, race and economic status are also important features that influence access to opportunity. Levinson proposed four 'seasonal cycles', which include pre-adulthood, early adulthood, middle adulthood, and late adulthood. Levinson, who originally studied 40 adult males between 35 and 45, is often criticised for being biased towards male thinking. Selecting careers and beginning a family mark the entry to early adulthood. Career advancement and its critical appraisal provide an evaluation of oneself at about age 30, and the next transition occurs at about 40, as individuals realise the limitations of their ambitions.

Adults deal with the concerns and issues of life at particular points; for example, during middle adulthood, people deal with their particular individuality and work towards cultivating their skills and assets as they move towards late adulthood. Therefore, in later years, the transition to late adulthood is a time to reflect upon successes and failures, and enjoy the rest of life. In later years, Levinson (1987) interviewed 45 women between the ages of 35 and 45. One-third were homemakers, one-third college instructors, and one-third businesswomen. In his analyses, Levinson found that women go through the same type of cycles as men. However, the life stages of women tend to be tied closer to the family lifecycle.

COGNITIVE DEVELOPMENT AND CHANGES IN THINKING

In this section, we discuss the perspectives of adult thought and related evolving processes in adult thought. It can be argued that the mind matures enough to handle complexities beyond the formal structures in thought, as individuals are placed in a complex set of life situations where they have to take decisions with regard to different age groups, social contexts and future aspirations. Formal operational thinking is absolute, and involves making decisions based on personal experience and logic. With cognitive maturity, young adults can reflect on their own thinking. They can now analyse their own thoughts, often referred to as meta-cognition.

Post-formal thought lies beyond Piaget's formal operational stage. This thinking is more complex, and involves making decisions spontaneously—'thinking on your feet'—based on signals from situational constraints and circumstances, integrating emotional guidance or pressure with logic to form context-dependent principles. For example, adolescents have a harder time with emotionally charged situations than adults.

Perry (1970) studied college students to get a glimpse of the evolving thinking skills of the adult mind in the making. He found that students gradually change their thinking in the face of reality and adult responsibility, and termed this change in thinking 'dualistic thinking' and 'relativistic thinking'. Often, younger students portray dualistic thinking by comparing truth with abstract standards and respecting authority figures. Dualistic thinking often reviews the information, or values and social directives, categorising them as right and wrong, thereby striking a balance between values and authority, right and wrong, good and bad, we and they. Truth is compared to abstract standards, and authority figures are respected simply because of their authority.

However, exposure to people from other religions, speaking many languages, and privy to various experiences allows for the acquiring of relativistic thinking. Adults then become more flexible, tolerant and realistic. As students' age and become aware of the diversity in opinion, they view knowledge as embedded in a framework of thought, and recognise relative truths on the basis of context. This transition in thinking may be unique to people pursuing an extended education, with all the diversity that they face in that environment. The underlying theme is adaptive cognition—thought that is less constrained by the need to find one answer to a question, and is more responsive to the context.

In recent years, there have been many thoughts on the diverse influences on adults, and how their skills and thinking expand, especially in the wake of digital devices. Longevity is on the rise, and there is a huge intervention by innovations, which positively influence adaptability. With the information boom, there is an attempt to explore the application of information to knowledge, and the latter's practical application. The shift from acquiring knowledge to using it is considered an important goal of mental activity by K. Warner Schaie. He categorised this shift in the following stages:

1. Acquisitive stage (childhood and adolescence) is the period of seeking, earning and skill-building.
2. Achieving stage (early adulthood) is the time when the skills learnt in the earlier stage are used as the means to achieve new goals in different life contexts. As individuals grow, they encounter particular situations like jobs, marriage and childbearing, which affect long-term goals. The application of knowledge to real-life problems creates needs, as well as an awareness of more than just a single right solution. How a person negotiates need-fulfilment or learns to be a team player are significant pathways. Skill and methods of cooperation may set a trajectory for the remaining life course.
3. Responsibility stage (middle adulthood). Adults are necessarily required to move towards roles that encapsulate responsibilities towards others, not only through care and nurturance, but also as mentors at work, role models while raising children, or caring for elderly parents. Reasoning now has to coincide with social obligations, boundaries, and averting the circumstances that one cannot change.
4. Individuals grow and have to take on appealing and leading roles. By being in this executive stage, they need to display an advanced level of thinking, keeping in mind the many complexities characterising people and responsibilities. Job responsibilities require monitoring with 'people skills', that is, taking people along and finding ways to motivate progress in business missions. There needs to be an understanding of the dynamics of institutional structures, incoming information, goals, and the personal needs of employees or family members.
5. The reintegrative stage, or late adulthood, resonates with many earlier views that describe late adulthood as a period of self-search and self-discovery. People in late

adulthood often re-examine and reintegrate their interests and values to create a satisfying life. There is no obligation to consider decisions in terms of consequences, or be selective about how they spend time and who they spend it with.

Identity and Self

Identity and creation of the self continue to develop throughout adulthood. An important aspect of identity in adulthood is how one integrates various aspects of the self. During adulthood, individuals move towards a mature sense of identity, based on taking control of their lives and developing ideologies. Young and middle adults might see themselves as improving with age, and expecting to get better in the future. Many cultural images, roles and responsibilities influence men and women to shape their views of themselves. Societies organise roles and certain tasks become gender-specific and are often adopted without resistance. However, there are instances of gender-role transgressions, when men and women might find themselves socially out of favour. In contemporary society, there is greater space for role diffusion and transformation in gender roles.

People's beliefs about the appropriate characteristics for men and women reflect shared cultural beliefs about masculinity and femininity. These can also be stereotypes; for example, men are regarded as stronger, more active and aggressive in many cultures, so collectively, such descriptions help form gender role identity. Jung (1933) proposed that during mid-life, women may place increased emphasis on achievement and accomplishment, while men may emphasise familial and nurturing concerns.

Besides the influence of gender roles on identity, individuals also experience a shift in primary orientation—a movement from being a son or a daughter to becoming a parent of a son or daughter. This shift begins when two individuals marry, and crystallises with the birth of a child.

Arnett and Tanner (2006), in their landmark book *Emerging Adulthood*, explore the changing patterns of adult life and its situatedness in contemporary sociality.

Recentring, a term introduced by Tanner, is a process that underlies the shift to an adult identity. It is one of the primary tasks of emerging adulthood. It is a three-stage process, in which power, responsibility and decision-making gradually shift from the family of origin to the independent young adult (Tanner 2006). Theorists have tried to explain this process of individuation with both interdependence and sustained connections with the family of origin.

In stage 1, the individual continues to be with the family of origin, but expectations of self-reliance and self-directedness begin to increase.

In stage 2, the individual is connected to the family, but is no longer with the family of origin. The individual might, however, still be financially dependent on the family. During this stage, individuals explore various opportunities, whether in education, relationships, or career. At the end of this stage, they move towards serious commitments, and try gaining the resources to support themselves.

Stage 3 is marked by independence from the family of origin, and commitment to a career, partner, etc. The individual retains close ties with the family of origin. The stages are similar to the identity formation process of adolescents as proposed by James Marcia.

Friendship

Although both family and friends are important to an individual's psychological well-being, some people are of the view that friends are often more important than family members. Another approach to friendship sees it as a relationship that is chosen, and not ascribed (as a family is). The sense of being desirable, which is elicited by friendships, enhances well-being and self-esteem. Gender differences persist in adult friendships. Women have more close friends than men, and their friendships are more intimate, compared to those of men. Cross-gender friendships are more common in adulthood. It gives both sexes the opportunity to understand the issues and concerns of the other gender.

According to Sternberg, intimacy—but not passion or commitment—characterises friendships. Friends normally come from similar backgrounds, share the same interests, and enjoy each other's company. Although many young adults feel the time pressures of work and starting a family, they usually manage to maintain at least some close friendships. As life responsibilities increase, time for socialising may decrease; however, an increase in the use of technological devices are somewhat decreasing the gap between friends. Friends are increasingly remaining connected to each other via social networking sites, and are virtually in touch with the lives of their friends, whom they often talk to.

Romantic Relationships and Marriage

Intimate and romantic relationships continue to be very important in adulthood. Adults see their partners as a base to which they can return for comfort and security, especially in times of stress. Several research studies have indicated that passion and sexual intimacy are very important in early adulthood, whereas feelings and loyalty dominate in the later years. Young adults of the current generation rate communication as an important characteristic of their relationships. Irrespective of the age and stage of adults, emotional security remains of utmost importance. Other aspects that young adults seek are love, respect, sexual intimacy, and loyalty. The collapse of a love relationship also feels tragic.

Across cultures, the most common way of selecting a mate is through arrangement, either by parents or professional matchmakers. However, with the boom in technology, the Internet now also serves as an important medium. In India, many marital relationships are fixed by parents, other relatives, or mediators. In such a case, the couple may be given limited opportunity to know each other. Despite the absence of familiarity, such relationships do last as girls and boys both accept the fact that their parents have done their best for them. In recent years, though. marriages—both 'arranged' and 'love marriages'—have often been short-lived.

Only when the couple start living together do they get to know each other well, and understand the seriousness of the relationship. Many urban couples now opt for live-in relationships, some of which culminate in marriage. However, as most such relationships are without the consent of the parents, they do not receive the necessary support if the relationship breaks down, and the absence of a strict law makes the recuperation tough, especially for girls.

In India, the institution of marriage is considered the best way to ensure the protection and optimal care of children. It offers intimacy, companionship, friendship, affection, sexual intimacy, and an opportunity for emotional growth, as well as a new source of identity and self-esteem. Many young adults now believe that traditional marriages, with their rigid gender roles, are no longer viable. They want to try and 'explore' this arena as well. The transition to married life brings in major changes in sexual functioning, living arrangements, attachments, and balancing intimacy with autonomy.

Some marriages that proved difficult during early adulthood become better during middle adulthood. Although the partners may have lived through a period of stress, they eventually discover a deep and solid foundation on which to strengthen their relationship. Also, at this stage the partners may have fewer financial worries, and more time for each other. Family ties, friendships and spousal relations need consistent and continuous interactions to thrive and bloom.

Family Ties, Transitions and Challenges

To form meaningful and trustworthy relationships, an individual needs to have a fully formed sense of self. Relationships that are warm and empathetic are long-lasting, trustworthy and harmonious. Several studies depict less committed relationships, emotional isolation and loneliness (which can turn to depression) for people with a poor sense of self. Erikson firmly believed that close and committed relationships are very important in an individual's life, and that people who are unable to form meaningful relationships remain alone and isolated.

During early adulthood, adults make every effort to ensure the well-being of their self and family. Soon, the stage of generativity versus stagnation, which occurs during middle adulthood, sets new goals for psychosocial development. Adults contribute to society in ways that will benefit future generations. Generativity refers to caring for others and giving back to the coming generation by caring and sharing. Stagnation refers to the failure to find a way to give back to society. These individuals may feel disconnected or uninvolved with their community, and with society as a whole. Those actively involved in contributing to home and community are successful, and feel a sense of accomplishment when they look back on their life.

According to Robert Sternberg, love consists of three components: passion, decision/commitment, and intimacy. Passion involves the intense feelings of physiological arousal and excitement present in a relationship, while decision/commitment involves the decision to love one's partner and maintain the relationship. Intimacy involves the sense of warmth and closeness in a relationship. Furthermore, intimacy can be expressed physically, psychologically—through sharing thoughts—and socially—through social activities with the same group of friends.

- Physical intimacy involves mutual affection and sexual activity.
- Psychological intimacy involves sharing feelings and thoughts.
- Social intimacy involves enjoying the same friends and types of recreation.

PARENTHOOD

Becoming a parent typically denotes taking up new responsibilities for one's self, and for others as well. Parenthood not only works towards fulfilling the needs of the child, but also has the self-fulfilling function of providing self-confidence and a sense of well-being. Adults also get the opportunity to face new challenges and show diverse competencies by taking up multiple roles. Every time a parent deals with a situation, s/he reflects on whether they have taken the right decision. But this does not mean that parents are only the givers of warmth and affection; they receive ample love and affection back from their children—the purest form of love.

Specific Place of Fathers

The role of fathers has been researched a lot in the caregiving process. In the traditional Indian context, fathers were considered the breadwinners and kept away from displaying love for their children. The equation has changed drastically, as most fathers are now equal partners in caregiving practices. According to Gore (cited in Anthony et al. 1978), the father's affective role is considerably circumscribed by social and cultural norms. Traditionally, he is to assume an authoritative rather than an affective role in his children's lives. It is only in later childhood that the father is known to become a salient agent in socialisation.

In a study on the father's role in infant care, Rajgopalan (1989) investigated the nature of father-infant interactions in urban, upper-middle class, nuclear families. She found that infants with employed mothers were usually left in the care of the grandparents, even if they lived separately. The fathers were also involved in routine caretaking of the children. The study clearly demonstrated that fathers are capable of being active and nurturing caregivers. In his 2013 study, Anand revealed that fathers played a major role in caring for their disabled children, and actively engaged with their children in routine activities. They were very supportive and shared the caring role with the mothers and other family members.

Parenting Concerns

Many parents experience the **empty nest syndrome** after their children leave home. In the absence of children—the focal point in their lives—they are often unable to reconnect easily with each other. They slowly move towards rediscovering their own individuality, separate from parenthood. In India, the lives of all family members revolve around the children; middle-aged parents may continue to live with both their grown-up children and their own ageing parents. There are many realities; in some cases, parents may feel overworked. Many parents also report feeling as though they give more than they receive in their relationships with their children.

In multi-generational families, grandparents' contribution in the care of grandchildren can lead to added pressure. Many elderly people report that they need more time to themselves to introspect, to indulge in leisure activities, and to mingle socially. If they have to take on the full-time role of grandparents, these opportunities shrink, leading to occasional feelings of resentment.

Sibling Relationship

Sibling ties are the longest lasting in most people's lives. Relationships with siblings who remain in touch can be central to psychological well-being in mid-life, when children get married or move into their own homes. For many, especially older, adults, relationships with siblings are among the closest. Some older adults end up providing care for, or live with, one of their siblings, especially when one sibling has no other caretaker. Research indicates that people with siblings believe that their siblings would provide help in a crisis, and would share their happiness, worries and sorrows.

WORK AND GENDER RELATIONS

Amina, a 26-year-old communication specialist, wonders about her career. Should she become a producer or would she be better suited as a public relations spokesperson? She thinks that her outgoing personality is an important factor that she should consider while taking this decision. Choosing one's work is a serious business. For some people, work is a source of prestige, recognition, and a sense of worth. For others, the excitement of creativity and the opportunity to give something of themselves makes work meaningful. But for most of us, the main purpose of work is to earn a living. Many factors influence whether an individual is satisfied with her/his job. People who love their work tend to stay in them for a longer time than people who do not. Early adulthood is a period of decision-making, and is even more critical for choosing a career path. Decisions about work go to the very core of a young adult's identity. The choice goes beyond determining financial status, sense of self-worth, and the direction an individual would take.

Many individuals experience emotional distress and low self-esteem when they are unable to get work, or are stuck in unsatisfactory work. It is seen that there is greater commitment to the job as one gets older. Younger adults, in their attempt to look for the right job, sometimes even experiment with work. Middle-aged adults may reach a peak in terms of position and earnings. Mental and physical capabilities are not a major concern for many middle-age adults who continue to work. For many, mid-life is the time of evaluation, assessment and reflection of the work they do and want to do in the future.

With an increasing number of women working out of the family, gender roles are changing in Indian homes. Many men have taken over the responsibilities for the home, children, and other household chores. In many homes, women earn more than their husbands and have actually taken on the role of breadwinner. In such families, men take pride and interest in home and childcare. In many traditional families, too, women have taken up such roles. However, it is seen that in most households, women juggle multiple roles.

PLANNING FOR RETIREMENT

Work creates a particular structure, rhythm and routine that individuals often miss when they do not work for a long time. The term 'retirement planning' involves a balanced approach to the process of retirement. Adults need to sit back, introspect, and answer questions such as: What would one do in the leisure time? How would one keep physically, socially and mentally active? Preparation is the key to successful retirement, and helps in a smooth transition from employment to unemployment. Research has shown that people who plan for retirement tend to be more successful in adapting to this major life transition.

This planning further aids in financial savings, increased possibility of a healthy lifestyle, exposure to new leisure activities, and most importantly, a positive attitude towards retirement. For instance, in India, irrespective of social class, families do plan to buy their own home after retirement. For people employed in government and private institutions, there is a fixed age of retirement. Some people take extensions or work as consultants in other projects to keep themselves occupied and active. Many decide to take a break from routine tasks and look forward to this new freedom, and might follow social or religious pursuits. Self-employed people need to decide the right time and age to retire. Research also shows that retirement impacts men and women differently; women generally look forward to retirement, as they feel they would be able to devote more time to the family and grandchildren. On the other hand, men start looking for an alternate work option as a preparation for retirement.

Civic responsibility refers to an active participation in the public life of a community in an informed, committed and constructive manner, with a focus on the benefit of the whole society. In adulthood, it includes:

- Following and showing respect for laws
- Establishing a balance between rights and responsibilities
- Community involvement in the decision-making process
- Recognising the human rights of each person
- Making oneself heard and voicing one's rights

These may also include more specific roles, such as voting, supporting causes, etc. Individuals who take up tasks as volunteers may want to meet their need to feel wanted, and it might also give them an opportunity for intellectual stimulation. As individuals move from adolescence to adulthood, they feel a strong need to maintain a balance between rights and responsibilities, and as a result participate in several activities that define their personal goals. The transition also reflects in their movement from personal goals to the larger goals of the society, and they start seeking answers to the various questions they encounter in their personal tryst with the larger principles governing their society.

SUMMARY

- This chapter discussed the physical, intellectual, social, and emotional facets of transition from adolescence into adulthood. It also discussed the rites of passage that prepare an adult to move through various life events, and the journey of adulthood—career, intimacy, nurturance, retirement—and successes and failure. It revisited the four stages of the traditional Hindu lifecycle—Brahmacharya, Grihasta ashrama, Vanaprastha and Sannyasa—and divided adulthood into three distinct stages, viz., early adulthood (20–40 years), middle adulthood (40–60 years), and late adulthood (60–80 years). The developmental tasks associated with adulthood, the various physical changes that accompany ageing, as well as changes in one's own body image and sexuality are dealt with in detail. The chapter also looked at the various theoretical perspectives on adulthood, before moving on to family ties, friendship and marriage, and then to the most important role of all, parenthood. Retirement, another important milestone in the lives of adults, is also discussed.

KEY TERMS

Adulthood – A period of optimum mental functioning, when an individual's intellectual, emotional and social capabilities are at their peak to meet the demands of career, marriage and children. Adulthood is commonly thought of as beginning at age 20 or 21. Middle age, commencing at about 40 years, is followed by old age, which starts at about 60

Transition – The process or a period of changing from one state or condition to another

Rites of passage – A ceremony or event marking an important stage in someone's life, especially birth, the transition from childhood to adulthood, marriage, and death

Identity – A major personality achievement, and a crucial step towards becoming a productive, content adult

Incontinence – Inability to control the passing of urine

Intimacy – A primary developmental task of adulthood, involving the ability to merge your identity with someone else's without losing yourself in the process

Isolation – The inability to form intimacy results in loneliness and despair

Dualistic thinking – A key feature of emerging or early adulthood, this involves dividing information, values and authority into right and wrong, or we and they, by comparing truth with abstract standards and respecting authority figures

Relativistic thinking – A key feature of emerging or early adulthood, this involves flexibility, tolerance and realistic thinking, which are associated with the context

Expertise – The acquisition of extensive knowledge and domain-specific concepts in a field or endeavour by specialising in a major stream or occupation

Creativity – Divergent thinking characterised by an innovative thinking style, tolerance of ambiguity, special drive to succeed, and a willingness to experiment and try again

Relationships – The way in which two or more people or things are connected, or the state of being connected, for instance in marriage, parenthood, friendship, etc

Generativity – A key feature of middle adulthood, characterised by making your mark on the world through caring for others, and creating and accomplishing things that make the world a better place

Stagnation – A key feature of middle adulthood, characterised by the failure to find a way to contribute to society

Empty-nest syndrome – This is the time when children leave home, leaving parents with feelings of grief and loneliness. Developmentally, the children are ready to be on their own, to attend college or university or get married.

EXERCISES

1. Among your family and friends, make a profile of about 10 people between the ages of 18–25. List out the courses, jobs or trainings they are associated with. Analyse their affiliations. Record their social relations, and the presence of any significant other. Try and understand the nature of work, daily rhythms and relationships.
2. Do a survey in a locality of the ages at which people retired from active work, or will retire. What are the retired people doing? Analyse the daily rhythms of life after active employment.
3. What is the transition from high school to college like?
4. What are some key physical changes that take place from young to middle adulthood?
5. What career challenges and changes might people experience in middle adulthood?
6. Identify any five adults and ask them to write about people they have held as role models. Analyse the responses for the kind of qualities that people identify as admirable and worth following.
7. Analyse from about 25 families how the couples chose to marry, and the ceremony that was held.
8. List several ways in which a couple, as new parents, can help each other make an effective adjustment to parenthood.
9. On his 50th birthday, Ram was asked how he felt. He replied, 'I feel calmer and more content than at any time in my life.' What positive changes might have contributed to Ram's response?

REFERENCES

Anand, A., 'Caring for Children with Disability: Role of Fathers', Unpublished Master's thesis, Department of Human Development and Childhood Studies, Lady Irwin College, University of Delhi, New Delhi, 2013.

Anthony, E. J., C. Koupernik and C. Chiland, *The Child in His Family*, Vol. IV, New York: John Wiley & Sons, 1978.

Arnett, J. J., 'Emerging Adulthood Theory of development from late teens through the twenties', *American Psychologist*, 55 (5), 2000, pp. 469–80.

Arnett, J. J. and J. L. Tanner, *Emerging Adults in America: Coming of Age in the 21st Century*, American Psychological Association, 2006.

Erikson, E. and J. Erikson, *The life cycle completed*, New York: W. W. Norton & Co., 1997.

Gilligan, Carol, *In a Different Voice: Psychosocial Theory and Women's Development*, Cambridge, Mass.: Harvard University Press, 1982.

Havighurst, R. J., *Human Development and Education*, New York: Longman Greens, Co., 1953.

Levinson, D. J., 'Seasons of a Woman's Life', Paper presented at the meeting of the American Psychological Association, New York, 1987.

Perry, W. G., Jr., *Forms of intellectual and ethical development in the college years*, New York: Holt, Rinehart & Winston, 1970.

Rajgopalan, J., 'The father and the infant: Patterns in caregiving', Unpublished Master's thesis, Department of Child Development, Lady Irwin College, University of Delhi, New Delhi, 1989.

Tanner, J. L., '*Recentering during emerging adulthood: A critical turning point in life span human development*', in Jeffrey J. Arnett and Jennifer L. Tanner (eds), *Emerging Adults in America: Coming of Age in the 21st Century*, American Psychological Association, 2006.

Online sources

http://ablongman.com/html/productinfo/berkcd7e/contents/0205449131_4.pdf (accessed 31 August 2013).

http://adultdevelopment.weebly.com/havighurst.html (accessed 19 January 2014).

http://highered.mcgrawhill.com/sites/dl/free/0070909695/120220/santrock_edpsych_ch02.pdf (accessed 28 August 2013).

http://mhhe.com/cls/psy/ch03/levinson.mhtml (accessed 27 January 2014).

http://sation.in/2012/02/sudden-infant-death-syndrome-sids/ (accessed 31 August 2013).

http://wahsa.org/agingprocess.pdf (accessed 21 January 2014).

http://www.britannica.com/EBchecked/topic/481644/psychological-development/5954/Adulthood (accessed 19 January 2014).

http://www.healthline.com/galecontent/neonatal-reflexes-1 (accessed 31 August 2013).

http://www.imamu.edu.sa/topics/IT/IT%206/A%20Conception%20of%20Adult%20Development.pdf (accessed 27 January 2014).

http://www.learningseed.com/_guides/1009_Infants_Physical_Development_Guide.pdf (accessed on 7 September 2013).

http://www.longestlife.com/ebook/change.html (accessed 21 January 2014).

http://www.mcgrawhill.ca/web_resources/sch/Chapter_4_Final.pdf (accessed 28 January 2014).

http://www.nlm.nih.gov/medlineplus/ency/article/002301.htm (accessed 7 September 2013).

http://www.nlm.nih.gov/medlineplus/ency/article/002395.htm (accessed 7 September 2013).

http://www.pearsonhighered.com/ormrod/humanlearning/pdf%20files/4_PiagetSensorimotor.pdf (accessed 7 September 2013).

http://www.thevisualmd.com/health_centers/child_health/infant_nutrition/cardiovascular_development (accessed 7 September 2013).

8

Ageing and the Elderly

HIGHLIGHTS

- Describes the changing competencies of the elderly: the interplay of physical strength, biological bases of diminishing functions, and their bearing on the social status of individuals.
- Discusses theories of ageing that present varying perspectives, to build an understanding of the varying dimensions of the elderly.
- Provides nuances of the everyday rhythms of elderly males and females, while also providing specific contexts.
- Government laws and provisions for the welfare of the elderly are listed.

The increasing presence of the elderly is a significant part of the recent changes in demographic configuration. The human population is ageing, and concerns for the care and well-being of the elderly are presenting new challenges. A growing increase in life expectancy and longevity are indicators of the health and well-being of nations. The human development index, which compares the progress of nations, also includes life expectancy as a measure of development, besides economic assets. Longevity is emerging, and is also in need of social planning. What is of interest is the way societies are recognising, adapting and evolving to meet the emerging needs of older people. With the presence of an increasing number of old people, societies need to ready themselves to understand the needs and issues related with the elderly.

Although many people maintain that old age is a state of mind, there are several life events that signal the beginning of late adulthood. There are both physical and social signs of ageing. Most societal features for everyday living are designed for the competencies of well-functioning adults. Ageing brings in many developmental changes and diminishing abilities, such as weakened eyesight and reaction patterns. Accompanying diminishing physical abilities are social limitations and regulations, such as retirement. Ageing is characterised by altered states in the occupational and financial domains, in physiology, and in health, including psychological and social domains. Such changes influence the well-being of elderly persons, and tend to lessen their physical and mental capacity to cope with the rigors of daily living (Prakash et al. 2007).

Developmental changes in late adulthood convey a decline in the overall functioning of organs, and hence in social competencies. The capacities of the elderly, as well as their ability to do things, are often impacted by reaction time, memory, vision, hearing, or mere mobility. The biological clock is now ticking in a slow rhythm; however, despite the degeneration in physiological functions, many individuals defy the waning phase of life and emerge triumphant. Historical figures around the globe provide evidence of the active, healthy lives led by the elderly. Poets, playwrights, and even sportsmen have been active well into their 80s. Gandhi's movement to lead India to freedom began in his mid-40s, and extended well into his late-70s. For instance:

At 94, Bertrand Russell was active in international peace drives.

At 93, George Bernard Shaw wrote the play *Farfetched Fables*.
At 84, Somerset Maugham wrote *Points of View*.
At 83, Aleksandr Kerensky wrote *Russia* and *History's Turning Point*.
At 82, Winston Churchill wrote *A History of English Speaking People*.
At 82, Leo Tolstoy wrote *I Cannot Be Silent*.

AGEING AND CONTEMPORARY INDIA

In recent times, too, there have been illustrious personalities whose skills and performances continued to be acclaimed in their old age. The legendary nonagenarian artist, B. L. Sanyal, actively participated and guided young students in the movement of the Society for the Promotion of Music Amongst Youth. The Indian film industry provides many examples of actors much beyond the age of 60—Zohra Sehgal continued to act well into her 80s, and sang her favourite song, 'Abhi to mein jawaan hoon' (I am still young) to a packed hall at the inauguration of a Drama Festival. Lata Mangeshkar, Amitabh Bachchan, Kamal Hassan, and Waheeda Rehman are some other luminaries who continue to enthrall audiences. Kurien Verghese and E. Sreedharan who spearheaded Amul Dairy and the building of the Metro in the national capital, respectively, worked well into their old age. The diverse roles performed by individuals can defy the stereotypical representations and expectations associated with age.

Although age and ageing are in many ways associated with role-taking, social expectations, and value orientations, many individuals deal with ageing in a unique way. There are certain trends, though, in the collective thinking regarding the role and position of the elderly.

Ageing is a natural biological phenomenon. Often, there is an assumption of reduced efficiency due to declining physiological functioning, which impacts competencies. Yet within societies are active and alert older individuals, whose age comes as a surprise to others. A diversity in the functional levels of the elderly is becoming increasingly apparent, as is the emergence of age-related dysfunctionalities such as dementia or problems related to mobility.

Box 8.1 Active at All Ages

One of the leading artists of contemporary India, B. C. Sanyal, lived for 101 years (1902–2003). He led the art movement and nurtured it in the difficult years after India's partition. He had by then made a name for himself in Lahore. He taught in many institutions and initiated an informal education in the arts. He kept his youthfulness through a diverse range of activities that involved the youth. In the latter part of his life, he was an active advisor to the Society for the Promotion of Indian Classical Music Amongst Children and Youth. Besides attending concerts and infusing simplicity in the nuances of music and dance, Sanyal Baba (as he was popularly known) attended Spicmacay conventions, stayed in dormitories, and remained accessible to the young. He would accompany groups of young participants on treks even in his 90s.

At the age of 101, Sanyal Baba was excited to start working on glass, as new techniques of working on glass were explained to him. The human spirit can defy all norms, including those set by declining body functions brought on by ageing.

Source: http://www.the-south-asian.com/april%202003/sanyal-1.htm

SOCIAL CONSTRUCTION OF AGEING IN INDIA

Ageing refers to inevitable biological and psychological processes, while old age is conceived as the psychosocial and cultural experience. In India, as we grow as individuals, three primary duties become part of socialisation—service towards elders in the family and society; duties towards God; and duties towards wise persons. Being an Indian by birth goes beyond a mere biological process; it is seen as a social birth scripted by the cultural significance of duty and service towards parents (or elderly persons in the family). The Manusmriti (Chapter 2.121) states: 'One who always serves and respects elderly is blessed with four things: long life, wisdom, fame and power.' Such cultural norms may serve two completely opposing functions. One is, of course, the social direction provided to individuals—to be respectful and caring towards the elderly—while the other is often a silence on any other (extra-familial) form of care for the elderly.

Most elderly in India were part of families, both as the respected head of the family, or living in the dwellings set up by their offspring. In certain situations, changing values and individual choices could lead to a clash between generations. A contentious interplay of intergenerational relationships may cause a break in the cultural regulation of service to elders by living with them. Longevity has introduced many more perspectives in the everyday lives of the elderly.

Indian society believes that the family is best suited to meet the needs of the elderly. Older people require assisted living, which it is assumed can generally be with the family. Out-of-family living contexts for the elderly are few, although not entirely absent—institutions like the Arya Samaj Vridhh Ashrama or ashrams run by religious leaders are examples. The government, too, has made provisions in the form of separate old-age homes for men and women. Non-governmental organisations such as Helpage India, geared towards the care and well-being of the elderly, have also made their presence felt in social networks. There is growing awareness of the increase in the ageing population, and their specific needs. Recent studies have provided data on the increasing number of institutions providing care for the elderly. There is state support and provision for emerging laws to assist the old (Situation Analysis of the Elderly in India 2011).

The Situation Analysis of the Elderly indicates a steady increase in the population of the elderly. In 1961, the elderly comprised 5.6 per cent of the population According to population projections, in 2026 the elderly will comprise 12.4 per cent of the population.

Till 2008, the literacy profile through formal schooling of the elderly was not gender balanced, as more males were literate—50 per cent males and only 20 per cent females were educated in schools. Perhaps the state emphasis on educating the girl child, coupled with different kinds of financial incentives, will correct the male bias and lead to greater gender balance.

A promising feature is that 40 per cent of men and women above the age of 60 were still working, defying the retirement age in many professions. There is also an increase in financial dependency—20 per cent elderly women are dependent on spouses, while 6–7 per cent men are dependent on their spouses. Around 70 per cent women are dependent on children; interestingly, about 85 per cent males are supported by their children. A slightly higher number of grandchildren, that is, 3 per cent, financially support their grandparents. The support from other quarters is 6 per cent for both elderly men and women.

Let us examine some of the developmental changes influencing the social and emotional state of the elderly.

Changing Social Perceptions of the Elderly

In India, in recent years, according to Lawrence Cohen (2003), writings about old age and ageing have been dominated by a powerful and seldom challenged narrative of the decline of the Indian joint family, and the consequent emergence of old age as a period of difficulty. Films like *Bagwaan*, starring the superstar Amitabh Bachchan, have further highlighted the dwindling role of the new generation vis-à-vis the elderly, and indicated a societal resolve to restore the primacy of the family in the care of ageing parents.

Historically, being an agrarian society, leadership roles were usually imposed on the head of the family, who became the decision-maker. With industrialisation and subsequent urbanisation, the reins of power shifted and were reshaped. Families moved away from group living to set up units in geographically distant areas. The oldest person was no longer the *karta* (legal term for Head of the Undivided Indian Family). Economic opportunities and new living arrangements created smaller units with different power systems.

There are certain interpretations of the elderly in sociological thinking. The experience and knowledge the elderly possess helps in cultural continuity, and in the sustenance of values and traditions. First, there is the approach of functional significance that views the elderly as a repository of experience and valuable information. Use has been made of this in agricultural projects in several states. The youth is very much part of the workforce; however, society places the elderly in central positions as mentors or advisors at the grassroots level.

It is natural for the youth to feel that the older generation does not allow them to exercise their skills. This second approach falls within conflict theory, which views ageing as problematic. There is societal pressure to minimise the role of older individuals and take away their privileges and power. Some of this relates to an absence of enthusiasm on the part of the young to participate and act. However, there could be a balance between the two approaches.

In a third interpretation related to features of age, there is a general perception of the youth as active and alert, while older people are viewed as weak, reflective and calm. Thus, the different age groups become part of their functional levels. The dominance of new media may contribute to isolating the elderly from mainstream action. Some societal efforts to defy the symbols of age can be noted in the inclusion of the elderly in advertisements related to digitised gadgets, such as photography and new cell phones, and connecting to the youth.

A completely different perspective is the 'emancipation approach', which provides a liberating dimension to the status of the elderly. It is the creation of a social identity with privileges tied to economic, political and psychological participation, rather than exclusion. Such features can be noted in reserved seats in public transport, travel concessions, particular celebrations such as school functions, and other forms of recognition of senior citizens.

INDIAN PERSPECTIVES ON AGEING: ASHRAMA THEORY

The Hindu tradition, backed by folklore, popularly recognises a belief in stages in the human lifecycle and division of life in different ashramas, referred to as the Ashrama Theory. Popular Hindu epics reiterate the ashrama system, where boys spent a good part of their childhood acquiring skills and competencies meant for a useful adult life. While popular epics are silent on the specific socialisation of girls, regional lore has many women icons, such as Kamala, Maitreyi, Gargi, and Savitri. Folklore and *Vratta Kathas* have stories about the heroic deeds of women, and their wisdom in holding on to family values, and protecting the family from danger and evil. The Manusmriti pays particular attention to this aspect of Indian life, and lists the four ashramas as:

- The First Ashrama: '*Brahmacharya*' or the Student Stage
- The Second Ashrama: '*Grihastha*' or the Householder Stage
- The Third Ashrama: '*Vanaprastha*' or the Hermit Stage
- The Fourth Ashrama: '*Sannyasa*' or the Wandering Ascetic Stage

Brahmacharya—The Celibate Student

This is a period of formal education. It lasts till the age of 25, during which the young male leaves home to stay with a guru and attain both spiritual and practical knowledge. During this period, he is called a *brahmachari*, and is prepared for his future profession, his family, and the social and religious life ahead. Modern-day schooling would be an equivalent stage. The Manusmriti also refers to *Vidya-arambha* as a Hindu milestone, heralding the onset of Brahmacharya.

Grihastha—The Married Family Man

This period begins when a man gets married, and takes on the responsibility for earning a living and supporting his family. During this stage, Hinduism supports the pursuit of wealth (*artha*) as a necessity, and indulgence in sexual pleasure (*kama*) under certain defined social and cosmic norms. In contemporary parlance, career choices, selecting a life partner, and beginning a family would correspond to this stage. This ashrama lasts till about the age of 50. According to the Laws of Manu, when a person's skin wrinkles and his hair greys, he should go out into the forest. However, in real life, most Hindus are caught up in their lives, and *mohmaya*, translated closely as 'web of family bonds', binds them to the joys and travails of family life, making Grihastha last a lifetime. Individuals also find it difficult to give up family involvement or release their roles to the young.

Vanaprastha—The Hermit in Retreat

This stage begins when a man's duty as a householder comes to an end. He has become a grandfather; his children are grown up, and have lives of their own. At this age, he should renounce all physical, material and sexual pleasures, retire from social and professional life, leave his home, and go to live in a forest hut, spending his time in prayers. He is allowed to take his wife along, but is supposed to maintain little contact with the family. Such a life is indeed harsh and cruel for an aged person, rendering this third ashrama nearly obsolete. Emotional bonds, economic requirements, and physical needs make living in isolation difficult. Total renunciation is difficult, especially in the present contexts.

Sannyasa—The Wandering Recluse

At this stage, a man is supposed to be devoted to God. He is a *sannyasi*, he has no home, no attachment; he has renounced all desire, fear and hope, duty and responsibility. He is virtually merged with God, all his worldly ties broken, and his sole concern becomes attaining *moksha*, or release from the circle of birth and death. When an individual dies, the funeral ceremonies (*Prêt karma*) are performed by his son and heir, one of the reasons fuelling the desire for a male child. A daughter does not perform this task ritualistically. Even in the changed social milieu, this duty is still largely a male act.

OTHER THEORIES ON AGEING

Literature from other parts of the world presents similar changing responsibilities with age. As individuals grow, each culture etches out roles and responsibilities. Often, the elderly manage to shift the responsibilities, thereby disengaging from active social roles, as suggested by the *sanyas* stage. In a way, societies tend tc both recognise decreasing physiological functions and consequently respect the changing nature of body competencies impacting social dynamics. Several perspectives have emerged and evolved to promote understandings of behaviour, and identify features that contribute to harmonious interaction patterns among different age groups.

Psychosocial Development

Erik Erikson attempts to understand life span development in eight stages, from infancy to late adulthood. Each stage is explained in terms of a certain milestone, which leads to a sense of psychosocial stability. This state of harmony prepares individuals to take on emerging challenges, as the body grows physically and provides new competencies. Erikson posits an explanation concerning the dynamic interactions between the individual and the social challenges that individuals have to negotiate and manage. An infant builds a sense of trust from the possibility of developing mistrust, as at this stage there is total dependency on others.

Individuals carve a social presence by facing and resolving different psychosocial challenges—gaining autonomy, building initiative, consolidating skills, developing an identity, exploring relationships, reflecting on the purpose of life, thinking about the journey so far. The final conflict of Erikson's theory, ego integrity vs. despair, involves coming to terms with one's own life. Individuals may make peace with their circumstances, while some may see their lives as a series of unfinished tasks, and give way to despair.

Box 8.2 Elderly Profile A

Mr Inder is 91 years old. He lost his wife in his early 50s. At this stage, he feels satisfied with the relationships he has been able to develop. The initial void left by his wife's death was filled by involvement with his two grandchildren, who responded with affection. His army background influenced his daily rhythms, which created a healthy life and gave him enough time to engage with family and build loving bonds. The grandchildren would often come to him to solve their issues in their growing years. He always lets them make their own choices, and so they willingly return to their non-judgemental grandfather, whom they can trust. He still goes for a short walk in a nearby park, and spends time with his age mates. He is always careful about his diet, and takes care of his health and medical conditions, like blood sugar levels. Adults who arrive at a sense of integrity feel complete and satisfied with their achievements.

Profile B

Mr Thakur, a doctor, decided not to work outside of home after his official retirement at the age of 60. He spent most of his time watching television, reading newspapers, and some reluctant time with his grandchild. He talks often to his friends over the phone, but makes no effort to meet them. His social interactions are minimal. His visits outside the home are only to the bank, or for other government-related paperwork. Five years after retirement, he feels physically weak and is on a high intake of dietary supplements to ensure good health. But the lack of physical movement and a social life has led him to feel isolated and physically weak. Over the years, his love of money has grown, and he is not satisfied with what he has achieved, or with his present life. He does not trust his family members either. Often, despair sets in, especially if dissatisfaction and disappointment are given centrality. Social interaction assists in enhancing perspective. Absence of activity leads to an absence of routine, which can be detrimental and taxing.

Source: Dimple Rangila.

Social Theories of Ageing

Certain other theoretical perspectives on individual roles and relationships have been explained by social theories, which analyse patterns of behaviour, and social and physical activities. Akin to the Indian Ashrama theory is the disengagement and activity theory, which look at behavioural change stemming from psychological and social changes. **Disengagement theory** describes the altered nature of relationships and social networks of older people initiated by oneself, or others. Disengagement may occur due to individual health or choice (dictated by social or economic factors). Disengagement is inevitable, and encompasses adaptive mechanisms to deal with altered situations.

Activity theory follows a proactive approach, which involves maintaining the activities and attitudes of middle age for as long as possible. Substitutes should be found for the activities and roles that one is forced to give up at retirement, and can take the form of familial, recreational, volunteer, and community roles. Being part of family and community life, with assigned duties, activities and social responsibility, provides satisfaction. Self-esteem and self-worth are derived through high levels of participation, and greater roles and responsibilities.

Box 8.3 Profile C

Shavikadevi, aged 88

Many elderly people live with their families. Shavikadevi lives with her daughter-in-law and grandson in an urban metropolis. She is the only stay-at-home member of the family unit of three. She wakes up at 6.30 AM and makes morning tea for herself and her daughter-in-law. After reading the newspaper, she helps to pack lunch for the two people going out to work. She has had a high chair made, which enables her to sit and make *rotis*. After her morning rituals, she gets the house cleaned and makes tea for the domestic help. Before lunch, she reads for a while or talks to different relatives and friends on the phone. When her daughters visit, she goes shopping with them. She enjoys watching the latest movies. An important part of her daily routine is watching television serials, which she enjoys discussing with her friends over the telephone.

Her grandchildren fondly say that she even irons their clothes. The family is in harmony across generations, as each takes an interest in the other, while also giving each other space. As observed, Shavika is well-blended as her role is positive. The lesson for changing dynamics is to adjust and adapt according to family dynamics.

Interview conducted in New Delhi by Asha Singh

Activity theory has a positive orientation, and advocates new roles and responsibilities for the elderly, rather than being simply labelled 'old'.

Labelling is damaging to the individual, as there is a danger of being viewed within the parameters of 'being old', with all actions viewed as symbols of the elderly. In modern society, there are dangers accompanying living excluded lives, with no inclusion in social activities.

In different residential localities, one sees an attempt to create a **subculture of the elderly.** Groups of older people meet in the evenings, chat, and form a network for their socialisation. The elderly also form laughing groups, yoga collectives, or participate in tuition groups for economically weaker sections in society. Such actions indicate an attitude of emancipation and empowerment.

Building on the Theory of Ego Integrity

Robert Peck (cited in Austrian 2013) analysed Erikson's explanation of ageing by examining the conflict of ego integrity vs. despair. He commented that during old age, there are three distinct tasks, each of which must be resolved for integrity to develop:

a. Ego differentiation versus work-role preoccupation is a task resulting from retirement. The elderly must seek ways to affirm their self-worth by investing in new pathways for involvement in relation to their skills. They must differentiate a set of family, friendship and community roles that are as satisfying as work life.
b. Body transcendence versus body preoccupation is simply building recognition of a decline in body functions. Older adults need to transcend physical limitations by relying and emphasising more on cognitive and social powers, which can be rewarding and satisfying.
c. Ego transcendence versus ego preoccupation is related to thinking of detachment and nurturing the skills of others. The elderly must find constructive ways to face the reality of death. Attaining ego integrity requires a continuing effort to make life more secure, meaningful and gratifying. Drawing on wisdom, they must reach out to others in ways that make the world better.

Socio-Emotional Selectivity Theory

Certain forms of behaviour are about deriving emotional satisfaction through social interactions. During old age, people become selective about what they do. With a limited income flow, there can be altered attitudes towards social life, spending habits, memory, and other goals. This theory is largely based on what motivates different individuals at different ages, and considers the influence of other factors, such as ideals and priorities.

Box 8.4 Profile D

Sarla and Sharda, both in their 70s, began to go on walks every evening. Soon, they would sit and talk about their homes or recall their youth, contrasting it with the lives led by youngsters now. Other elderly ladies soon began to join them, and the group became bigger. In fact, such groups of the elderly (of both genders) are present in most residential colonies. They often plan picnics and go for movies. They enjoy their time together and look forward to sharing more stories. Conversations also refer to common television programmes and the high points of the different serials they watch.

Profile E

Mrs Kanta is aware of the peer group of the elderly. However, she finds herself a misfit, as she likes to paint or do clay modelling and write poetry. She is lonely, as she does not have company with whom to share her flights of imagination. She waits for conversations with her grandchildren, who are able to appreciate her artistic work, but cannot provide a continuous presence to maintain her social web.

Source: Asha Singh.

One of the major aspects of socio-emotional selectivity theory is how individuals with different perspectives of time behave socially. People who perceive time as relatively unlimited are more likely to want to meet new people and attempt to build new friendships and relationships, in spite of the emotional risks. People who perceive time as limited, on the other hand, are more likely to spend their time focusing on relationships that they consistently find pleasant and emotionally fulfilling. This is representative of the theory's concept of a bias towards the positive.

SUCCESSFUL AGEING

The quality of life and relationships, together with good mental health, are the key variables that must be considered when examining the concept of successful ageing. Life years, or the absence of disease, are no longer the means of measurement, and perhaps the best and most comprehensive description is: 'A person is considered to be ageing successfully when that person reaches their own potential and possesses a level of physical, social and psychological well being with which they are content' (www.misa.ie/successful-ageing; accessed 5 January 2015).

While it is expected that cognitive, physical and emotional disabilities will occur at some point in many older people's lives, ample proof exists showing that these disabilities can be modified through early detection and intervention. Many of these factors are potentially modifiable in mid-life and beyond, for example, through social engagement, regular exercise, and adaptive coping skills. In Indian society, cultural values and traditional practices emphasise that elderly members of the family be treated with honour and respect. The families of aged persons are expected to ensure care and support. However, recent changes in the size and structure of families have caused the re-arrangement of roles and functions of other members.

Changing Profile of Longevity

Several factors, such as improved medical care and advancing technical support has led to better investigations and cure mechanisms, thereby increasing survival and life expectancy. There have been dramatic gains in the average life expectancy, that is, the number of years that an individual can expect to live, due to multiple factors—slow biological ageing, improved nutrition, medical treatment, sanitation, and safety. Life expectancy varies with socio-economic status, ethnicity and nationality. Although women outnumber men by a greater margin, differences in the average life expectancy between the sexes decline as elders advance in age. Surveys indicate that the population of the elderly has increased from 5.63 in 1962 to 6.58 in 1991, and by 2021, it will increase by 9.87. Kerala, Punjab and Tamil Nadu will have a higher number of the elderly.

INDIAN SOCIETY AND THE ELDERLY

In each society, there are ways in which the elderly pass on responsibilities to younger members in the family. In business families, economic responsibilities are shared, and sons learn by watching their father or uncles. Informally, the mantle of leading the family comes to the next generation. Such a transfer of economic power may be smooth, or cause divisions among brothers. It is often noticed that business disputes impact social dynamics within families. There can be many ways of arriving at solutions, both acrimonious and harmonious. Sometimes families separate, while many families report that they live in two or three-storeyed houses, where the sons live with their families and function as independent units. The elderly parents stay with each son in turn, and all come together for festivity and celebrations.

At times, the elderly may maintain an independent unit for themselves. The everyday rhythms of elderly individuals depend on temperament, family support, and, to a very large extent, economic status. A combination of these factors contributes to social dynamics, interaction patterns and relationships. Individuals who continue to be active may command more respect, while increased dependency may impact interactions and social position. Power structures and economic assets associated with elders may also dictate the attitudes of family members. The elderly often create their wills, and are advised to employ a lawyer to assist them.

Societal Recognition of the Elderly

Traditionally, in India, the aged enjoyed a place of honour and respect in the family and community. The elderly were treated as repositories of experience, skill and wisdom. With the breakdown of the joint family system, there has been a decline in the role and status of the aged population. Over the years, the population of the elderly has become the fastest growing segment in the world population. Family is considered the most important social unit, with special significance for elderly people. Across fraternities, elderly people are recognised for their contribution in their respective fields. They are looked upon for suggestions and advice from people of all age groups.

Old age is considered one of the stages of human development, wherein a person attains wisdom, maturity, and social and economic stability, with social recognition and emotional fulfilment. This is to lead to the last phase of life—spiritual salvation. Parents are placed at par with not only the great gurus, but also at times with God. Service to parents has been considered a debt; children have to repay their parents for giving birth to them.

Due to socio-technological changes, changing values, dual-career families, etc., the position of the elderly has declined. In a youth-based culture, there is a strong stereotype of the aged, resulting in society looking down on older people. A negative age discrimination persists against the elderly. The elderly consequently suffer marginalisation, alienation, and poor living arrangements, with fewer choices of careers (Ramamurthi 2003). D'Souza (1969), in his paper presented at the 8th International Congress on Gerontology, stated that the structure of society has been undergoing a fundamental change, under which older persons are being dislodged from higher status.

Box 8.5 Social Status of the Elderly in the Media

Television serials have been focusing on family dramas, a theme popularised by the first serial *Humlog*, telecast on the public channel Doordarshan. The serials have captured the diversity of the Indian ethos—ranging from R. K. Narayan's *Malgudi Days*, set in south India, to *Balika Badhu* in Rajasthan, to several stories from Gujarat, the stories present a well-respected and cared-for icon of the elderly. Stories flesh out the roles of family heads, an elderly male or female usually in control of the family's economic and social decisions.

Most younger members are presented as being in awe and fear of the family monarch. This fear and power leads some members to manipulate and distort reality for the individual good. The dynamics of good and evil are represented and balanced. The dominant aspirational image is of family-based care and residence for the elderly. Depiction of the elderly in institutions are few and far between.

Among films, *Bagwaan* provides a riveting portrayal of the changing status of the elderly. It presents a classic model of modern life, where retirement from active service takes away economic independence, which impacts on the social position of the elderly.

Retirement and Changed Social Dynamics

With improvement in the health and well-being of the elderly, there has been an increase in the age of retirement from active employment in various fields. However, for the service and working class, retirement brings psycho-social changes in the lives of individuals. There are state facilities for pension and other forms of financial assistance; however, the absence of a daily rhythm and routine may leave individuals with a temporary loss of purpose. Family support and positive interactions are necessary to preserve a sense of identity and status. In contemporary times, increase in life span and improved healthcare allows for post-retirement jobs and positions.

Retirement is a one-time event and a milestone, but it has many processes associated with it. Retirement, with its altered routines and economic resources, brings changes into the everyday lives of people. Individuals with financial security, an active interest in voluntary work, sound educational qualifications, good health, and the company of a spouse adjust best to retirement, and experience the greatest satisfaction. In present times, individuals either seek re-employment or complete termination from work activities. Individual temperament plays a significant role in adjusting to retirement and related issues.

Many couples wait for a spouse to retire to indulge in their hobbies, and assume that their marriages will be happier, given the greater freedom to pursue their dreams. Increase in marital harmony and satisfaction will, however, depend on how individuals carve out their relationships with care and understanding. For example, although couples may intend to share the housework, the patterns established early in marriage might continue, with wives cooking meals and doing the household chores. Women often state that 'wives never **retire** from household work as men do from working outside the home'. Although husbands may pitch in, women remain primarily responsible for housework. Significant changes do occur in spending patterns and expenses. The most common sources of retirement income are pensions, savings, investments, and income from employment. Medical expenses also increase with age, and are a source of worry for many ageing families.

The Population Census 2001 and the results from the NSSO Survey on Employment-Unemployment (2007–08) reported nearly 40 per cent of people aged 60 and above were still working. This included 19 per cent women and 60 per cent men. In rural areas, 66 per cent aged men and 23 per cent aged women contributed actively to the economic process. This proportion was less for the urban elderly, with 39 per cent men and only 7 per cent of elderly women being active in economic production (Situation Analysis of the Elderly in India 2011).

HEALTH AND WELL-BEING OF THE ELDERLY

Statistical data indicates a pronounced increase in longevity. People are living longer and staying healthy for a longer time. Yet, the body does go through many physiological changes, and declines in the functioning of different systems. This impacts the competencies and skills of the elderly. The following section describes the changes in the different domains.

Physical Development

Several physical changes can be observed during late adulthood. These changing capabilities are closely related to the process of advanced ageing. With degenerating organ systems impacting physical functioning, many daily activities are curtailed. Symptoms of organ degeneration appear prominently in middle adulthood, and become more pronounced as people progress through late adulthood. The body's organ systems work less efficiently under the general effects of ageing. For quite a while, individuals continue to function, despite the declining efficiency of organs and the body in general; however, problems occur when the decline becomes dramatic, later in the stage.

Changes in Weight and Height

In middle adulthood, men begin to lose weight, and this continues through late adulthood. Elderly women also lose weight during this stage, due to several factors such as lower metabolism and decreasing physical activity. Many individuals revert to less food consumption, which, combined with lower metabolism and activity, also results in reduced muscle and tissue mass, and hence weight. Loss in height is caused by the compression of the spinal column, and the softening of muscle and bone tissue. The changes result in a characteristically stooped posture, with the head held forward and down from the body.

Changes in Bodily Systems

The body declines in physical functioning, bringing in numerous changes that result in changed patterns in life and living. We are familiar with older people losing their teeth at night, or using a walking stick.

Teeth: Not all elderly people experience a total loss of teeth; this happens to a sizeable minority between the ages of 65 and 74. Good and proper care of one's teeth can avoid many dental problems in old age. At times, lack of economic resources mean that dental problems cannot be addressed, leaving many old people with no dentures or poorly fitted dentures. Consequently, they may eat easy to chew foods, leaving out vegetables, fruits and meats from their diet. Such poor eating habits lead to malnutrition.

The muscular and skeletal systems: With age, changes in muscle and bone functioning restricts mobility. Difficulty in mobility is a result of a loss of elasticity in muscle tissue, reducing flexibility and causing stiffness. Elderly people are often prescribed calcium, as there is a thinning of bones. Bone density assessment is a positive step for proactive health management. As people grow older, bones begin to grow thin, which is why older people are more prone to fractures. This condition is known as osteoporosis, which means porous bones. This fragile state of bones can lead to easy bone breakage, and is a condition more common in women. Arthritis and rheumatism are the most prevalent musculoskeletal disorders among the elderly. Back pain also increases in frequency and intensity, reflecting a deterioration of the vertebrae.

Reduced height: The bones in the spinal cord are in the form of cubes, which shrink with age. This flattening of bones leads to a reduced length of the spinal cord, which is what causes stooping and reduces the height of older people. Elderly people begin to look shorter due to changes in bone density.

The cardiovascular system: Middle adulthood also brings changes, with the heart and blood vessels becoming more vulnerable in late adulthood. Fatty materials accumulate in the heart muscle and arteries (atherosclerosis), the heart valves thicken, and hardening of the arteries, also known as arteriosclerosis, becomes more pronounced. Changes in cardiovascular functions may cause high blood pressure, extra stress on the heart, and related cardiovascular problems. Older people also develop a slower heart rate, leading to a decreased level of oxygen in the blood, which is why elderly people tire more easily and cannot endure stress as well as younger people. Exercise assists the maintenance of body functions by activating blood flow. Regular exercise has been found to be beneficial in maintaining cardiovascular responsiveness.

The respiratory system: As mentioned earlier, in late adulthood the capacity of the lungs decline, which considerably impacts the capacity to inhale and exhale. The elderly become prone to lung disorders and respiratory infections like emphysema and pneumonia, which is an inflammation of the lungs. Pneumonia is a particular risk for an elderly person with prolonged illness, as physical inactivity prevents the lungs from clearing themselves. Poor lung efficiency leads to poor circulation and lowering of resistance to infection, all factors that increase the chances of pneumonia. A common serious respiratory condition among the elderly is cancer of the lungs. The elderly must be encouraged to take walks and do breathing exercises to maintain healthy lungs, and ward off disease.

The digestive system: Like all systems, the digestive system needs to be kept active, or problems such as gall bladder malfunction, or hernia, or constipation increase through adulthood. Gastritis, heartburn, or constipation or hemorrhoids are common disorders among the elderly. Many elderly individuals rely on laxatives for regular bowel movements, which is more an outcome of dietary practices than of the ageing process. A light diet with more fibre can stimulate digestive processes, avoiding a dependence on laxatives.

The urinary system: The urinary system, comprising kidneys, bladder and urethra, becomes susceptible to infection and disorders in elderly people. Ageing is accompanied by a decrease in the blood flow through the kidneys, as well as a gradual lowering of the kidneys' efficiency in removing waste from the blood. People of a advanced age sometimes develop an inability to retain urine in the bladder; this condition is known as urinary **incontinence.** Lack of voluntary urine control is a very real and embarrassing problem. Certain exercises, like contracting the urinary tract muscles, helps in strengthening voluntary bladder control. Many of the problems can be moderated through exercise, which can enhance the reduced blood flow.

The brain and central nervous system: A general belief about the elderly is that their reactions are slow, that is, information processing takes longer and therefore 'reaction time' is not as quick as earlier. Certainly, the brain and the central nervous system undergo developmental changes with ageing. There is both a slowing of nerve cell transmission and a decrease in the number of nerve cells.

A decreasing efficiency of different organs and slower flow of blood together impact the transmission of oxygen to the brain, which produces the slowing in reaction time. The changes in oxygen flow may influence reflexes, and delayed reaction time can affect perception and memory. Progressivly slower reaction times endanger the safety of elderly people.

Changes in sensation, perception and motor skills: The ability to adjust and adapt through the lifespan depends on the capacity to receive and process information gained through the senses. The area of the brain that regulates sensory messages declines in efficiency, and elderly people experience sensory deprivation. Mental alertness and contact with reality receives an enormous setback with such deprivation.

Vision suffers many changes, such as the need for an increase in the threshold of light needed to stimulate retinal cells, as well as a decreased sharpness of vision or acuity as a result of changes in the lens, pupil size and focusing ability. There is decrease in accommodation, that is, ability to focus, and a decrease in the adaptation to dark and light environments. Several age-related changes occur in the structure of the eye, and some common problems of old age are cataract and glaucoma. Changes in the accommodation of light, less amount of light passing through the eye, and yellowing of the lens are some of the causes of cataract and other eye diseases.

Hearing: We sometimes notice a complete withdrawal from social interaction, which may stem from a significant sensory change in hearing. Psychologically, hearing loss can reduce the ability to have communicate satisfactorily with others Hearing handicaps increase considerably with age. The loss of hearing of high-frequency sounds, first noticed during middle adulthood, continues. Loss of hearing in the mid to low-range frequencies becomes more likely with age.

Taste and smell: During late adulthood, the number of taste buds decreases, leading to a need for stronger stimulation to enjoy different flavours. At times, elderly people remark that food tastes bland, and add salt, pepper, and other condiments to improve its flavour. This is really an extra effort to stimulate the perception of taste. Taste and smell perception decline in old age. Changes in smell are primarily responsible for the reported changes in food preference and enjoyment.

Changing Lifestyle

Health is central to psychological well-being, and individuals do change their rhythms and routines in tune with the altered capacities of their bodies. In response to the physical changes of late life, the elderly change their diets to increase their intake of certain nutrients needed to protect the bones and immune system, and prevent free radicals. The quantity and quality of food may have to be altered as there may be a decline in physical activity, in the senses of taste and smell; even chewing may be difficult. Older people often eat light food as changes in the digestive system make the digestion of proteins and other nutrients difficult.

Along with appropriate nutrition, exercise is a powerful health intervention. Exercise increases lung capacity and blood circulation to the brain, which helps preserve brain structures and behavioural capacities. Some elders value the intrinsic benefits of exercise, and feel stronger and more in control, and stay healthier and more energetic. It is also noted that exercise can minimise the physiological changes associated with ageing and contribute to health and well-being. Common chronic diseases like type 2 diabetes, stroke, etc., can be prevented through regular exercise. Exercise can be used to counteract the side effects of standard medical care, and thus improve disease outcomes and quality of life.

Certain changes in the environment can prevent injuries and accidents resulting from the decreased body functioning and sensory inputs. No mental or physical disability is part of the ageing process, although their incidence increases with age. Hearing aids can enhance hearing, thereby influencing social interaction. Changes in the house, such as bars in the bathroom, adjusting the height of the bed for comfort, can improve mobility. The elderly can be given training for balance, corrective eye surgery, and walking sticks. It must be remembered that in late adulthood, the chances of unintentional injuries increase manifold. A slight fall in the bathroom may lead to a fractured bone. Efforts must be made to prevent falls, with anti-slip tiles/mats in bathrooms and rooms.

Cognitive Functions

In recent years, more people are living to a ripe old age. Their greatest fears are the possibility of physical immobility and losing their mental capacities. At times, some people are afflicted with dementia, a set of disorders occurring almost entirely in old age. Dementia brings in many disjointed behaviour patterns. People may lose a sense of time; many aspects of thought and behaviour may be impaired, disrupting everyday activities. Dementia may strike both men and women, and rises with age. The most common form of dementia is known as Alzheimer's disease. In this illness, there is both structural and chemical brain deterioration, and a gradual loss of aspects of thought and behaviour. People with Alzheimer's suffer severe memory problems. Most often there is loss of recent memory, followed by distant memory, too.

Box 8.6 Profile of Persons with Dementia

Profile F: A 45-year-old scientist reported that his 82-year-old father, who had been an executive engineer with the government in the 1950s, would hallucinate. He would have imaginary conversations with Winston Churchill, or at times would reorganise the Indian States.

Profile G: Mr Arora found that his father experienced delusions and imaginary fears. He would often wake up at night and imagine that some people were trying to break into the house. He would cry and state that he was not being taken care of by his family, even in the presence of loving caregivers. Over time, he lost the ability to comprehend and produce speech.

Profile H: Seventeen-year-old Radha avoided visiting her friend Meena's as Meena's grandfather insisted on reading poetry to any friend who visited. The youngsters were keen to discuss current issues or play games, but 75-year-old Mr Gaur would only want to read his own poetry or text that made no sense to the youngsters. Slowly, he was avoided by most people as he had lost the skills to listen.

Source: Dimple Rangila.

In old age, individuals sometimes suffer paralytic attacks or strokes. Stroke is the loss of blood supply to the brain and may cause neurological damage, altering memory or speech or movement, depending on the part of the brain that has been attacked. In such situations, individuals need assistance in living and a lot of care. In severe cases, institutional living is often advised.

Changing Dimensions of Memory

Memory is a cognitive skill that helps in the retention of information. Two important features are working memory and processing speed. Research indicates an increase in working memory during childhood, adolescence and early adulthood, reaching a peak at 45 years, and declining from 57 years. This increase and decrease is both related to remembering new information and maintaining the memory of old information. There are various aspects to remembering, which is the active component of memory. Episodic memory deals with remembering events or important experiences, while there is memory for knowledge of the world, called semantic memory.

An individual's long-term memory systems include memory of facts and experiences, also called explicit memory. Studies have shown that younger adults have better episodic memory than older adults. Older adults remember older events better than recent events. As people grow, they develop a tendency to recall their earlier experiences, which is an outcome of a strong relation to episodic memory. Although older adults often take longer to retrieve semantic information, they usually can do so as it may entail making inferences. Arriving at information is implicit memory, which is less likely to get affected with age. Thus, while older adults are more likely to forget the name of a familiar person, they will not forget how to drive a car.

The elderly find it difficult to remember time-based tasks, such as taking medicines or switching off the water pump, but are more likely to remember event-based tasks, such as sharing a newspaper article with a friend. One reason ascribed to this is the decline in physiological functioning and the brain. Training and using pneumonic devices can improve older adults' memory.

NEEDS AND CONCERNS OF THE ELDERLY

1. Issues of health: There is an absence of good quality, age-sensitive healthcare for the elderly in India. Poverty exacerbates the disadvantage, with a lack of support and poor accessibility. Inadequate information, little knowledge, and misplaced trust in only private healthcare puts healthcare out of the reach of people.

2. Economic insecurity, arising out of a lack of finances or non-availability of pension, leaves the elderly unable to sustain themselves. Many older people either lack the opportunity and/or the capacity to be as productive as they were.
3. Isolation from the mainstream and lack of active participation brings in a deep sense of loneliness. This problem is often imposed inadvertently by the families/communities in which the elderly live, and might further lead to deterioration in the quality of life.
4. Neglect: At times, older people suffer neglect and rejection due to specific conditions, and become a burden on caregivers. Neglect occurs especially in the cases of those who are weak or dependant, and require physical, mental and emotional care and support.
5. Abuse: Vulnerability may expose the elderly to abuse. A family member may wilfully or inadvertently harm an elderly member of the family. Often, the elderly are abused of their finances, in addition to emotional and mental abuse. The best form of protection is prevention by raising awareness of the needs and declining functions of the elderly. Another major aspect is preparation for old age. A large number of people enter this stage with little awareness of what it entails. There should be greater government and non-government efforts in this regard as well.

Social Groups and the Elderly

With changes in society, some natural support systems emerge to address issues and concerns. Support groups may be informal, or may take the form of institutions. One example of informal support is evening groups. In residential colonies, groups of the elderly are observed sitting in parks every evening, and there is increased participation in welfare associations. The elderly also engage in exercise and form yoga clubs, laughter clubs, and sometimes even open coaching centres for the children of domestic helps. There is an attempt to keep themselves fuelled by activity, unless failing health restricts mobility. It is not unusual to find elderly people out on walks, assisted by a helper.

Support Groups

With an increasing presence of elderly and diversity in occupations, a greater number of older people may have to be self-reliant and self-supportive. There has been an increase in pensions, and more institutions for assisted living have emerged to meet the needs of the elderly, although family remains the major source of care.

Nursing care or Companions: Professionals have come together to provide care within families or for individuals staying independently. There are paid services for nursing, as well as routine care and assistance for the everyday activities of the elderly.

A more recent development is that of 'providing companions'. Young people have come together to offer companionship and outings. Such facilities are a boon for those elderly whose children live in different countries, and are not easily accessible socially.

Leisure

Recreation is healing, as it restores states of vigour and alertness through pleasurable activity. Through social activities, elderly people get to interact with others in society. Social interaction makes a positive impact, creating feelings of self-worth and inclusion. This further improves physical health and mental well-being. Leisure activities have a therapeutic effect on mind and body, especially for the elderly. It is important to identify recreational areas according to people's varying needs and choices.

Although leisure activity varies according to age and period in the lifecycle, the choice of activities depends on a number of factors—income level, interest, personality, health status, transportation, education, etc. Each factor plays a significant role in the choice of leisure activities. The personal value derived from recreational activities cannot be quantified, as it may even provide an opportunity to explore specific creative talents. It also allows physical, emotional and intellectual expression and exploration. Its social and cultural value provides for different needs, enjoyment in this special phase of life, forging new friendships, etc.

For some people, the leisure activity might fulfill an economic need as well. It also provides community support for the elderly through the formation of RWAs, old-age homes, senior citizen associations, daycare centres, etc. The satisfaction that the elderly get from leisure activities goes a long way in promoting well-being and quality of life. Sometimes, leisure takes the form of engaging with religious groups, or mere self-engaging.

Religion and Spirituality in Old Age

Older adults may turn to spirituality and religion when they meet difficult life changing events and experience personal loss. Their reaction to these events may cause distress, and temporary or chronic psychological conditions. Mental health interventions may include or add to one's faith or practice of spirituality in times of difficulty. Coping patterns and skills develop over a lifetime.

Research confirms that religious values, beliefs and traditions can provide a meaningful thread of integration, which enhances adjustment processes. However, it seems that the importance of religious beliefs and practices in late life is a function of the transmission of religious teachings from one generation to the next.

SOCIAL DYNAMICS AND THE ELDERLY

All individuals do not have one uniform social web in which they find themselves during this last phase of life. Besides economic and ethnic differences, there are factors such as family configuration, and support by siblings, spouse, or friend or neighbourhood groups. The family is often redefined.

The Importance of Families

The family is as important in later life as it is during childhood. It is an important support group that creates joy and a sense of belonging through shared time together, and expressions of love and affection. The family also provides assistance, such as financial support or help with chores, through all life's changes. The quality of family relationships is established in the early years of marriage and parenthood, and carries over into the later years. Older people with healthy marriages and positive relationships with their children enjoy their family lives in later years. The elderly with strong family relationships often feel they can turn to family members for assistance when needed. As older people experience losses in life—such as the death of close friends or a spouse—and changes in health or mobility, family remains the biggest support.

Marriages in Later Life

Older married couples have many opportunities to enjoy their lives together and grow closer. In addition, spouses provide extraordinary companionship and support when health and mobility decline. Married couples with vital relationships are most likely to experience continued, positive interactions within marriage. Those who enjoy spending time together and can confide in each other usually maintain a close and giving relationship as they age. However, those couples who are unsatisfied in the earlier years of their marriage tend to have a negative experience later in life.

Widowhood

Widowhood brings about many changes in finances, physical and emotional health, and social support. These changes often last years after the death of a spouse. Becoming widowed usually means a significant decline in income. Over time, however, the financial situation levels off or improves, especially for the middle-aged and remarried. Physical and emotional health is often affected by the loss of a spouse. They also show symptoms that are characteristic of depression, such as sadness, tearfulness, insomnia, and appetite and weight loss. Men and women experience similar emotional difficulties after the death of a spouse. As time progresses, however, they adjust, and the negative effects of the loss decrease.

Social contacts are an important resource because they provide support during the period of adjustment. Social contacts, as well as good health and participation in recreation, are associated with feelings of well-being among the widowed.

Widows and widowers tend to continue the social patterns they had established in marriage. Women are more likely than men to talk with friends and close relatives, and to turn to their children in times of crisis. This pattern continues in widowhood. However, both men and women experience continued and frequent contact with friends and family members.

Parent-Child Relationships

In old age, parents want to have caring and sharing ties with their family. They view their children as friends, and remain interested in their activities and welfare. As most Indian parents believe that 'children will always remain children no matter how much they grow up', they are always concerned and worried about their children. We sometimes think of older people as needing help or attention from younger family members; but in fact, giving is an enduring part of the parental role. This ability to give to their children has a positive impact on the older parents' own well-being. Parents enjoy feeling needed and loved, and are flattered when asked for advice. Those who feel competent as a parent and have open, affectionate communication with their children feel good about themselves.

Throughout life, give-and-take across the generations is a sign of family well-being. Older parents can continue to provide care for their children and grandchildren for as long as they can. Middle-aged children do receive love and aid from their parents, and can also help their parents as needed.

Grandparenthood

Becoming a grandparent is usually a positive experience. The bonds between mothers and daughters are usually strengthened as they share the experiences and activities of parenthood. Grandparenthood can be a source of fulfilment and happiness because it gives older adults a meaningful role in maintaining family stability, traditions and values, and a joyous chance to relive life and indulge grandchildren.

Grandparents have always been looked upon to give love, protection and support. In India, grandparents are notionally an integral part of any family, whether nuclear or joint. Grandparents living as part of the family are considered a strength; members look to them for support in almost all spheres of life. In a study, Rangila (2004) found that grandparents played a major role in the care of grandchildren with disabilities. They were very supportive, shared the caregiving role with the parents, and took a lead role in the socialisation of the children. Despite a few inter-generational differences, the grandparents were found to be fairly involved in the lives of their disabled grandchildren.

Punia (2012) concluded that children also see a safe refuge in their grandparents, as most mentioned sharing a special bond with their grandparents, even listing the activities they did together.

Sibling Relationships

Older adults with at least one living brother or sister usually have contact on a weekly or monthly basis, particularly if they live near each other. For older adults, sibling relationships are unique and important. Often, this is the only continuous family relationship that endures from childhood to old age.

Sibling bonds developed in early childhood continue through life. Siblings provide companionship and emotional support, needed material resources, and guidance in old age. Sharing a family history is a foundation for continued interaction throughout life, and serves a special purpose in old age. A number of studies have found that all siblings feel a greater sense of closeness in later years, reducing feelings of conflict and envy and deepening their approval and acceptance of one another.

Friendship in Old Age

Researchers have uncovered three broad themes underlying adult friendships. The most frequently mentioned is the affective or emotional basis of friendship. This includes self-disclosure, and sociability and compatibility—our friends keep us entertained and are sources of amusement, fun and recreation. Most older adults, even those who live alone, have some friends and acquaintances to whom they can turn in emergencies. Although contact with friends tends to decline with age, the majority of older adults have at least one close friend with whom they are in frequent contact. In fact, older persons may turn more to friends and neighbours for immediate assistance than to family, in part because friendship involves more voluntary and reciprocal exchanges between equals, consistent with social exchange theory. To the extent that friendships can satisfy social and material needs, and allow for reciprocity in relationships, they can compensate for the absence of a partner and can help ease a sense of loneliness. Women tend to have formed more, and closer friendships throughout life.

Wisdom

Wisdom is not inevitably a product of old age, although reaching an old age increases the chances of acquiring the life experience and emotional maturity that nurture wisdom. Wisdom is generally defined as accumulated learning, that is, knowledge, the ability to discern inner qualities and relationships, insight, good sense, and judgement. These qualities are gained and enhanced through experience. Life experiences alone give older people an edge in the arena of wisdom and insight. In India, older people have always been respected as sources of wisdom, and it is this that makes older persons respected in society as well as in their respective families. However, with the changed socio-economic and demographic scenario, older persons are being marginalised in society, and the younger generations have fewer opportunities of benefiting from the wisdom of old age.

Attitude Towards Death

Although death is a familiar concept at all ages, it become a real issue during old age. Individuals at different stages of life view death differently. Young adults avoid thinking about death, despite an abstract understanding of the concept. As they finish their education/training and embark on their careers, marriage or parenthood, they are eager to live their lives rather than think of death. In middle adulthood, the realisation of death makes an appearance. Often, after the death of a parent, there is an awareness of being the 'older generation'. Awareness of finite time may lead individuals to take stock of careers, marriage, relationship with children, friendships, and values, and the way they spend their time and energy.

In late adulthood, there is less anxiousness about death. As the years pass by and elderly people lose friends and relatives, they start reorganising their thoughts and feelings to accept their own mortality. It is not uncommon to hear older people discuss death, either directly or indirectly. At times, older people talk about reducing their material goods, as they feel no one would look after them after they are gone. People across cultures view death differently. It is almost impossible for older people to avoid the question of their own death. Some older people may fear death and some may take it as inevitable, but no one can be neutral towards it. Those elderly who have been sick or bedridden for a long time seek death as a release.

In Indian culture, rules and regulations govern the activities of family members after a death, preventing them from undertaking certain activities for a specific period of time. Variations in the customs surrounding death are reflected in some of the oldest monuments on earth, such as the pyramids in Egypt and the Taj Mahal in India. Socio-culturally, too, death can be viewed in many ways.

People across cultures hold different views on life after death. Different religions have their own vision of death. The core concept in Hinduism spells out the cycle of birth and rebirth. Hence, followers tend to view their present life as part of a long cycle of existence on earth, with birth and death being the markers that separate one life from the next. Death is viewed as a passage to the next life. The soul *(Atman)* moves from one life to the next, and this journey terminates only when the soul has reached a certain level of spiritual progress. Hindus, Sikhs and Jains perceive the liberation of the soul as the ultimate goal, and human life is seen as an opportunity to achieve spiritual upliftment.

Box 8.7 Explorations into Death

In a conversation on issues related to death with an elderly couple, 86-year-old Yashji said, 'When you have reached my age, you think death is a natural thing and you are always ready to accept it.' His wife added, 'I would hope that my death wouldn't be too difficult for my family. I am concerned if I become bedridden, I would be a burden on my children. so I want to die peacefully in the presence of my loved ones.' Similar findings were revealed by Punia (2012), who found that elderly people had a lot of expectations from their family members. They wished to live a dignified life. They did not want any pity and hoped that their wisdom, gained through experience, would be fully utilised by the younger generation. Their main apprehension at this stage of life was fear of becoming bedridden and totally dependent on others.

Source: Dimple Rangila.

NATIONAL POLICIES AND PROGRAMMES FOR THE WELFARE OF THE ELDERLY

The Government of India has set up many provisions for the care and well-being of the elderly. We are familiar with the reservation of seats in buses and metros; shopping malls may have designated areas where spots are reserved. Brief descriptions of government facilities and provisions for the welfare of the elderly are given below.

Administrative Set-up

The **Ministry of Social Justice and Empowerment** is the nodal ministry that focuses on policies and programmes for senior citizens, in close collaboration with state governments, non-governmental organisations, and civil society groups. The programmes aim at providing easy access for the welfare and maintenance of destitute and needy senior citizens. There is movement towards assistance through old-age homes, daycare centres, mobile medicare units, etc.

Relevant Constitutional Provisions

Article 41 of the Constitution provides that the State shall, within the limits of its economic capacity and development, make effective provisions for securing the right to work, to education and to public assistance in cases of unemployment, old age, sickness and disablement, and in other cases of undeserved want. Further, **Article 47** provides that the State shall regard the raising of the level of nutrition and the standard of living of its people, and the improvement of public health as among its primary duties.

Legislations

The **Maintenance and Welfare of Parents and Senior Citizens Act, 2007,** was enacted in December 2007 to ensure need-based maintenance for parents and senior citizens, and their welfare. A general improvement in healthcare facilities over the years is one of the main reasons for the continuing increase in the proportion of the population of senior citizens. Ensuring that they do not merely live longer, but lead a secure, dignified and productive life, is a major challenge.

The **National Policy on Older Persons (NPOP), 1999,** was announced in January 1999 to reaffirm the commitment to ensuring the well-being of older persons. The Policy envisages State support to ensure financial and food security, healthcare, shelter, and other needs of older persons, an equitable share in development, protection against abuse and exploitation, and the availability of services to improve the quality of their lives. The primary objectives are:

- to encourage individuals to make provisions for their own, as well as their spouse's old age;
- to encourage families to take care of their older family members;
- to enable and support voluntary and non-governmental organisations to supplement the care provided by the family;
- to provide care and protection to vulnerable elderly people;
- to provide adequate healthcare facilities to the elderly;
- to promote research and training facilities to train geriatric caregivers and organisers of services for the elderly; and
- to create awareness about elderly persons to help them lead productive and independent lives.

The Maintenance and Welfare of Parents and Senior Citizens Act, 2007, was enacted in

December 2007 to ensure need-based maintenance for parents and senior citizens, and their welfare. The Act provides for:

- Maintenance of parents/senior citizens by children/relatives made obligatory and justiciable through Tribunals;
- Revocation of transfer of property by senior citizens in case of negligence by relatives;
- Penal provision for the abandonment of senior citizens;
- Establishment of Old Age Homes for Indigent Senior Citizens;
- Adequate medical facilities and security for senior citizens;

A Central Sector Scheme of Integrated Programme for Older Persons (IPOP) is being implemented since 1992, with the objective of improving the quality of life of senior citizens by providing basic amenities like shelter, food, medical care, and entertainment opportunities, and by encouraging productive and active ageing through providing support for the capacity building of government/non-governmental organisations/Panchayati Raj Institutions/local bodies, and the community at large.

Under this Scheme, financial assistance up to 90 per cent of the project cost is provided to non-governmental organisations for establishing and maintaining old-age homes, daycare centres, and mobile medicare units. The Scheme has been made flexible so as to meet the diverse needs of older persons, including reinforcement and strengthening of the family, awareness generation on issues pertaining to older persons, popularisation of the concept of life-long preparation for old age, facilitating productive ageing, etc. Some of these are:

- Maintenance of Respite Care Homes and Continuous Care Homes;
- Running of Daycare Centres for Alzheimer's Disease/Dementia Patients;
- Physiotherapy Clinics for older persons;
- Helplines and Counselling Centres for older persons;
- Sensitising programmes for children, particularly in schools and colleges;
- Regional Resource and Training Centres of Caregivers to the older persons;
- Awareness Generation Programmes for Older Persons and Caregivers;
- Formation of Senior Citizens Associations.

The **International Day of Older Persons** is celebrated every year on 1 October.

Schemes of Other Ministries

I. Ministry of Health and Family Welfare

The Ministry of Health and Family Welfare provides the following facilities for senior citizens:

- Separate queues for older persons in government hospitals.
- Two National Institutes on Ageing at Delhi and Chennai have been set up.
- Geriatric Departments have been set up in 25 medical colleges.

II. Ministry of Rural Development

The Ministry of Rural Development has implemented the National Old-age Pension Scheme (NOAPS). For persons above the age of 65 belonging to a household below the poverty line, central assistance is given towards pension of Rs 200 per month, which is meant to be supplemented by at least an equal contribution by the States, so that each beneficiary gets at least Rs 400 per month as pension.

III. Ministry of Railways

The Ministry of Railways provides the following facilities to senior citizens:

- Separate ticket counters for senior citizens aged 60 and above at various PRS (Passenger Reservation System) centres, if the average demand per shift is more than 120 tickets;
- 30 per cent and 50 per cent concession in rail fare for male and female senior citizens, respectively, of 60 years and above.

IV. Ministry of Finance

Some of the facilities for senior citizens provided by the Ministry of Finance are:

- Income tax exemption for senior citizens aged 65 years and above, up to Rs 2.40 lakh per annum.
- Deduction of Rs 20,000 under Section 80D is allowed to an individual who pays medical

insurance premium for his/her parents, who are senior citizens aged 65 and above.

- An individual is eligible for a deduction of the amount spent or Rs 60,000, whichever is less, for medical treatment (specified diseases in Rule 11DD of the Income Tax Rules) of a dependent senior citizen aged 65 and above.

V. Department of Pensions and Pensioner Grievances

A Pension Portal has been set up to enable senior citizens to get information regarding the status of their applications, the amount of pension, documents required (if any), etc. The Portal also provides for the lodging of grievances.

VI. Ministry of Civil Aviation

The National Carrier, Air India, provides concession up to 50 per cent for male senior citizens aged 65 and above, and female senior citizens aged 63 and above in air fares.

SUMMARY

- This chapter discussed the changing competencies of the elderly: the interplay of physical strength, biological bases of diminishing functions, and their bearing on the social status of individuals. It also discussed the various theories of ageing, which present varying perspectives, to build an understanding of the varying dimensions of the elderly, and with special reference to India, focused on the social construction of the elderly in India, and Indian perceptions of ageing. It focused on the nuances of the everyday rhythms of elderly males and females, while also providing specific social contexts. Special emphasis has been paid to the health issues of the elderly, including physical and physiological changes, changing lifestyles, and cognitive and memory functions. The needs and concerns unique to the elderly have been talked about, as well as the importance of support groups, leisure, religion and spirituality, and the role played by the family. The relationship with children and grandchildren during old age has been discussed, as has notions of and attitudes toward death. Finally, the last section focused on the national policies and programmes for the welfare of the elderly that have been implemented by various ministries in the government.

EXERCISES

1. Go around your neighbourhood and do a brief survey of the number of the elderly. Note their activities, their qualifications, interests, and schedule in a typical day. Analyse the survey results for male-female ratio, age range, occupation, and current interests. Take any four to six people and identify the patterns and differences in their lifestyle and interests. Study their living arrangements to identify similarities and differences.
2. Discuss the status and role of the elderly in contemporary India.
3. Identify four women and four men of 70 or older, living in at least two different non-family contexts, to understand their views on life. Make a note of the available facilities and list the activities chosen by the elderly. Understand the nature of conversations and the patterns of bonds between the different members who stay together.
4. Identify a group of the elderly in your neighbourhood. Make a note of the different kinds of activity groups. Try and interview one or two members of the group to understand interactions and the nature of conversations, and how they sustain the group. Do they have disagreements? How do they resolve them?
5. Discuss the portrayal of the elderly in popular media.
6. Comment on the bodily changes and physiological functioning of older people.

7. Take a walk in the evening in two localities to note the group activities of the elderly in the area. Interview groups about their leisure-time activities and interests. Try to collect a demographic profile of living arrangements and contribution to household functioning. Classify and analyse the information to see patterns.
8. Describe some of the changed activities and roles that elderly people have adopted.
9. List the constitutional provisions and some of the privileges in Indian society for senior citizens.
10. Write an essay on ideal societal provisions for senior citizens.
11. What are the social support groups in local residential areas that you are familiar with? Describe their activities.

REFERENCES

Austrian, S. S., *Developmental Theories Through the Life Cycle*, New York: Columbia University Press, 2013.

Cavanaugh, J. C. and F. B. Fields, *Adult Development and Aging*, Australia: Wadsworth, 2002.

Cohen, L., 'Metaphor and Alienation', *Anthropological Quarterly* 76(2), 2003, pp. 343–50.

D'Souza, 'Changes in Social Structure and Changing Roles of Older People in India', Paper presented at the 8th International Congress on Gerontology, Washington, D. C., 1969.

Lemme, B. H., *Development in Adulthood*, Boston: Allyn and Bacon, 1999.

Papalia, D. E., C. J. Camp, and R. D. Feldman, *Adult Development and Aging*, New York: The McGraw-Hill Companies, Inc., 1996.

Prakash, O., L. N. Gupta, V. B. Singh, A. K. Singhal, and K. K. Verma, 'Profile of Psychiatric Disorders and Life Events in Medically Ill Elderly: Experiences from Geriatric Clinic in Northern India', *International Journal of Geriatric Psychiatry*, 22 (11), 2007, pp. 1101–05.

Punia, N., 'Perceptions of old age through a developmental lens', Unpublished master's thesis, Department of Child Development, Lady Irwin College, University of Delhi, New Delhi, 2012.

Ramamurthi, P. V., 'Ageing in India—Some critical issues', in A. B. Dey (ed.), *Situational Analysis: Planning for the Future*, New Delhi: Rakmo Press, 2003.

Rangila, D., 'Grandparents' Role in the Socialisation of Children with a Disability', Unpublished master's thesis, Department of Child Development, Lady Irwin College, University of Delhi, New Delhi, 2004.

Online source

http://www.medrounds.org/encyclopedia-of-aging/2005/12/achievements-at-advanced-age-action.html.

Notes on the Editor and Contributors

THE EDITOR

Asha Singh is Reader, Human Development and Childhood Studies, Lady Irwin College, University of Delhi. She has also been active in the corporate life of the institution. She takes a keen interest in combining the use of performing arts in mainstream education as a resource. Asha Singh has written about the use of Arts in pedagogy, as well as developed curricula for courses in Theatre in Education, the National School of Drama, CBSE(i), and IGNOU. She conducts workshops with teachers in the areas of theatre, play, and communicating with parents.

THE CONTRIBUTORS

Vinita Bhargava is Associate Professor, Department of Human Development and Childhood Studies, Lady Irwin College, University of Delhi. Dr Bhargava has been Chairperson of the Coordinating Voluntary Adoption Resource Agency (CVARA) since 1996. As founder-member of the Central Adoption Resource Agency (CARA) and 'NOC' committee member for screening applications for inter-country adoptions, she has contributed significantly to national policies on adoption. She is the author of *Adoption in India: Policies and Experiences*.

Shradhha Kapoor is Associate Professor, Department of Human Development and Childhood Studies, Lady Irwin College, University of Delhi. Her areas of interest are childcare, gender, parenting, family studies, and early childhood education. Dr Kapoor is on the Editorial Board of *Navtika*, a journal in early childhood education.

Punya Pillai is Assistant Professor, Department of Human Development and Childhood Studies, Lady Irwin College, University of Delhi. Her areas of interest include culture and cognition, children's ideas and theories about the world around them, and Indian thinking on family and the individual.

Dimple Rangila is Assistant Professor, Department of Human Development and Childhood Studies, Lady Irwin College, University of Delhi. She is currently enrolled as a doctoral student at the Central Institute of Education, University of Delhi. Her research areas include children's narratives and the role of storytelling in primary classrooms, early childhood care and education, disability, parenting and socialisation.

Savita Sagar is Assistant Professor, Department of Human Development and Childhood Studies, Lady Irwin College, University of Delhi. She is currently enrolled as a doctoral student at the University of Delhi. Her research interests are adolescence and emerging adulthood issues, gender and development, and parenting and caregiving practices in Indian families.